Psychology in the Classroom

A Teacher's Guide to What Works

Marc Smith and Jonathan Firth

Routledge
Taylor & Francis Group

LONDON AND NEW YORK

First published 2018
by Routledge
2 Park Square, Milton Park, Abingdon, Oxon OX14 4RN

and by Routledge
711 Third Avenue, New York, NY 10017

Routledge is an imprint of the Taylor & Francis Group, an informa business

© 2018 Marc Smith and Jonathan Firth

The right of Marc Smith and Jonathan Firth to be identified as authors
of this work has been asserted by them in accordance with sections
77 and 78 of the Copyright, Designs and Patents Act 1988.

All rights reserved. No part of this book may be reprinted or reproduced
or utilised in any form or by any electronic, mechanical, or other means,
now known or hereafter invented, including photocopying and recording,
or in any information storage or retrieval system, without permission in
writing from the publishers.

Trademark notice: Product or corporate names may be trademarks or
registered trademarks, and are used only for identification and explanation
without intent to infringe.

British Library Cataloguing in Publication Data
A catalogue record for this book is available from the British Library

Library of Congress Cataloging in Publication Data
A catalog record for this book has been requested

ISBN: 978-1-138-05967-2 (hbk)
ISBN: 978-1-138-05969-6 (pbk)
ISBN: 978-1-315-16342-0 (ebk)

Typeset in Galliard
by Swales & Willis Ltd, Exeter, Devon, UK

Psychology in the Classroom

Written by experienced classroom practitioners who are experts in the field of psychology, *Psychology in the Classroom* provides a thorough grounding in the key principles of psychology and explores how they can be applied to teaching and learning. It draws on both classic and cutting-edge research, offering practical advice on commonly overlooked or misunderstood concepts that contribute to positive academic outcomes. It aims to show the value of psychology in enabling teachers to make and justify everyday classroom decisions.

Designed to equip teachers with the skills to identify and tackle common issues that affect students' learning, each chapter highlights key areas of research and discusses how lesson planning and material design can be informed by the psychological concepts presented. It covers core areas essential for improving learning, including:

- memory and understanding;
- creativity;
- motivation;
- independent learning;
- resilience;
- cognition; and
- self-theories and mindsets.

Full of advice and strategies, *Psychology in the Classroom* is aimed at both new and experienced teachers, across primary, secondary and post-16 education, providing them with practical ways to apply these psychological principles in the classroom. With an emphasis on understanding the theories and evidence behind human behaviour, this book will allow you to reflect critically on your own classroom practice, as well as making simple but valuable changes.

Marc Smith is a freelance writer, chartered psychologist and Associate Fellow of the British Psychological Society. He has taught in secondary schools across the north of England since 2004 and writes for publications including *The TES* and *The Psychologist*.

Jonathan Firth is a teacher, researcher and a chartered psychologist. He has written several school psychology textbooks, and is currently working in teacher education at the University of Strathclyde, as well as doing a PhD on the practical applications of memory research to teaching.

Contents

Acknowledgements

This book is the result of a process of engagement with both psychology and education throughout our careers, and a gradual realisation of the links between the two. Although there have been too many friends and colleagues along that journey to thank all of them individually, we would like to acknowledge the support of the psychology teaching community in the UK, in particular Mark Healy, with whom we have both presented at a number of conferences and teaching events, and who was instrumental in developing the initial idea for the book. We would also like to thank Fiona Firth for support and publishing advice during the development of the project, as well as Kieran Dhunna Halliwell for sharing ideas and for peer reading an early draft. Finally, we also wish to express our thanks to the education team at Routledge, who have been an absolute pleasure to work with.

Introduction

Psychology is the study of the human mind and human behaviour. Its areas of interest include both the workings on an individual's mind and the way that people behave in pairs and groups. Its theories and research touch on processing abilities such as memory and thinking, as well as more emotional issues such as motivation and curiosity.

In any field of human action and interaction, therefore, the study of psychological principles can potentially be applied to problems that people face. The world of education is just such a field – how people behave and learn in the classroom can be analysed and explained in terms of the psychological processes involved. This book aims to help both new and experienced teachers to understand these processes, helping them to apply them in the classroom in practical ways that will make a positive difference to learners.

As a scientific subject, psychology relies on practical research and tests hypotheses via experiments, trying to establish an objective picture of how mental processes work. Just as in other sciences, this means that there will be situations where common-sense assumptions eventually have to give way to a body of evidence. The drive for research findings to underlie teaching practices – to make education more 'evidence-based' – reflects an increasing desire to scrutinise the educational status quo, and to question whether common teaching practices are actually the best way to impart knowledge and understanding, to motivate young people for lifelong learning, and to foster positive learning behaviours.

This means that popular ideas about how people learn and behave – including some older scientific theories – can be scrutinised and compared to current research knowledge. Your own professional knowledge of learning and thinking can be developed and informed by this process.

Through reading this and other books on the psychology of education, your planning and thinking can become increasingly evidence-based. This shouldn't in any way threaten your professional autonomy to make those decisions that you think are in the best interests of your learners. Indeed, an informed professional is in a better position to both make and justify educational decisions, rather than having practices imposed on them.

Some teachers may feel that they are too busy to learn about psychology, and that feeling is understandable. The profession is facing a crisis of workload and conditions while wages stagnate, with thousands of good teachers leaving the profession. However, there are two main counter-considerations to the argument that we are too busy to learn about the evidence:

- *Many of the ideas in this book will make teaching easier and reduce stress.* Learning better means that more gets done in the same amount of time, and is therefore more efficient. Better results cut the stress level for teachers, too. Higher-achieving, more motivated and resilient learners are easier and more pleasant to teach. When learners understand their own learning processes, are highly motivated and work well independently, this again reduces the workload.
- *A deep understanding of classroom processes is important to the profession.* Deep, research-based knowledge about learning is one of the key things that sets a professional teacher apart from a student helper or classroom volunteer, and is what puts the teacher in the position to make high-stakes choices about their learners and about the curriculum. Concurrently, there is personal satisfaction and a confidence boost to be gained from improving one's professional skill level and delivering classes more effectively. An empowered, skilled professional is also in a better position to negotiate working terms and conditions.

Who is this book for?

This book is for teachers in all sectors and at all stages of their career. While a teacher would ideally learn many of the psychological principles discussed in this book towards the start of their career, there is also a great deal to be said for developing a reflective and evidence-based approach as one progresses through the years of a teaching career. This book will give you a primer on many key considerations, and make you aware of a great many theories and concepts, but the best way to understand the issues in depth is to regularly engage with new findings and debates in the psychology of education. The knowledge gained from reading this book will set you up to do so by making it much easier to read and act on relevant new research, and to be sceptical about educational fads.

It should be clear that this book places an emphasis on understanding the theories and evidence behind human behaviour, but we are not for a minute suggesting that classroom experience is unimportant. As one of the first major psychology researchers, William James, wrote:

> I say moreover that you make a great, a very great, mistake if you think that psychology, being the science of the mind's laws, is something from which you can deduce definite programs and schemes and methods of instruction for immediate schoolroom use. Psychology is a science, and teaching is an art; and sciences never generate arts directly out of themselves. An intermediary inventive mind must make the application, by using its originality.
>
> (James, 1899, p. 23)

In other words, it is important to understand the science of how the mind works, but this is only a start – this knowledge must be applied to a particular educational context by you, the teacher. A solid understanding of the mind is therefore a part of our professionalism, but only a part. Informing ourselves about psychological and educational research can be an empowering force, allowing us to make judgements confidently and in full knowledge of both the facts and the uncertainties highlighted by current psychological research. This book is therefore not going to tell you how to teach your classes, but to provide a grounding in the psychological background that underpins what happens in the classroom. We therefore see a sound knowledge of psychological theory as necessary but not sufficient for the teacher's 'art'.

How to use this book

The book is divided into eight relatively discrete topics, and the chapters can therefore be read in any order. Each can function as a stand-alone guide. It is presented in this way to make it easier to tackle the issues one at a time, perhaps prioritising the areas that are of most relevance to your teaching context. However, they are ordered in what we feel is a logical progression – beginning with the fundamentals of how individuals think and reason, and moving on to areas more concerned with social interaction and long-term outcomes. If you do intend to read all of the sections, it may therefore be best to read them in the order they are presented.

Also, as with any area of psychology, there are considerable overlaps between different topics. For example, there are separate chapters on memory and creativity, but it is acknowledged that these (and other) areas are intermeshed. It would be beneficial for the reader to check back to the other chapters periodically, and to consider how the various topics could affect each other in your teaching context. For example, what are the implications of mindset on independent study? How could the limitations of student cognition play a role in motivation? Such connections are productive areas for a teacher to reflect upon, and perhaps to research independently.

As well as using the book for your own professional development, it could be used to structure staff development within a department or team. One option would be to use a 'book group' format – setting each chapter in turn as a piece of reading, and following it up with a group discussion. If there is sufficient time, further sessions could be allocated to the books suggested for further reading, or colleagues could read and report back on one or more relevant research articles. The suggested further reading titles, it should be noted, have been chosen because they are accessible and well-researched – they don't necessarily reflect our viewpoints! We have also tried to ensure that the bulk of the choices are primarily education-focused, and that they are up to date.

The structure of each chapter in this volume comprises an introduction, a section that tackles several theoretical concepts and how they apply to the classroom together with one or more psychological theories and their implications, and finally a discussion of how practical tasks such as lesson planning and materials design can be informed by the psychological ideas presented.

The chapters cover the following issues:

1 *Memory and understanding.* This chapter presents the fundamentals of how people learn and retain information in the memory. It explains the main types of long-term memory, as well as many of the factors that affect whether information and concepts are retained in memory or not.

2 *Cognition.* This chapter looks at how learners take in and use information in the here and now – issues concerning thinking, processing and working memory. It looks at the key role of attention and what psychologists call 'executive function'. Applications to the classroom are founded on Baddeley's working memory model, which sees working memory as dynamic but limited.

3 *Self-theories.* This chapter describes non-academic components within the individual that impact learning outcomes. Self-esteem, self-concept and beliefs about intelligence can both help and hinder students, and identifying these can foster a more appropriate view of learning.

4 *Creativity.* This chapter looks at what psychology can tell us about the processes of creative thinking, including association, incubation and divergent thinking, and presents a view of creativity that is based on transferring knowledge and skills to new contexts.

5 *Emotions.* This chapter looks at the often-overlooked influence emotions have on academic outcomes. Emotions, both positive and negative, can impact learning in a number of unexpected ways, and helping students to nurture the most adaptive emotions can improve both well-being and learning outcomes.

6 *Resilience, buoyancy and grit.* Often misunderstood, resilience is a complex construct with many variations. This chapter helps teachers to identify those aspects of resilience that are more useful to academic outcomes and those that can help promote general well-being.

7 *Motivation.* This chapter investigates different types of motivation and why some motivational interventions fail. While the emphasis is on intrinsic motivation, the chapter also discusses the best way to motivate using extrinsic factors.

8 *Independent learning.* This chapter identifies concepts from psychological research that suggest more effective ways to structure independent learning, including revision and homework. It also

looks at the debates about active learning and discovery learning, and proposes evidence-based ways of structuring and supporting project work to take account of student metacognition.

About us

Marc and Jonathan are both experienced teachers who have studied and taught psychology, as well as engaging with research, and writing articles and textbooks. Through teaching psychology as a school subject, we both became interested in the many links that exist between its subject matter – thinking and behaviour – and the teacher's day-to-day role. We felt that our many years working in the field of psychology had given us an insight into matters of importance to teacher professional development that would be useful to share with our colleagues throughout the teaching profession, particularly given the shortage of such information from other reliable sources.

In Marc's case (Chapters 3, 5, 6, 7), he began with an interest in how students cope with failure and why some appear more able to bounce back. This led down a path that incorporated both resilience and the emotions that appear more prevalent in the most resilient students. His interests have expanded to include both academic achievement and student well-being, and how the two interact. Jonathan (Chapters 1, 2, 4, 8) became interested in the psychology of education through looking at how to present information so that it would be better remembered by his students. This led to practical classroom-based research into the spacing effect and alternative approaches to homework.

We have therefore teamed up to write a book that combines our complementary areas of interest: unlike some existing volumes, it doesn't focus just on cognition or just on identity, but combines these and other key areas of interest, and it draws on our psychology expertise as well as on our years of classroom experience. It aims to be both intellectually stimulating and highly practical. We really hope you enjoy it.

Reference

James, W. (1899). *Talks to Teachers on Psychology: And to Students on Some of Life's Ideals.* New York: Henry Holt.

Memory and understanding

How does information enter the memory, to be remembered and understood over the long term? This chapter explains the key psychological processes and concepts involved. In particular, it covers:

- The types of long-term memory there are, and why there are so many misconceptions about memory.
- Schemas, and the role of meaningful information in recall.
- The importance of learner attention levels, and of context.
- How the spacing effect and retrieval practice effect can be applied.
- Applications of key theories of memory to lesson and course planning.
- What constitutes good learning habits on the part of learners.

Memory is essential to the process of education. If our learners don't remember anything (i.e. if our teaching activities do not have a lasting impact on their abilities), then why do it at all?

In fact, to say that our teaching should have an effect on memory is a very minimal ambition. We want it to have a positive effect, and one beyond that which would have been achieved if we had not done anything at all; after all, children will always learn something, whether they are at school or not. As teachers, then, what we do in the classroom can be seen in terms of the long-term changes that our activities engender in learners, allowing them to develop and retain knowledge, understanding and skills that they will be able to transfer to new situations.

It is important to clarify that psychology uses the term 'memory' very broadly to include any lasting change in thought processes or behaviour. It does not imply meaningless memorisation, and this chapter is certainly not advocating more rote repetition of isolated facts. As will be seen, meaningful connections between prior knowledge and new learning is an essential facet of learning, making it much more likely that new concepts or skills will be retained. The term also applies to a learner's beliefs, understandings and skills, not just their factual learning.

If our work as teachers is to have positive and long-term effects on our learners, it is essential that we understand how human memory works. However, the research literature into memory is large and complex, and many findings are counterintuitive. In addition, the research has developed rapidly in recent years, and despite the value of professional judgement, we cannot rely just on intuition when the effects of an intervention may not be apparent to learners or teachers, or may not manifest itself until a later point. This chapter aims to help teachers to understand the science of memory, and to show how it can be applied in everyday classroom situations.

Why key aspects of memory are not intuitive

What exactly is meant by memory being 'counterintuitive'? Memory defies expectations, we cannot reliably figure out how it works just from experience, and this is especially true of long-term memory (henceforth LTM) (Bjork, 2011). We cannot fully understand human memory simply through our own subjective experience; how the human brain takes in and stores information is primarily a matter of fact, and this field of study continues to yield surprises after decades of careful experimentation. Developing a professional understanding of how memory works is made more difficult in that the results, by definition, are not immediate, and there are important instances where short-term gains are a very unreliable guide to long-term learning (Soderstrom and Bjork, 2015).

It is also hindered by a set of misleading everyday analogies that liken the human mind to a computer's data processor. We talk of 'encoding' information to memory, 'storage', 'processing' and 'retrieval'. In reality, human memory is not a simple means of recording information, and things we have learned do not stay there in memory in the same format until we are ready to recall them. In short, human memory is very different from a hard drive or video recorder!

Some examples of inaccurate popular assumptions include:

- *We remember things more or less as they were shown to us.* There is now a large body of evidence to show that information is distorted as soon as we begin to remember it, and some of our 'memories' never actually happened (Loftus, 2005).
- *Children are like 'sponges', and remember things better than adults.* In studies of eyewitnesses to a crime, it has been shown that children are highly susceptible to leading questions and false information (Schacter, 2001).
- *The more you repeat something, the better you will remember it.* It is now known that short-term memory is not a reliable gateway to LTM. Going over things repeatedly results in increased confidence without long-term improvements (Kornell et al., 2011), while simply repeating information does not guarantee entry to LTM (Dempster, 1996).

Structure of long-term memory

LTM can be defined as an evolved group of neurocognitive systems involved in the permanent storage of information, understandings, skills and actions in order to retrieve them for future use. It is therefore very broad, involved in everything that draws on previously learned skills and knowledge, and therefore in almost everything we do, from preparing breakfast to discussing politics. In school, learners are drawing on memory when they read, play sports and follow rules, as well as in more obvious situations such as memorising the lines to a play or answering an exam question. And as will be seen in Chapter 4, retention of factual knowledge also plays a key role in creativity.

A complication with understanding LTM is that it is responsible for several apparently quite different functions. Figure 1.1 helps to illustrate

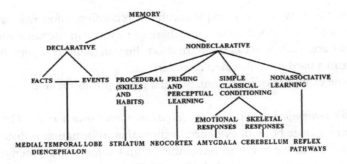

Figure 1.1 Subsystems of LTM with associated brain areas
Source: Squire (2004)

this point by showing some of the different subsystems of LTM, together with the separate brain areas that they are associated with.

As can be seen, there are different types of LTM associated with different functions. Importantly for the teacher, LTM can be split into declarative memory (they know it and can explain it) and non-declarative memory (they have learned it, but cannot necessarily explain how or when; an improvement at playing a musical instrument is one example, as is an emotional association). Therefore, although learning in schools is often linked especially to declarative memory for facts and events, other types of LTM such as memory for procedures and skills are important too, particularly in certain disciplines. However, there are also more basic associative and emotional learning processes that should not be ignored.

As can also be inferred from the diagram, encoding things to LTM involves a change in one or more of the relevant brain areas. Although the details of how this happens are still not fully understood by neuroscientists, we know that it must happen. All of our thoughts and behaviour arise from brain processes – the interaction of neurons, primarily – so if you think differently, remember something new or improve at a skill, a physical change must have taken place within your brain. As might be imagined, this process can be relatively slow, and needs to be consolidated over time. It's not essential for teachers to have a detailed understanding of neuroscience, but it is worth keeping in mind the general context: all of the memory processes described throughout this book involve the brain, and while a pupil can retain and process unfamiliar information over the short term, no new learning is possible without permanent changes taking place on a neural level.

What are the key principles of memory and understanding?

Clearly, a person's ability to form new memories for facts and events – more broadly termed their declarative LTM – plays a key role in most learning situations. This section looks at several key principles of this memory system, all of which are immediately applicable in the classroom.

Meaning

LTM preferentially encodes and stores meaningful information (Baddeley, 1966). This is why when recounting a story or joke, we remember the gist, not the exact words used when we first heard it. The clear implication of this factor in memory is that if learners do not fully understand things, they are unlikely to remember them over the long term. Meaningful processing of information is often referred to as *deep processing*, in contrast with the processing of more superficial details such as what information looks or sounds like (see the next section of this chapter).

Meaningful information is not stored in separate units (as might happen on a computer hard drive), but is structured into well-integrated groups and categories known as schemas. These schemas guide us by filling gaps and providing assumptions. New information is best remembered if it can be linked to an existing structure; if we have some understanding of a topic already, it is easier to learn more about it than if we are complete beginners.

Schema knowledge is not based on memory for single events, but is the representation of more general and abstract characteristics of objects and categories. For example, a learner may recall being shown a video of Mount Etna erupting, but their schema for a volcano will draw on this and many other experiences that allow them to make generalisations, such as that volcanoes are usually mountains, they can erupt but are sometimes extinct, etc.

Research into the structure of memory and schemas suggests that our expectations can lead to information being distorted. If something that is presented is partially familiar, learners may unintentionally distort and misremember it to fit their assumptions. This was found in a classic study by researcher Frederick Bartlett, the first British professor of psychology, who read Native American folk tales to his Cambridge University students and then tested their recall. He found that they missed out the more confusing parts, added bits that were not in the originals, and overall distorted the stories to make them more like stories from their own culture. What this suggests for the more everyday teaching context is that learners who lack fundamental knowledge will not be able to take in new, more advanced knowledge – and when they do take in ideas, their understandings may be flawed and inaccurate.

The concept of schemas links well to the dominant idea in education of how knowledge is formed – social constructivism. This states that rather than being an individual process of learning an objective set of facts, knowledge is based on developing understandings partly through interaction within a social and linguistic context (Vygotsky, 1978; see also Chapter 8).

The importance of meaning implies that activities which prompt learners to think about and process meaningful information should be encouraged. This could include tasks where learners categorise information, draw hierarchies, make links and distinctions, explain concepts to others, or spot errors, for example.

Teachers often like to deliver material in discrete chunks so as not to overload learners, but it is important that links to other information are made salient too, in order to activate and develop schema knowledge. The meaningful foundations for learning must be in place; individual isolated facts are easily forgotten, while knowledge that is integrated within a well-understood structure will be retained.

Learners can be encouraged to draw diagrams that show how areas of topic material link together, while tasks that involve drawing on several areas of learning in a real-world context can help them to develop a more interconnected structure of understanding.

Engagement and attention

Being engaged and making a mental effort plays a curious role in memory. While it may seem obvious that learners who are making more of an effort will remember better, a classic research study by Hyde and Jenkins (1973) suggested that meaningful processing plays a larger role. In their study, some learners were asked to try their best to learn a list of words for a later test, while another group were not told about the test, but were asked to state how much they liked the items on the list. It was the latter group who remembered the words better.

Nevertheless, on a more basic level, learners must at least devote *attention* to the task at hand (with some exceptions; see Chapter 2) in order to process new meaningful concepts at all, and too much new information presented at once – such as long lists of words or a large number of PowerPoint slides – is likely to lead to information overload and a failure to encode much of the information to memory.

Boosting the attention level of pupils is not always easy, and depends on an interaction between the learner and the material; people pay more attention if they are interested. It certainly helps to make things relevant to individual learners, activating their schemas and finding analogies that they can relate to. This does not imply that we need to tailor teaching to a pupil's particular 'learning style'; in a review of the popular idea that teaching is most effective when it matches their preference for visual, auditory or kinaesthetic information, Pashler et al. (2008) found virtually no evidence that supported this hypothesis, and many studies that contradicted it.

Emotion also plays a key role in prompting attention. Pupils tend to pay more attention to things that attract them on an emotional level – from amusement to curiosity, and even disgust. Things that are funny, surprising or rude tend to be better remembered than things that are bland or repetitive. This doesn't mean that we need to shock our learners every day or that everything has to be funny, but we should be wary of making the presentation of content overly standardised; things that are predictable have less emotional impact, just as you would probably remember every holiday you've been on, but not every occasion that you have travelled to work.

A mild degree of short-term pressure (e.g. an in-class competition or time limit) can boost performance. This is based on a principle known as the *Yerkes-Dodson law*, which states that people's performance, including learning, is best at a medium level of arousal (see Figure 1.2).

Attention levels also vary throughout the day, and are linked to fatigue – people take in information less effectively when tired. Evidence is also accumulating (e.g. see Rasch and Born, 2013) that one of the primary functions of sleep is to help to stabilise and consolidate long-term memories in the brain. In a large-scale study, Wolfson and Carskadon (1989) found that pupils who slept for longer and more regularly (i.e. not catching up at the weekend) were significantly

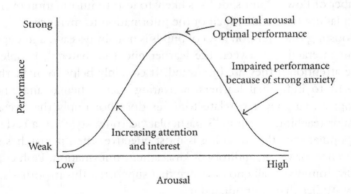

Figure 1.2 The Yerkes-Dodson law shows that performance on tasks such as learning are optimal at a medium level of arousal

more likely to get A grades. Aside from this, attention levels vary across the day as part of our circadian rhythms, meaning that learning will be more effective in the middle of the day than early in the morning or late at night.

The human memory appears to have evolved to pay extra attention to information that will be useful to us in the future. Why, after all, do humans have a flexible LTM, rather than the more instinctive/imprinting-based systems seen in fish and birds? The likelihood is that in our evolutionary past, there was an advantage in having the flexibility to remember a range of things that could aid survival. A number of recent findings have shown that LTM works more effectively in situations that are relevant to life or death, and those that concern animate rather than inanimate objects (Nairne et al., 2013). One example study compared memory for items in three scenarios: on grasslands surrounded by predators, moving to a new home, or (the control condition) just rating the pleasantness of the words, with the former leading to the best recall rate. Soderstrom and McCabe (2011) found a similar effect in a scenario involving being 'in a city being attacked by zombies', suggesting that this evolutionary preparation may be a fairly general ability to focus more on things that seem relevant, dangerous or useful.

Catching learners' attention is a skill that comes partly with teaching experience, but a great deal of it involves stimulating curiosity via simple strategies. One example is to avoid starting lessons with a set of facts, but instead to begin with the questions or problems – for example, what difficulties were renaissance artists trying to overcome when they developed the techniques of linear perspective? Prioritising active research tasks and personalising topics by presenting them via real-life stories can also help to boost attention and engagement.

Teachers don't usually have much control over student sleep or lesson timing, but should encourage good and regular sleep habits. Consideration should be given to learners' well-being, and homework should be designed to be as brief as possible, to avoid learners having to stay up late working on it.

Survival processing is in its early stages in terms of lab investigation, and as yet it is hard to see how it can be broadly applied in the classroom. Can we persuade pupils to 'imagine you need to know this quote from Macbeth to avoid being eaten by a lion'? One promising angle from the work of Wilson (2016) has found that the memory benefit of survival tasks seems to link to the degree to which they require creative thinking. In other words, figuring out whether words and objects would be useful in a survival situation can be seen as a novel problem-solving task. It's therefore probably not necessary to invent scenarios that involve life-or-death situations; learning activities that combine novelty, curiosity and problem-solving will stand a very good chance of being retained in memory.

Context

Pupils learn things in context rather than as separate bits of information. It is easier to recall things in the same context than in a novel context. This is why if we see a person in an unfamiliar place, such as meeting a neighbour on holiday, it can be hard to put a name to the face (i.e. to retrieve the name from our memory). However, the context where learners retrieve information (e.g. the exam hall, the workplace) is often different from where it was learned, and if a lot of information is learned in the same context, it will be easily confused (Smith et al., 1978).

Teachers should keep in mind that learners are not taking in facts in isolation, but as a holistic bundle that includes the social context and sensory information such as their surroundings. They will remember information more readily if the surroundings of recall match those in which things were memorised, but when the context where they will need the information in future is unpredictable, it is best to study in varied contexts. This includes not just the physical surroundings, but factors such as seeing the information in the context of a different topic, working with different people, or even when you are in a different mood.

Spacing

The spacing effect (also known as distributed practice) is the very well-established but little-used principle that for any material, information is better remembered if there is a larger rather than smaller interval between the first time it is studied and the second (Cepeda et al., 2008). Covering anything intensively therefore, such as revising a topic several times within a weekend, will lead to more rapid forgetting than introducing a delay. Having two study sessions spaced apart will be far more effective than a single session – in fact, the larger the gap, the better, within certain limits.

The reason for this effect is a matter for debate, but it may draw on some of the principles already discussed: a time delay before restudy changes the context, boosts attention, and gives the learner more time to consolidate the first learning event via sleep. It also allows more time for forgetting, which (counterintuitively) might actually be helpful, because it makes the second study session more effortful, leading to it having a bigger impact (Pyc and Rawson, 2009).

Spacing interacts with another memory effect known as *interleaving*. This is the finding that new information typically leads to more durable learning if it is mixed or shuffled with other information, rather than being presented in a block of similar items. For example, Kornell and Bjork (2008) presented learners with images of paintings by 12 artists, and then tested their ability to recognise the artists' style via previously unseen paintings. Contrary to the researchers' expectations, participants learned to recognise the various painting styles more quickly when they were interleaved than when they were presented together as a block. Rohrer et al. (2015) applied a similar principle in a school context, and found that maths exercises where problems were set in blocks of the same type – the typical arrangement in most contexts – led to poorer outcomes over a three-month period than when the problems were interleaved.

The research into spacing suggests that teachers should avoid teaching concepts and skills in a single session, instead splitting the learning time across two or more separate occasions (i.e. it suggests a reorganisation and reordering of when tasks are done). Rawson and Dunlosky (2011) helpfully state this more specifically: learners should practise concepts until they have got them right three times, and then study them a further three times at times that are spaced out over days or weeks.

In terms of whole topics, Rohrer (2015) notes that although learning is already spaced out to an extent, learning a topic over a greater rather than smaller number of weeks (while keeping overall learning time constant) appears to lead to better retention. Teachers could therefore consider extending the duration of topics rather than teaching them in an intensive block, and/or conducting review and extension after a time delay rather than immediately after the topic is first taught.

It will occur to many teachers that interleaving of new target learning items can be difficult and lead to confusion. Kang (2016) notes that in the very early stages, practice of a single item can be helpful, but after this initial learning phase, interleaving of material actually boosts learners' ability to discriminate between easily confused items and ideas. However, teachers need to be careful to keep learners on side, as strategies that make learning more difficult affect motivation.

Retrieval

Getting information into memory ('encoding') is of course essential, but it does not guarantee that we can get it out again when needed – such as in an exam or real-life situation. Retrieval is the term used to mean accessing our memories and recalling the facts and skills, and could include many types of event: performing a piece of music, making a link between new information and something previously studied, or answering a multiple-choice question are all examples of retrieval.

As well as the eventual end result for pupils in exams, retrieval is very useful as a study strategy – people learn better when they are tested than when revising more passively. As a learning strategy, this is commonly known as retrieval practice, and is considered one of the most effective educational interventions (Dunlosky et al., 2013), along with spacing.

It should be noted that the use of retrieval practice is not the same as formative assessment – a method of using performance to identify weaknesses and priorities (although the two can complement each other). Retrieval practice helps because the active use of learned information appears to consolidate that memory and make it less likely to be forgotten (Karpicke et al., 2014). A good example comes from an experiment by Roediger and Karpicke (2006), which gave groups of learners a text to learn (see Table 1.1). One group was given three additional chances to read the text, a second group was given two additional chances followed by a test, and a third group was simply tested three times (the test involved writing down everything they could remember from the text).

After a memory test five minutes later, Group 1 did slightly better – no surprise, given that they had seen the text more often. However, one week later, the findings were much more surprising – at this point, it was Group 3 who did the best, remembering around 60 per cent of the key ideas compared to close to 40 per cent among Group 1, with Group 2 midway between the two. These findings show that while repeatedly reading or hearing information has an impact on learners, its effects are very short-lived, and it is largely useless as a long-term learning and revision strategy. It also shows how easy it would be for students or teachers to be misled by short-term gains into thinking that permanent learning has taken place.

Table 1.1 Summary procedure of the Roediger and Karpicke experiment, which showed the benefits of testing one's memory rather than rereading

Group 1	Study	Study	Study	Test
Group 2	Study	Study	Study	Test
Group 3	Study	Test	Test	Test

A number of learning activities involve retrieval. Any activity where learners are having to use previously encoded knowledge and understanding or skills will cause them to retrieve this from memory, including giving a talk, answering a teacher's questions, discussing an issue in class, peer teaching, or essay writing (especially when done 'closed book'). The strategy can also be combined with spacing – retrieval that is spaced out over time is likely to have greater benefits than spaced restudying.

It might be assumed that a test should be done as soon as possible to obtain the benefits described above and to prevent forgetting. However, making a test too easy could reduce its beneficial effects, as follows from the point made about retrieval effort above. For this reason, retrieval will be more effective when delayed by at least a few minutes, and preferably repeated on subsequent days. There is also some evidence that retrieval practice will have the most benefit when it involves 'free recall' – such as writing or explaining something rather than choosing among options, such as in a multiple-choice test, though both are better than simply rereading (McDaniel et al., 2007). However, McDermott et al. (2014) found no difference between short-answer and multiple-choice tests in a study of science and history learning with 12–13-year-old school pupils, but supported the idea that either type of low-stakes test has a significant impact, boosting later exam grades. The difference (or lack of it) may depend on the difficulty of the particular test, and the extent to which it prompts active retrieval from memory. These findings again demonstrate that making learning tasks more challenging can have benefits.

There is of course a debate about the use of tests in education, and the use of large-scale standardised tests is controversial. However, when it comes to short, low-stakes, teacher-generated tests done on a regular basis, the evidence is clear – retrieval helps, and is better for consolidating LTM than when learners are passively presented with the information again.

A theory: levels of processing in memory

The concepts in the previous sections cover the basic apparatus of LTM. For information to be remembered, it must be encoded, a process that relies on forming meaningful connections to other memories. New learning is more durable in memory when practice is interleaved with other concepts or skills, involves retrieval rather than by rereading/reteaching, and is spaced out over time rather than immediate. These can be considered the basic conditions of learning and remembering, and should guide teachers when thinking about the kind of tasks to use in the classroom.

There have been many theories of LTM proposed, and some are very complex without being especially helpful to the teacher. The levels of processing model (Craik and Lockhart, 1972) is one of the more useful ones, as it explains how items that are processed on the basis of meaning were more deeply processed, and therefore better remembered than more superficial forms of learning (e.g. by sound or appearance).

This was demonstrated experimentally by Craik and Tulving (1975). They presented lists of words together with questions, such as the following, each requiring a yes or no answer from their research participants. For example:

1   Is this word a type of fruit? GRAPE. Yes/No

2   Is this word in capital letters? HOUSE. Yes/No

3   Does this word rhyme with dip? CHIP. Yes/No

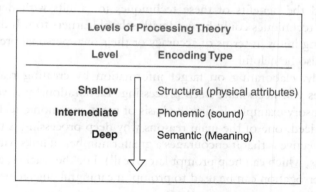

Figure 1.3 The levels of processing model, which focuses on whether information is processed meaningfully

The findings of the study were that even though the participants had paid attention to all of the items in order to process them and answer the questions, items that were linked to a meaning-based question, such as number 1 in the example above, were better remembered. This fit with the prediction of the theory that meaningful items are more deeply processed, leading to better LTM recall.

Using the theory

Importantly, it is not the words themselves that led to better recall in the Craik and Tulving experiment, but the activity that learners were prompted to do. This has implications for the way new material is presented in class – what matters is not the concepts that learners have to tackle, or even the specific worksheets or PowerPoints that a teacher uses, but the activity that a class has to undertake. This is what makes the key difference to encoding the information into LTM.

There are a variety of teaching techniques and activities that could lead to deeper processing. The essential point is to link information in a meaningful way, which generally means connecting it to schema knowledge (which, of course, varies slightly depending on the learner). Tasks that require learners to sort information into categories is inherently meaningful, as is using it for creating stories; Craik et al. (2007) explored the benefits of these techniques for adults with dementia, and the techniques could be used with school learners too. Judging or evaluating items in terms of accuracy or their own personal preference would also be helpful.

Finally, elaborating on target information by creating real-world examples will necessitate deep processing. Elaboration by developing multisensory examples is also the basis of many mnemonic techniques (and indeed, one of the main reasons why deep processing is thought to be effective is that it encourages a greater number of links with other concepts, which can help prompt later recall). For the teacher, elaborative interrogation can be used to prompt meaningful engagement with an idea. The use of 'how' and 'why' questions during classroom discussion, tutoring or teacher questioning therefore fits very well with this theoretical framework.

It should be noted that the theory has its limitations. It doesn't account for other key variables such as the learner's interests or the learning context, or explain the circumstances under which the learner will spontaneously engage in deep processing. However, it is useful in guiding us as teachers to ensure that the focus of a learning task is on meaningful connections rather than superficial processing.

Using the principles of memory and understanding

So far, this chapter has explained how key factors in memory can have a major impact on how well skills and ideas will be remembered and understood. The following section explains how planning decisions that teachers make can take account of these ideas.

Lesson planning

When preparing a lesson, a teacher will usually consider the quantity of information to be covered and decide how much detail will be appropriate for a given lesson, bearing in mind the limited time available to cover the syllabus. We know that good knowledge is essential for understanding, but we may be concerned about overloading learners with too many facts and ideas.

One initial consideration is to make target information stand out in terms of meaning and emotion. Lessons are often quite repetitive in structure – pupils sit in the same place, and listen to the same teacher in the same surroundings. A school day or class that is very distinctive (the school trip, the day you studied outside, the day a famous author visited the school) will tend to stand out amid otherwise forgettable lessons.

This can also be linked to the principle of context discussed above – learning that occurs in multiple contexts will be more easily accessed at a later date than learning from a single context.

If the above suggestion sounds like a recipe for mayhem, there are other ways of making information stand out. Books and teaching materials typically illustrate information with cartoons and photographs, and this fits with another well-established encoding principle: *dual coding*, the idea that learning information through two modalities (e.g. visual and auditory) boosts recall (see Clark and Paivio, 1991). Teaching the same idea in different ways, through both explanation and activities, can help, as well as gradually reinforcing the points with reading or other activities, which will lead to connections naturally forming in varied contexts.

Clearly, we also need to introduce the most important ideas when learners are most receptive to them. A very reliable finding in psychology is that for any series of items, people typically remember the first few items and the last few, and are much more likely to forget the ones in between (Murdock, 1962). This can easily be demonstrated in the classroom by asking pupils to remember 20 words that are read out one at a time, or 20 objects that are shown one after the other on a screen (see the demo task below). When it comes to classes, learners are likely to remember their first day and their final few classes, but remember the others less well, and the same applies within a class or activity.

This demonstration aims to show the serial position effect – most people remember items at the start and end of the list, and forget many of the other items. Hopefully, it should also demonstrate the importance of distinctiveness – an unusual item in this example stands out from the rest of the list and may be better remembered. Improved memory for unusual items is called the 'Von Restorff effect'.

Although the demonstration focuses on short-term memory, the serial position effect has been demonstrated in LTM too; Tulving (1983) notes that episodic LTM – our memories for life events – also shows this phenomenon. The obvious implication for teaching would

Task

Read the following list of items out loud. Then close the book, take a piece of paper, and write down all of the items that you can remember:

- Banana
- Phone
- Hat
- Mustard
- Business
- Sign
- Laptop
- Cake
- Pocket
- Gate
- Wheel
- Stairs
- Switch
- Mexico City
- Toothbrush
- Guitar
- Lane
- Blanket
- Paper

be to ensure that the messages that we give at the beginning and end of a lesson are the most important ones. Rather than using up the focused attention learners paid at the start to ask them about their weekend, take the class register or tell them a funny story, a teacher might begin with three or four crucial learning points for the lesson even before saying anything else at all, then take time for administrative or pastoral functions midway through, when learner attention levels have dropped.

Course planning

Beyond the structure of a single lesson, most of us are faced with the problem of how best to deliver a fixed syllabus over an inflexible period of time. If we are fortunate, we may have some control over tasks and timing, allowing us to exercise professional judgement regarding the order in which to present tasks, tests and revision activities. As the spacing effect implies that a time delay leads to superior learning, we can therefore ensure that learning of a particular concept is divided into at least two parts, spaced apart over a term or year.

A popular and understandable reason for not spacing things is a sense of neatness of teaching a single subtopic/text/theory in a single lesson, and perhaps the worry that covering the subtopic in more than one lesson essentially amounts to teaching it twice, and would therefore take too long. However, it should be emphasised that all experiments on spacing keep other variables constant, including the learning time. In fact, even if *less* time was spent on the material overall, spaced learning would still be more effective, and it could therefore be seen as a partial solution to an overly busy curriculum.

Another issue is that a brief or incomplete explanation may be ineffective, and Kang (2016) notes that despite the benefits of interleaving, it tends to be better to learn a new concept or skill in a block during the early stages. At times, a full explanation cannot be practically split into two or more shorter chunks. It may even be the case, though, counterintuitively, that an incomplete explanation has a more powerfully positive effect on memory than a complete one, rather like the lasting emotional impact of a cliffhanger in a TV show. Early research by Russian scientist Bluma Zeigarnik (1927) found that restaurant staff remembered incomplete orders better than ones that had already been delivered to the table, and were therefore mentally finished. This *Zeigarnik effect* may link to the increased attention given to unfinished tasks, and was supported in a study of the workplace showing that workers were more likely to think about incomplete than complete tasks when they got home (Smit, 2015). This could be applied to teacher explanations.

In judging when to return to material after a spacing interval, it appears that the optimal amount of time to be left between the first and second study session depends on when the eventual test/use of material will occur. Rohrer and Pashler (2007) concluded that the time between studying and restudying should be around 10–30 per cent of the time between the first study session and the final test/exam. Cepeda et al. (2008) looked at longer intervals of up to 350 days, and found a 5–10 per cent delay to be optimal. As they put it, 'The interaction of gap and test delay implies that many educational practices are likely to be highly inefficient' (p. 1095).

Overall, then, people tend to restudy too soon, and a gap of 10 per cent or a little more will work well within most school courses. As a practical example, that would mean waiting 20 days or more before review/testing on a topic if the exam was 200 days away. However, if we want our learners to gain enduring benefits from their work that they will apply to life and to their future studies, it would be best to have even longer spacing intervals, even *after* a course is complete. This could in part be achieved by broad interest-based reading of relevant information, as well as cross-curricular research projects. Küpper-Tetzel et al. (2014) point out that material is typically not reviewed a single time during the school year, but studied on three or more occasions, with decreasing gaps as a test approaches. However, their research suggested that for long-term retention, an expanding schedule (with the spacing gaps gradually increasing in size) or a fixed/regular schedule (e.g. reviewing once per month) were more effective.

The serial position effect, discussed above, also applies not just to a task or single lesson, but to a course as well. Rather than working through syllabus material in more or less the order that it is given by the exam board, another approach might be considered: tackle the most important points at the start and end, and the least important (the ones least likely to be in the exam or of long-term benefit to learners) towards the middle of the learning time.

Many of these points have implications not just for the classroom, but also for homework. Most obviously, there is much to be gained by spacing and interleaving homework tasks, by ensuring that they prompt learners to retrieve information or test themselves rather than reread, and by promoting links to meaningful, real-world examples. Homework is typically presented immediately after learning a concept, and often involves practice of the same tasks done in class (or doing something entirely unrelated). From a spacing effect perspective, it would be preferable to set a homework task several days or even weeks after the task was done in class, promoting the spaced retrieval of key ideas and, in effect, building revision into the course plan.

Judging task difficulty

Difficulty is another area where the workings of human memory are rather counterintuitive. It might be assumed that making a classroom task easier would help students to encode items into memory; in fact, a body of research has started to show quite the opposite – that making things harder for learners can actually increase long-term recall. Bjork and Bjork (2011) have called these obstacles *desirable difficulties* – an obvious example already described is retrieval practice rather than rereading information.

Spacing is also a form of desirable difficulty – it is more effective to revise after a gap, even if this means that you have forgotten some information, rather than straight away. Ironically, it appears that forgetting and relearning is more effective over the long-term than trying to maintain things in memory. This may be in part because consolidation tasks that are too easy result in reduced attention levels as we develop a false sense of mastery (Kornell et al., 2011). This doesn't mean that we should make things unnecessarily complex, but that our pupils may actually be learning more if it seems hard – even at times confusing or difficult – than if they are comfortable and too quick to think, 'Yes, I get it'.

Examples of ways in which desirable difficulties could be created in the classroom include:

- questioning learners after a 30-minute delay rather than immediately;
- interrupting a reading exercise with another task, then returning to it;
- having pupils summarise a topic in a very limited word count;

- presenting a new text as a gap-fill/close reading;
- not helping immediately if a pupil is struggling;
- asking learners to summarise a concept with textbooks closed rather than open;
- giving homework on a topic one month later rather than the same week;
- giving a short, low-stakes test rather than summarising a topic; and
- having learners rather than the teacher summarise each subtopic.

All of these things will promote learning through forcing learners to recall, think and use information (although some may resist such strategies as they tend to be more effortful!). It may concern teachers that structuring these desirable difficulties, such as having students test themselves rather than reread, will lead to more mistakes. This is true, but this should not be seen as a major problem. As Dweck (2006) has said, an openness to mistakes is part of a growth mindset – learners who view errors as useful feedback are likely to make more progress over the long term than those who stick to easier tasks in order to avoid making mistakes (see Chapter 3). It might concern teachers that incorrect guessing will somehow ingrain the mistake, but research by Kang et al. (2011) found no evidence of this – when forced to guess when unsure, students did no worse on a later test.

An important professional consideration for any teacher is that the desirability of a difficulty can be an interaction between the material and the learner themselves; it is, of course, possible to make things too difficult (McDaniel and Butler, 2011). McNamara et al. (1996) varied the difficulty of a biology text by removing key information. They found that learners with good knowledge remembered the text better after this increase in difficulty level but low-knowledge readers did worse. A simple explanation for the above and similar findings is that the text was already difficult enough for the weaker learners. If we assume that there is an optimum difficulty level, a given task may be too hard for some and too easy for others. This links to the

Yerkes-Dodson law, discussed above – people perform best when the level of challenge is neither too low nor too high. Ideally, therefore, a class set-up will push stronger learners out of their comfort zone, while allowing others more time and space to learn well. However, it doesn't mean that we should be deliberately hard on learners – this could lead to stress without adding desirable difficulty to learning tasks.

Revision and review

A common complaint among school learners is that much of what they do for their exams involves 'short-term' memorisation. Although their terminology is wrong (short-term memory in psychology research relates to immediate recall), their point is nevertheless valid – much of what is studied via cramming at exam time is simply forgotten within a few days or weeks of the exam. This links to another old and very reliable finding in psychology: the *forgetting curve*. New learning is subject to extensive forgetting, which is especially rapid in the initial hours or days.

As can be seen from Figure 1.4, a typical set of information could be subject to over 80 per cent forgetting inside as little as a month. On the other hand, if forgetting can be arrested for a month or so (e.g. by using quizzes and feedback) after two to four weeks the curve levels off, meaning there is a good chance that material will still be remembered six months or a year later.

Rapid initial forgetting may be one of the key reasons why the spacing effect is so effective. It also implies that failing to space is going to lead to a dramatic drop in what our learners are able to do, even within just a few days. In short, learning without spacing is tremendously inefficient! If pupils go over something within a single study session (sometimes called 'overlearning'), the repeated presentations of the information may boost short-term performance but have very little effect on LTM beyond a certain point (Landauer, 2011). Imagine applying more than

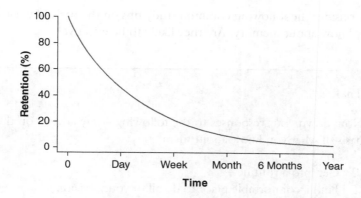

Figure 1.4 The forgetting curve displays the rapid loss of information from memory after it is initially learned

one coat of paint to a wall – the first coat needs to dry first before a second can effectively be applied. This concept was supported by Cepeda et al. (2008), who found that spacing works best when it takes place over days, rather than within a single day.

Positive learning habits

When learners are working through tasks or studying, whether in the classroom or elsewhere, they are likely to rely on inaccurate assumptions about memory, such as the idea that repeated rereading will be effective. As mentioned at the start of the chapter, learners also tend to underestimate the effect of their own actions on learning, and overestimate innate ability. In the broader context of learning, they may be influenced by study advice that they have heard or read over their years of schooling, too much of which, although well meaning, is likely to lack a foundation in research evidence. This becomes particularly important towards the later years of study as they prepare for exams, and in situations where learning takes place more independently.

Consider the following common study tips on the basis of what you now know about memory. Are they likely to be effective?

Task

Note down your responses to the following study advice, on the basis of what you know about memory:

1 Get into a routine.
2 Find a comfortable place to do all of your revision.
3 Use coloured pens to highlight notes.
4 Drink at least 2 litres of water per day.
5 Make mind maps.
6 Form an initial letter acronym/mnemonic.
7 Copy sections from your textbook on to notecards.
8 Have a relaxing bath.
9 Study with a group of friends.
10 Get an early night before your exams.

Feedback on task:

1 The value of a routine depends on what it is that the learner is routinely doing. Routines that involve ineffective studying (such as simple rereading of notes) are best discouraged. Good routines can certainly help to overcome the inertia and procrastination that many learners struggle with, but it is important to keep the level of variability high and avoid always studying material in the same way.
2 From a memory point of view, it would be best to learn in many different places, rather than to form an association with a single place (see the section on context, above).
3 Highlighting doesn't prompt recall from memory, and Dunlosky et al. (2013) describe its overall efficacy as 'low',

---

although Yue et al. (2015) argue that minimal and strategic use of colours to highlight different types of information could potentially promote deep processing.

4 We do know that a good diet and keeping hydrated can be beneficial for concentration (e.g. Gajre et al., 2008), but it is a myth that 2 litres of water is necessary (McCartney, 2010).

5 Mind maps do have potential as a study technique; they are visually distinctive (promoting dual coding) and require meaningful links to be made. They are better for an overview of course structure than for detailed knowledge; detailed knowledge is better revised via self-testing. If they are used, they would be best constructed 'closed book' to benefit from this testing effect rather than simple copying.

6 Mnemonics are primarily a recall technique rather than a learning technique, and do nothing to support the development of meaningful schema knowledge. They also have diminishing returns (how many times can we use 'one is a bun', for example?), but can be a helpful short-term prompt for lists of verbal information.

7 Notecards/flash cards can be very useful, but are best for summarising (requires deep processing) and self-testing. Although a little bit of incidental learning may occur, copying sections from a textbook is not an effective exam study strategy as it can be done without engaging with the meaning.

8 It is important to relax at least some of the time – among other things, stress is harmful for memory (McEwen and Sapolsky, 1995). However, this should probably not be the main focus of study advice.

9 Studying together can be motivating but also distracting, as the presence of others will divide our attention (see Chapter 2), harming the encoding of new information. However, peer testing and peer teaching can be very effective (Hattie,

(continued)

(continued)

2013), perhaps in part because both involve retrieval practice, or because of their potential for feedback.

10 As mentioned earlier, evidence is accumulating that sleep plays a critical role in memory consolidation and also affects attention levels. A student can choose to go to bed earlier and time their revision for the optimal benefit. To promote better-quality sleep, students would be best advised to limit screen time, especially in the hour immediately before going to sleep (Chang et al., 2015; Hysing et al., 2015). However, going to bed unusually early the night before an exam might just lead to worry and insomnia.

If you found this task difficult, don't worry – this simply reflects how we need factual evidence in order to give reliable advice to learners, to ensure that their time is not being wasted on ineffective strategies. In some cases, more research is still needed to provide a fuller picture of how learning works, but we can at least apply general principles based on memory research rather than rely on subjective assumptions. Learner revision tasks should therefore be guided by the same aspects of memory that influence classroom activities, as described in this chapter – a given amount of time spent on revision will be more effective if it is spaced out over several sessions, if concepts and skills within each subject discipline are interleaved rather than studied in a block, and if revision focuses on retrieval (e.g. self-testing or practice essays rather than rereading of notes). As learning depends on context, it would also be better to repeat material in a different context, which could include practising it in different formats, as a varied context limits the extent to which recall is context-specific, making it easier to transfer learning to new situations. Chapter 8 looks at issues relating to revision and independent learning in much more detail.

Conclusions

Memory is a key aspect of learning, and depends on forming meaningful schema knowledge to which new material can be linked. There are a number of effective interventions, such as retrieval practice, spacing and interleaving, that can relatively easily be applied to classroom tasks and materials without any need to fundamentally alter teaching materials or the way that teachers manage their lessons. Importantly, teaching that takes account of the science of memory does not require more time to do, and may even save time due to its greater efficiency. A key reason why its principles are not already more widely used is that both teachers and learners tend to misjudge the way that the human memory operates, being misled by short-term gains and avoiding effective strategies that make learning feel more effortful. An evidence-informed approach to planning classes and activities led by the teacher can begin to make systematic use of these principles, to the benefit of learners' overall levels of attainment and understanding.

Further reading

Make It Stick: The Science of Successful Learning by P. C. Brown, H. L. Roediger and M. A. McDaniel (Harvard University Press, 2014)
This is written as a popular science book, but two of the co-authors are memory researchers, and it expands upon and illustrates many of the principles that have been discussed in this chapter.

From the Laboratory to the Classroom: Translating Science of Learning for Teachers edited by J. C. Horvath, J. M. Lodge and J. Hattie (Routledge, 2016)
This edited volume contains chapters by active researchers in many of the issues that have been discussed in this chapter. Written in a way that is aimed at teachers, it is light on technical language and statistics, making it much more accessible than many other collections.

Making Good Progress? The Future of Assessment for Learning by D. Christodoulou (Oxford University Press, 2017)
Making a strong argument that educational success depends on accumulating factual knowledge, this accessible book examines and rethinks the popular 'assessment for learning' approach to feedback.

Memory by A. D. Baddeley, M. W. Eysenck and M. C. Anderson (Psychology Press, 2014)
A thorough and up-to-date guide to all aspects of the psychology of memory and cognition. Essentially an academic textbook, but very accessible and full of engaging activities.

Learning as a Generative Activity: Eight Learning Strategies that Promote Understanding by L. Fiorella and R. E. Mayer (Cambridge University Press, 2015)
This work focuses on the development of meaningful conceptual knowledge, drawing on evidence from e-learning and innovative classroom research to summarise eight key practical strategies for classroom use.

References

Baddeley, A. D. (1966). Short term memory for word sequences as a function of acoustic, semantic and formal similarity. *Quarterly Journal of Experimental Psychology*, 18, 362–365. doi: 10.1080/14640746608400055

Bjork, R. A. (2011). On the symbiosis of remembering, forgetting, and learning. In A. S. Benjamin (ed.), *Successful Remembering and Successful Forgetting: A Festschrift in Honor of Robert A. Bjork* (pp. 1–22). New York: Psychology Press.

Bjork, E. L. and Bjork, R. A. (2011). Making things hard on yourself, but in a good way: creating desirable difficulties to enhance learning. In M. A. Gernsbacher, R. W. Pew, L. M. Hough and J. R. Pomeranz (eds), *Psychology and the Real World: Essays Illustrating Fundamental Contributions to Society* (pp. 56–64). New York: Worth.

Cepeda, N. J., Vul, E., Rohrer, D., Wixted, J. T. and Pashler, H. (2008). Spacing effects in learning: a temporal ridgeline of optimal retention. *Psychological Science*, 19(11), 1095–1102. doi: 10.1111/j.1467-9280.2008.02209.x

Chang, A. M., Aeschbach, D., Duffy, J. F. and Czeisler, C. A. (2015). Evening use of light-emitting eReaders negatively affects sleep, circadian timing, and next-morning alertness. *PNAS*, 112(4), 1232–1237. doi: 10.1073/pnas.1418490112

Clark, J. M. and Paivio, A. (1991). Dual coding theory and education. *Educational Psychology Review*, 3(3), 149–210. doi: 10.1007/BF01320076

Craik, F. I. and Lockhart, R. S. (1972). Levels of processing: a framework for memory research. *Journal of Verbal Learning and Verbal Behavior*, 11(6), 671–684. doi: 10.1016/S0022-5371(72)80001-X

Craik, F. I. and Tulving, E. (1975). Depth of processing and the retention of words in episodic memory. *Journal of Experimental Psychology: General*, 104(3), 268–294.

Craik, F. I., Winocur, G., Palmer, H., Binns, M. A., Edwards, M., Bridges, K., et al. (2007). Cognitive rehabilitation in the elderly: effects on memory. *Journal of the International Neuropsychological Society*, 13(1), 132–142. doi: 10.1017/S1355617707070166

Dempster, F. (1996). Distributing and managing the conditions of encoding and practice. In E. L. Bjork and R. A. Bjork (eds), *Memory* (pp. 318–339). San Diego, CA: Academic Press.

Dunlosky, J., Rawson, K. A., Marsh, E. J., Nathan, M. J. and Willingham, D.T. (2013). Improving students' learning with effective learning techniques promising directions from cognitive and educational psychology. *Psychological Science in the Public Interest*, 14(1), 4–58. doi: 10.1177/1529100612453266

Dweck, C. S. (2006). *Mindset: How You Can Fulfil Your Potential*. London: Robinson Books.

Gajre, N. S., Fernandez, S., Balakrishna, N. and Vazir, S. (2008). Breakfast eating habit and its influence on attention-concentration, immediate memory and school achievement. *Indian Pediatrics*, 45(10), 824–828.

Hattie, J. (2013). *Visible Learning: A Synthesis of Over 800 Meta-Analyses Relating to Achievement*. London: Routledge.

Hyde, T. S. and Jenkins, J. J. (1973). Recall for words as a function of semantic, graphic, and syntactic orienting tasks. *Journal of Verbal Learning and Verbal Behavior*, 12(5), 471–480. doi: 10.1016/S0022-5371(73) 80027-1

Hysing, M., Pallesen, S., Stormark, K. M., Jakobsen, R., Lundervold, A. J. and Sivertsen, B. (2015). Sleep and use of electronic devices in adolescence: results from a large population-based study. *BMJ Open*, 5(1), e006748. doi: 10.1136/bmjopen-2014-006748

Kang, S. H. (2016). The benefits of interleaved practice for learning. In J. C. Horvath, J. M. Lodge and J. Hattie (eds), *From the Laboratory to the Classroom: Translating Science of Learning for Teachers* (pp. 79–93). London: Routledge.

Kang, S. H., Pashler, H., Cepeda, N. J., Rohrer, D., Carpenter, S. K. and Mozer, M. C. (2011). Does incorrect guessing impair fact learning? *Journal of Educational Psychology*, 103(1), 48–59. doi: 10.1037/a0021977

Karpicke, J. D., Lehman, M. and Aue, W. R. (2014). Retrieval-based learning: an episodic context account. In B. Ross (ed.), *Psychology of Learning and Motivation, Vol 61* (pp. 237–284). Waltham, MA: Academic Press.

Kornell, N. and Bjork, R. A. (2008). Learning concepts and categories: is spacing the 'enemy of induction'? *Psychological Science*, 19, 585–592. doi: 10.1111/j.1467-9280.2008.02127.x

Kornell, N., Rhodes, M. G., Castel, A. D. and Tauber, S. K. (2011). The ease-of-processing heuristic and the stability bias dissociating memory, memory beliefs, and memory judgments. *Psychological Science*, 22(6), 787–794. doi: 10.1177/0956797611407929

Küpper-Tetzel, C. E., Kapler, I. V. and Wiseheart, M. (2014). Contracting, equal, and expanding learning schedules: the optimal distribution of learning sessions depends on retention interval. *Memory & Cognition*, 42(5), 729–741. doi: 10.3758/s13421-014-0394-1

Landauer, T. K. (2011). Distributed learning and the size of memory: a 50-year spacing odyssey. In A. S. Benjamin (ed.), *Successful Remembering and Successful Forgetting: A Festschrift in Honor of Robert A. Bjork* (pp. 49–69). New York: Psychology Press.

Loftus, E. F. (2005). Planting misinformation in the human mind: a 30-year investigation of the malleability of memory. *Learning & Memory*, 12(4), 361–366. doi: 10.1101/lm.94705

McCartney, M. (2010). Waterlogged? *BMJ (Clinical Research Edition)*, 343. doi: 10.1136/bmj.d4280

McDaniel, M. A. and Butler, A. C. (2011). A contextual framework for understanding when difficulties are desirable. In A. S. Benjamin (ed.), *Successful Remembering and Successful Forgetting: A Festschrift in Honor of Robert A. Bjork* (pp. 23–47). New York: Psychology Press.

McDaniel, M. A., Roediger, H. L. and McDermott, K. B. (2007). Generalizing test-enhanced learning from the laboratory to the classroom. *Psychonomic Bulletin & Review*, 14(2), 200–206. doi: 10.3758/BF03194052

McDermott, K. B., Agarwal, P. K., D'Antonio, L., Roediger III, H. L. and McDaniel, M. A. (2014). Both multiple-choice and short-answer quizzes enhance later exam performance in middle and high school classes. *Journal of Experimental Psychology: Applied*, 20(1), 3–21. doi: 10.1037/xap0000004

McEwen, B. S. and Sapolsky, R. M. (1995). Stress and cognitive function. *Current Opinion in Neurobiology*, 5(2), 205–216. doi: 10.1016/0959-4388(95)80028-X

McNamara, D. S., Kintsch, E., Songer, N. B. and Kintsch, W. (1996). Are good texts always better? Interactions of text coherence, background knowledge, and levels of understanding in learning from text. *Cognition and Instruction*, 14, 1–43. doi: 10.1207/s1532690xci1401_1

Murdock Jr, B. B. (1962). The serial position effect of free recall. *Journal of Experimental Psychology*, 64(5), 482–488. doi: 10.1037/h0045106

Nairne, J. S., VanArsdall, J. E., Pandeirada, J. N., Cogdill, M. and LeBreton, J. M. (2013). Adaptive memory: the mnemonic value of animacy. *Psychological Science*, 24(10), 2099–2105. doi: 10.1177/0956797613480803

Pashler, H., McDaniel, M., Rohrer, D. and Bjork, R. A. (2008). Learning styles: concepts and evidence. *Psychological Science in the Public Interest*, 9(3), 105–119. doi: 10.1111/j.1539-6053.2009.01038.x

Pyc, M. A. and Rawson, K. A. (2009). Testing the retrieval effort hypothesis: does greater difficulty correctly recalling information lead to higher levels of memory? *Journal of Memory and Language*, 60(4), 437–447. doi: 10.1016/j.jml.2009.01.004

Rasch, B. and Born, J. (2013). About sleep's role in memory. *Physiological Review*, 93, 681–766. doi: 10.1152/physrev.00032.2012

Rawson, K. A. and Dunlosky, J. (2011). Optimizing schedules of retrieval practice for durable and efficient learning: how much is enough? *Journal of Experimental Psychology: General*, 140(3), 283. doi: 10.1037/a0023956

Roediger, H. L. and Karpicke, J. D. (2006). Test-enhanced learning: taking memory tests improves long-term retention. *Psychological Science*, 17, 249–255. doi: 10.1111/j.1467-9280.2006.01693.x

Rohrer, D. (2015). Student instruction should be distributed over long time periods. *Educational Psychology Review*, 27, 635–643. doi:10.1007/s10648-015-9332-4

Rohrer, D. and Pashler, H. (2007). Increasing retention without increasing study time. *Current Directions in Psychological Science*, 16(4), 183–186. doi: 10.1111/j.1467-8721.2007.00500.x

Rohrer, D., Dedrick, R. F. and Stershic, S. (2015). Interleaved practice improves mathematics learning. *Journal of Educational Psychology*, 107(3), 900–908. doi: 10.1037/edu0000001

Schacter, D. (2001). *The Seven Sins of Memory*. New York: Houghton Mifflin.

Smit, B. (2015). Successfully leaving work at work: the self-regulatory underpinnings of psychological detachment. *Journal of Occupational and Organizational Psychology*, 89(3), 493–514. doi: 10.1111/joop.12137

Smith, S. M., Glenberg, A. and Bjork, R. A. (1978). Environmental context and human memory. *Memory & Cognition*, 6(4), 342–353. doi: 10.3758/BF03197465

Soderstrom, N. C. and Bjork, R. A. (2015). Learning versus performance: an integrative review. *Perspectives on Psychological Science*, 10(2), 176–199. doi: 10.1177/1745691615569000

Soderstrom, N. C. and McCabe, D. P. (2011). Are survival processing memory advantages based on ancestral priorities? *Psychonomic Bulletin & Review*, 18(3), 564–569. doi: 10.3758/s13423-011-0060-6

Squire, L. R. (2004). Memory systems of the brain: a brief history and current perspective. *Neurobiology of Learning and Memory*, 82(3), 171–177. doi: 10.1016/j.nlm.2004.06.005

Tulving, E. (1983). *Elements of Episodic Memory*. New York: Oxford University Press.

Vygotsky, L. S. (1978). *Mind in Society: The Development of Higher Psychological Processes*. Cambridge, MA: Harvard University Press.

Wilson, S. (2016). Divergent thinking in the grasslands: thinking about object function in the context of a grassland survival scenario elicits more alternate uses than control scenarios. *Journal of Cognitive Psychology*, 28(5), 618–630. doi: 10.1080/20445911.2016.1154860

Wolfson, A. R. and Carskadon, M. A. (1998). Sleep schedules and daytime functioning in adolescents. *Child Development*, 69(4), 875–887. doi: 10.1111/j.1467-8624.1998.tb06149.x

Yue, C. L., Storm, B. C., Kornell, N. and Bjork, E. L. (2015). Highlighting and its relation to distributed study and students' metacognitive beliefs. *Educational Psychology Review*, 27, 69–78. doi: 10.1007/s10648-014-9277-z

Zeigarnik, B. (1927). Das Behalten erledigter und unerledigter Handlungen. *Psychologische Forschung*, 9, 1–85.

2 | Cognition

How do our learners take in and process information when tackling classroom tasks in the here and now? What limits are there on their processing abilities, and how can teachers manage their presentation of information to maximise success? This chapter explains these issues from the perspective of psychological concepts and research. In particular, it covers:

- Working memory – its structure and limitations.
- The role of executive function in how a learner plans and organises their response to a task.
- Distractions and mind-wandering.
- Biological, age-related changes to executive function and working memory.
- Lesson planning that accounts for learners' cognitive abilities and limitations.

The term 'cognition' is widely used in teaching and teacher education nowadays, amid the movement that aims to make educational practices more evidence-based. But what exactly does this term mean? *Cognition* can be defined as thinking and reasoning, and therefore it is relevant to a wide range of learning processes in the here and now. In other words, it describes whatever activities are going on in a person's mind at any given time.

Cognitive psychologists study a huge range of processes, including stereotypes, language, visual perception, and many other aspects of our daily lives, not all of which we are fully aware of ('cognitive science' is broader still, including fields such as linguistics and artificial intelligence). Encoding information to LTM is one cognitive process, but it is not the only one relevant to learning. It is also important to consider what learners think about, how they process and deal with learning tasks, and to address situations where they are not focused on learning at all.

There are two closely interlinked cognitive processes that form the heart of cognition in the here and now: *thinking* and *attention*. These provide a kind of gateway to the other aspects of cognition that affect education – information and ideas must first be noticed (attended to) and thought about or processed on some level before they can start to contribute to a person's learning and knowledge. This chapter will explain how these processes operate, and how they can guide teachers' decisions.

Attention and thinking

Attention has always been a major concept in classroom practice (who hasn't been reprimanded at some point in their life for not paying attention?) and cognitive psychologists use the term in essentially a similar way to its everyday meaning. From a cognition point of view, however, attention has certain key characteristics that can be studied scientifically and which can inform the design of teaching activities. It also plays an essential role in other cognitive processes such as memory. Curiosity is a key driver in attention that can be observed from early infancy (Gopnik, 2016), and the resulting intrinsic motivation – finding things interesting for their own sake – has been shown to affect memory on a neural level, due in part to increased attention (Gruber et al., 2014).

One key facet of attention that is of immediate relevance to teachers is that it is considered to be a limited resource, which can be subdivided between one or more tasks. In other words, the more attention taken up by one task, the less that is available for others. This feature has broad-ranging implications for how to design lessons and activities in order to ensure that learners are focusing on learning, rather than on demanding but non-essential activities.

Thinking is such a broad term that researchers often divide it into several subprocesses. However, overall, the important consideration for educators is that information must be processed after it has been paid attention to. In other words, we need to know about what learners are doing when working on a task, how thinking works, and what implications this has for learning, discussion, group work and intelligence. Such an understanding can guide teachers to better support learners and lead to more successful learning.

What are the key principles of cognition?

Working memory

Up until the 1960s, the term *short-term memory* (or 'primary memory') was used to describe temporary memory lasting for a few seconds. However, this term misleadingly suggests that when a learner receives in the here and now, it is simply passively retained, when in fact they may use the information and manipulate it in various ways while completing a task. The term has also come to be used inaccurately in schools and society more broadly; many people incorrectly suggest that revision for exams involves short-term memory, but in fact any retention of information over hours or days actually depends on LTM (although it may well involve using it ineffectively, in a way that is rapidly forgotten).

The term *working memory* has begun to be used instead over recent decades. An important change in emphasis is that working memory is assumed to be responsible for processing abilities and completion of tasks (e.g. having a conversation or following the steps of a recipe). Nevertheless, it is still generally seen as having a limited capacity, meaning that only a small amount of information can be taken in and held at a given time, and that this information can be rapidly forgotten if nothing is done to ensure that it is transferred to LTM.

Examples of tasks that can be done by working memory include almost anything that a learner processes while in the classroom (e.g. keeping things in mind for a few seconds before writing them down, or listening to an explanation). In maths, it might involve a learner temporarily storing one part of a problem while they solve another (e.g. if they have to mentally multiply 12 × 15, they may initially multiply the digits together while retaining other parts of the problem and their progress through them on a mental 'to do' list).

It's also important to appreciate that working memory can deal with many different types of information, including both images and words. In the early history of our species, our verbal working memory capacity probably evolved in order to allow us to hold a conversation, while the visual-spatial store processes objects and movements in a real-world environment. It can also be used to imagine the same activities, such as when visualising how two sticks could be joined together.

Working memory abilities vary between individuals and improve throughout childhood. Gathercole et al. (2004) showed that the main components of working memory increase steadily in their capacity between ages 5 and 14 (it's worth noting that they didn't find the sudden increases that might be expected if cognitive development occurs in a series of stages, as proposed by Piaget's theories).

The development of working memory is particularly critical at a young age, as it sets up a young learner for tasks throughout the rest of their education. Children below the age of 8 will really struggle with some tasks that are easy for their older schoolmates, such as mental arithmetic and dictation. It is vital to practise activities that draw on working memory at this age, but there is no need to make it arduous; activities such as classroom games that involve mentally juggling more than one item will naturally stretch and develop working memory abilities. If a child in mid-primary school still really struggles with tasks such as repeating back a short list of words or numbers, it would be worthwhile to refer them to a speech and language therapist.

For groups of pupils in their teenage years, differences in working memory capacity will no doubt be present, and these are likely to correlate with academic success. It will be more difficult to address deficits at this stage, as the key biological developments have already taken place, and studies of 'brain training' activities suggest that they do not transfer well to situations beyond the specific tasks being practised (Simons et al., 2016). Nevertheless, anyone who is essentially able to function in everyday life does have the basics of working memory in place, as it is essential for daily tasks, from getting dressed to holding a conversation. Therefore, when older learners struggle to focus on complex tasks, this may be due to lack of background knowledge, or so-called non-cognitive factors such as issues with motivation (Farrington et al., 2012).

Overall, psychologists are increasingly becoming aware of how much the working memory is influenced by experience. As neuroscientist Sarah Jane Blakemore has argued, it is possible to get much better at non-verbal reasoning through regular practice – a finding that speaks against the idea that abilities are fixed in an individual, or that some learners are incapable of succeeding (Amass, 2017).

The rest of this section looks at a number of cognitive abilities that all pertain to working memory in one way or another, while the following section describes a theory of how its components operate as a whole system.

Executive function

The abilities to plan, make decisions, analyse progress, set goals, inhibit harmful actions and check whether or not we are on track – psychologists typically call these coordinating abilities our 'executive functions' (or 'function', collectively). One way of defining executive function is to include any cognitive abilities that involve the control of other, simpler abilities (Logie, 2016). When interacting with others, the ability to 'mind-read' (i.e. accurately surmise what they are thinking) appears to depend on executive function (Carlson and Moses, 2001). This set of abilities is vital to a great many actions, including regulating our own learning. They are largely domain-neutral, meaning that they apply to many different types of task, and therefore that a learner who is good at setting goals or staying on task in one setting will also tend to be good at it in a different situation, other things being equal.

Executive function depends on attention, but is not the same thing – attending to a complex task is necessary but not sufficient to complete it. In a way, attention can be viewed as the fuel of executive functions, as these processes tend to demand a lot of attention in order to run, although some researchers (e.g. Hassin et al., 2009) have argued that at least some of the processes must operate with minimal conscious awareness.

They are also highly dependent on the biological development of the brain throughout the early part of the lifespan, and in particular on the *prefrontal cortex*, a large area at the front of the brain. Executive functions develop rapidly between ages 5 and 8, with planning and task inhibition skills emerging alongside greatly improved problem-solving. Planning continues to increase steadily throughout adolescence, while other executive functions improve much more gradually beyond age 11 (Romine and Reynolds, 2005).

It is hardly contentious to suggest that younger children can struggle to control their own behaviour. What may be more surprising is that the essential biological development underpinning executive function continues much later than was previously thought. Although the overall size and shape of the prefrontal cortex is complete by adolescence, its interconnections and functional abilities continue to change until at least our early twenties, with increasing levels of myelinated nerve fibres (often called the 'white matter' of the brain) connecting different areas together, and allowing more rapid and efficient cognitive processes, while the overall number of connections decreases (Blakemore and Choudhury, 2006). It is a striking thought that most people will not only have finished their compulsory education, but may also have completed their further studies, by the time their brain's executive functions finish maturing.

A further complication is that adolescents' decision-making processes are strongly influenced by the presence of peers – helping to explain why the knowledge and cognitive abilities to understand risky behaviour such as drug taking and drink-driving are often insufficient to prevent them taking these risks in social situations (Steinberg, 2007). Indeed, the importance of social development from puberty onwards may be a major reason why the brain undergoes major changes at this point in the lifespan. Blakemore and Mills (2014) refer to adolescence as a sensitive period for social development, which fits with the idea that the human brain as a whole evolved its large size due to the pressure to maintain information about our complex social groups (Dunbar, 1998).

Perhaps most importantly, brain development throughout later childhood and adolescence presents major educational opportunities as well as challenges: 'If early childhood is seen as a major opportunity – or a sensitive period – for teaching, so too might adolescence . . . the adolescent brain is malleable and adaptable – this is an excellent opportunity for learning and creativity' (Blakemore and Mills, 2014, p. 200). Certain things can impact on the executive functions of self-control and planning, most obviously stress and fatigue (Arnsten et al., 2012). People concentrate less well and are more stressed and frustrated in situations with a lot of random background noise, and over the longer term, children exposed to chronic background traffic noise show poorer levels of reading comprehension (Cohen et al., 1973; Stansfeld et al., 2005).

A study of early primary school children by Ching (2017) showed a curious relationship between executive function and stress, in the context of maths anxiety. As might be expected, young learners with better developed executive abilities are able to use more advanced strategies when tackling maths problems, and therefore achieve more highly in maths. However, despite their abilities, such pupils were found to be more vulnerable to the effects of anxiety – it made a bigger difference to their achievement. This may be because intrusive thoughts linked to anxiety interfere with executive functions, and perhaps also consume limited working memory capacity. In contrast, the simpler strategies chosen by lower-achieving students were not greatly affected by maths anxiety.

As sleep deprivation can harm executive function, we need to be aware of the impact that fatigue can have on education, in addition to its role in LTM, discussed in Chapter 1. There is increasing evidence that young children are going to bed later than in the past and attending school tired, something that has been tentatively linked to increased screen time disrupting the release of the sleep hormone melatonin. For example, Chang et al. (2015) studied the effects of light-emitting e-reader screens, finding that they not only delayed sleep, but also affected levels of essential REM sleep and reduced participants' alertness the following morning.

A teacher may be limited in terms of what they can do to influence noise and tiredness, but there are some interventions that can be considered. Some schools have experimented with barefoot learning to reduce noise (Saner, 2016), and for particular pupils with additional sensory needs, special arrangement may be worthwhile, such as doing some or all of their learning in quieter environments or online.

Attention levels vary through the school day, tending to be higher in the mid-morning. However, as a child ages, their body's circadian rhythms adjust to a later timescale, meaning that most adolescents find it comfortable to stay up late. With a fixed school start time, this will impact on their functioning the next day. Later start times for older year groups may not always be an option in your context, but it is worth bearing in mind that many teenagers are operating in a state comparable to jet lag, and may struggle to maintain attention even when motivated. When learners have important choices to make, such as when planning their study time or reflecting on teacher feedback, it is best to avoid times when they are especially tired, as well as limiting the influence of peers by setting tasks to be done individually.

The neuroscience of executive function is even more directly relevant to pastoral care than to classroom teaching. An awareness that teenagers are prone to taking risks and making unwise decisions is nothing new, but perhaps we do not fully allow for this in curriculum choices, with learners making important decisions about subject choice at a relatively young age (in contrast to Finland, for example, where a broad curriculum is mandatory until age 15). Taking risky decisions, especially where group pressure is a factor, should be seen as the norm, and PSHE may benefit from evidence-based lessons about how pupils' behaviour and choices are likely to differ when surrounded by peers.

Distractions and mind-wandering

As mentioned above, the term 'attention' is used in cognitive psychology in a similar way to its use in everyday life – it is largely synonymous with 'focus'. If people do not pay attention, then they will fail to take in information, impacting on later performance or memory.

Of course, it is much easier to devote our attention to tasks in some circumstances than others, and attention is likely to dip over time – either on a difficult activity, or simply over the course of a normal day. Maintaining constant focus on a task that is not meaningfully engaging puts stress on the learner and pushes the limits of their cognitive resources, leading to frequent errors or slips (Grier et al., 2003). What we pay attention to is only partially voluntary – it is very easy to be distracted by something with more immediate significance, stealing attention away from learning tasks, and therefore important for teachers to limit distractions where possible.

Besides external distractions, learners' attention can lapse as they become lost in thought. *Mind-wandering* is essentially just research terminology for what is more commonly known as daydreaming – those moments where a pupil ceases to focus on their surroundings or the task at hand. In other words, it is a state that is likely to occur when a learner fails to sustain their attention, but has not been distracted – perhaps they are staring out of the window, or doodling, or just thinking about what they did yesterday. To put it more technically, mind-wandering is a state where thoughts are focused internally. It is particularly likely to occur during a low-demand activity.

When it comes to listening to teacher explanations or lecture-style classes, it is sometimes claimed that people only learn from the first 10 minutes, and although this is an oversimplification (Wilson and Korn, 2007), it does appear that learners of all ages are prone to mind-wandering during teacher talk. In an experiment on university students that featured lecture-style material, Risko et al. (2012) found a rate of around 40 per cent of mind-wandering overall, with this rate increasing later in the lecture. Of course, the age of learners makes a difference; one of the main explanations of mind-wandering is that it is the default state, and that executive functions of planning and goal direction are required to remain on task when learning (Pachai et al., 2016). This ability therefore tends to improve with age, but is subject to large individual differences and varies with the nature of the task.

Minimising distractions is standard teaching practice, but it's useful to understand the psychology behind this – and worth giving learners a cognitive explanation for it can be harmful, as pupils are otherwise likely to overestimate their own ability to multitask successfully. Internet use during learning time is negatively associated with test performance, at least among university students (Ravizza, 2014). This fits with what we know about working memory and attention being limited, and appears to be true for both low and high achievers. Learners are also likely to underestimate the extent to which other people observe their behaviour, such as teachers being able to spot covert phone checking – a research finding that has been amusingly termed the 'invisibility cloak illusion' (Boothby et al., 2017).

Mind-wandering is best seen as a natural side effect of thinking and learning, and is probably inevitable; it constitutes as much as 50 per cent of people's thinking time, so it's not going to disappear, regardless of what teachers do. Controlling it is a metacognitive skill that requires effort (Smallwood et al., 2007), and the ability to do so will therefore increase with age and will be greater in some individuals than others. Teachers should be aware that some situations – such as reading and lengthy explanations/demonstrations – are especially likely to trigger mind-wandering.

Focus on a task appears to be especially challenging for learners with poorer executive functions, but this can be addressed by altering task difficulty; Xu and Metcalfe (2016) found that being given tasks that are challenging but not too difficult – those in what psychologists sometimes refer to as the region of proximal learning – led to reduced mind-wandering (see Chapter 8, as well as the points made in Chapter 1 about individual levels of challenge and desirable difficulties). One classic study of school pupils across 12 schools by Edmiston and Braddock (1941) recommended that to boost engagement, teaching activities should prioritise relevance, increase levels of student participation, ensure that students have been well prepared for the task, and ensure clarity of instructions. It also recommended combining both verbal and visual aspects of learning.

Mind-wandering would appear to be an unambiguously bad thing for education, and it certainly has an impact on the ability to encode new information to memory. However, mind-wandering may have its benefits. Baird et al. (2012) found that when doing a creativity test, learners who did a simple task during a short break – promoting mind-wandering – subsequently did better than those who did either a demanding task or no task at all. There may therefore be hidden benefits to defocusing for a short while, and mulling over prior events.

It is also likely that most learning tasks are more effective if they are not too intensive for too long – learners may require a period of time where new information can be consolidated and integrated with previous learning, while prolonged intensive focus may cause stress, harming executive functioning (McEwen and Morrison, 2013). Taking into account these considerations, a practical approach could be for teachers to make it clear to learners when total focused attention is required, and otherwise tolerate occasional short periods of mind-wandering, such as during long writing or research tasks.

Habits such as doodling are seen by many teachers as a distraction, but a curious finding by Andrade (2010) showed that learners who were doodling were better able to concentrate on a listening task. It may therefore make sense to tolerate and even encourage doodling, fiddling with objects (as long as it is not distracting for others) and other routine habits; they may relax children, while the minimal cognitive load involved might be a price worth paying for keeping them better focused on the learning task at hand.

Automaticity

As discussed above, a key characteristic of attention is that it is limited at any given time, meaning that the more we divide our attention, the poorer task performance will be. However, this is modified by another important phenomenon – *automaticity*. This means that as a task becomes more familiar, the amount of attention it requires reduces, until we can do them without having to give them much thought, if any at all. Indeed, it may well be the case that the bulk of a person's cognitive processes take place largely automatically, without a conscious decision to do the task in question; according to Bargh and Chartrand (1999, p. 462), 'most of a person's everyday life is determined not by their conscious intentions and deliberate choices but by mental processes . . . that operate outside of conscious awareness and guidance'.

In the classroom, automaticity means that a learner's attention will largely be focused on new or highly complex tasks (e.g. learning a new theory or teaching a concept to a peer), while many other simpler processes (e.g. sipping from a bottle of water) can take place in the cognitive background. A key educational example is the way that simple spellings or multiplication sums – initially effortful for a child – become quick and easy with practice. This frees up the child's attention span to focus on more complex tasks for which these simpler skills are essential building blocks.

Other examples of tasks that can become largely automatic include:

- throwing, pouring, and other physical skills;
- playing a familiar musical sequence;
- reciting the alphabet; and
- categorising simple objects.

As specific skills become automatic, the overall level of demand of a learning situation can be increased. Nevertheless, there are limits – to become automatic, something needs to be routine, so things that are highly creative or novel do not become automatic. Even advanced learners can't generate random numbers or write a poem automatically.

Also, automaticity has its drawbacks – mistakes and flaws can also become automatic. Processes such as stereotyping (a form of categorisation), flawed study strategies, and harmful assumptions can all take place with very little conscious attention. Because of the reduced level of attention paid to them, it becomes increasingly hard for a learner to even notice that they are doing them, and they are therefore difficult to correct. A major example of this – familiar to most teachers – are the spelling and grammatical errors that appear to have become ingrained despite corrective feedback.

Arguably the most important example of automaticity from an educational point of view is reading. The development of this skill is a key aim throughout curricula worldwide. Given the huge volume of vocabulary items and the near-infinite combinations into which they can be arranged, memory researchers such as Landauer (2011) have suggested that most language learning takes place implicitly rather than through effortful study (this makes a lot of sense when you consider how much language learning occurs before the age of 2). The implication is that it is exposure to a lot of reading in context, rather than in-depth study of grammatical structures or vocabulary, that leads to reading becoming automatic and fluent (Krashen, 2009; Nation, 2017).

In terms of the contrast between automatic and more deliberate thinking, teachers can encourage both modes of thought; problems benefit from being both estimated quickly and then worked out more methodically. Doing the former can provide a useful element of quality control, flagging up missteps in the slower process. According to fuzzy-trace theory, a gist-based representation is not a degraded version of the more precise mental process, but a largely separate mode of thought that occurs simultaneously, and has separate properties (Reyna, 2012). However, it is important to bear in mind that in most contexts the ability to make quick and accurate estimates depends on experience, and will therefore benefit from deliberate practice over time (Ericsson, 2008).

When it comes to correcting automatic mistakes, the key obstacle is that the correction depends on paying attention – precisely the process that is being bypassed with increased automaticity. A pupil may pay attention to their feedback on an essay and be aware that they made particular spelling mistakes, but this does not stop them from repeating the automatic mistakes next time around. Think, for example, of how often you hear someone incorrectly say 'dice' as a singular, even if they know the correct word is 'die', or how often well-educated people mistakenly use 'it's' as a possessive. It is essential to slow down the problematic action, flagging up the mistake at the time that the task is being done, and slowly going through the replacement action until it becomes more automatic than the error. At the very least, the learner needs to slow down and focus attention on the area that is causing a problem, engaging a more conscious decision-making process (e.g. stopping to think whether the correct spelling is 'there', 'their' or 'they're'). This is standard practice in sports and music instruction but arguably less so in language and maths, where feedback tends to be given after a whole task has been completed.

The pace of a curriculum can make things worse rather than better – attention is focused on the new task, and anything that can be is delegated to automatic processes, leading to habitual errors becoming increasingly automatic and ingrained. Many primary teachers will focus on fluency in creative writing and ignore spelling, deciding quite correctly that trying to be correct in spelling will be a distraction from the task itself. On the other hand, the earlier habitual problems are tackled, the easier they are to solve, and it might be best to avoid practising mistakes, as undoing these habits will lead to more work in the long run. An alternative could be for young children to engage in oral storytelling prior to developing more accurate writing skills.

Automaticity is basically a good thing – without it, we'd struggle to cope with day-to-day life. Everything from getting dressed to reading to driving a car involves automated processes. Despite the habitual errors that can creep in, we shouldn't lose sight of the fact that we really do want learners to do the basics such as reading and arithmetic automatically. With years of experience, it's even possible to develop highly complex pattern recognition processes via quick, accurate, automatic judgements that we have little control over (Gladwell, 2006), and which are often just as accurate – or more so – than more protracted thought processes. One study found that for a reliable connection between people's own reports of their personality and short video clips of their body language observed by others, a 30-second clip was just as effective as a five-minute-long version (Ambady and Rosenthal, 1992).

One factor in increasing reading, besides pure exposure and practice, is a child's level of background knowledge. As they read, a learner is constantly (and automatically) accessing stored knowledge from their memory in order to understand the text. Moss (2008) has argued that due to an emphasis on stories in the early years, learners get insufficient practice of reading non-fiction, harming their ability to develop a broad background knowledge. Non-fiction texts can provide practice of reading while building knowledge, thus boosting automaticity of reading in two ways simultaneously. Providing a broad choice of reading material and tapping into existing interests can help to motivate young learners to enjoy non-fiction (Moss and Hendershot, 2002).

Cognitive load

Cognitive load has become a popular concept in education, though it is arguably less well-accepted among cognitive psychologists. This is because it does not describe a precisely defined process, but more of a general limitation that educators should consider – the essential idea being that people learn better if their limited cognitive capacity is not overloaded.

Drawing again on a computer analogy of the mind, Sweller (1994) has suggested that we have limited processing power, and using this on non-essential tasks will harm learning. This is similar to the concept of limited attention discussed above, but it is broader, as it covers all aspects of cognition – in particular, both working memory and executive functions are assumed to be included. Essentially, it implies that the level of detail and complexity should be 'just right', neither underusing or overloading the mind's limited capacity. This is the case because students are novices, and therefore when learning they rely more on limited working memory capacity more than on stored schema knowledge (Sweller et al., 2011). What determines the load of a task is its level of interactivity, which is based both on how many elements the task has, and how well related these are in the learner's understanding. If a learner's schema knowledge allows them to chunk elements into a single item, this reduces the cognitive load – and therefore the cognitive load of a task depends partly on knowledge and prior experience.

Sweller's ideas are supported by a range of evidence. For example, research into individual differences in pupils shows that high-knowledge learners tend to take in new information better than low-knowledge learners (Bransford et al., 2000), but this effect can disappear or even be reversed when the new information is given in greater detail. In one study, pupils' learning from a simulation about chemistry was compared when components were represented with verbal labels (e.g. a picture of a burner labelled 'temperature') or by the word alone. High-knowledge students actually did *worse* with the pictorial aid (Lee et al., 2006). The conclusion can be that these learners actually benefit from sparser sets of information, as details can add extraneous cognitive load. In contrast, a less detailed explanation would be harder for the less knowledgeable learners to understand, so for them, more details were beneficial.

These ideas fit well with some aspects of traditional educational practice, where more advanced pupils are expected to learn with less support in the way of examples and illustrations, even if it remains unintuitive that such details would result in worse performance. A limitation of the concept is that it fails to make a clear distinction between different cognitive processes that can happen simultaneously, instead treating working memory as a single system that stops functioning when it is too full. While popular in the late 1960s (e.g. Atkinson and Shiffrin, 1968), a unitary model of working memory has long been superseded by models that are more explicit about separate processes within working memory (e.g. Baddeley's model described in the following section of this chapter), for example visual and verbal components of working memory. There is also a lack of consistency in terms of how to measure the cognitive load of a task, leading to uncertainty about its effects (Naismith and Cavalcanti, 2015).

The basic premise here is that it is important not just to minimise unnecessary demands, but also to ensure that learners' mental efforts are focused on processes that are relevant to the intended learning. Sweller et al. (2011) refer to this as intrinsic rather than extraneous cognitive load. The efforts that learners make should focus on the educational target, avoiding unnecessary processing. For example, this could mean avoiding spelling homework tasks where the aim is to learn the spellings of target words, but much effort is expended in generating context-free novel sentences containing these words.

One counterintuitive assumption of the theory is that providing learners with a problem-solving task can actually be harmful, as learners must maintain both the task and the goal in their limited working memory. In other words, having to remember the aim uses up limited working memory capacity, so learners may actually learn better if they are given a task to do without being given the aim or goal. What's better, though, according to Sweller et al. (2011), is to give learners a worked example. This shows the problem together with all of its steps. It demonstrates the correct solution and the steps to reach it. By reducing the cognitive load, a worked example allows more of the mind's processing power to focus on learning. As learning progresses, however, problem-solving can start to be introduced.

One problem with this idea is that research into LTM suggests that at times, making things difficult for learners results in more durable learning (see Chapter 1). It is therefore over-simplistic to conclude from the concept of cognitive load that our job is always to simplify things for the learner. However, it is certainly valuable to ensure that classroom tasks focus on intrinsic cognitive load, and minimise extraneous demands. It is also useful to recognise that the difficulty of a task can be very high for a beginner as even a few separate elements within a task can overtax working memory.

Metacognition

Metacognition is a slightly ambiguous term, with some educators using it so broadly that it seems to cover any kind of thinking and processing that takes place during learning. However, a stricter definition is that it refers to any type of thinking about thinking. This could include, for example, thinking about our own memory abilities, or about the processes we use when solving a problem, or about our own planning and organisation skills. In terms of classroom activities, metacognition includes monitoring our own learning activities (e.g. noticing errors and keeping track of the steps taken when solving a problem – the latter example is known as metacognitive monitoring).

These abilities may seem rather similar to the executive functions described in the previous section, but there are important differences. Any executive function has a 'meta' equivalent when the learner thinks about or reflects on that function – so, for example, planning is an executive function, while thinking about one's own planning process is a form of metacognition. These processes do depend on attention and executive function, though, and therefore will be difficult for certain learners (e.g. the very young, those who are overly tired or distracted, or those who are struggling with the subject matter and require nearly all of their attention just to complete the task).

Additionally, metacognition draws heavily on knowledge and beliefs – especially beliefs about learning, which can be flawed. Metacognitive monitoring can be inaccurate because introspection is a poor way of understanding thinking (which is why psychology largely abandoned it as a research method over a century ago!). Sometimes, learners may have very little awareness of how they solved a problem, even when they got the answer correct. A good example of the role of beliefs comes from a study by Glenberg and Epstein (1987), where students were shown two texts – one about music and one about physics. Learners were experienced in one subject but not in the other. Their judgements of their own understanding of the text proved to be more accurate about the subject that they had less knowledge in. In other words, it is easy for a learner to overestimate their understanding based on such factors as beliefs about their own abilities. And as mentioned in Chapter 8, learners overestimate the quality of examples that they generate themselves.

Most teachers will wish to ensure that learners can accurately assess their own progress – something that education researchers have called 'visible learning' (Hattie, 2012; Rinaldi and Gardner, 2001). Indeed, Hattie's meta-analysis of the efficacy of interventions gives prominence to accurate self-assessment and formative evaluation – techniques that provide feedback to a learner and that prompt them to think about their own learning processes.

Some educators appear to see metacognition as a kind of silver bullet for all educational problems – it's certainly too much to expect that this alone will lead to all learners becoming more motivated and spotting all of their own mistakes. Additionally, promoting metacognition may directly conflict with the desire to reduce extraneous cognitive load, and teachers may prefer to focus purely on a learning task rather than asking learners to reflect on their own work.

On the other hand, metacognition can undoubtedly help with self-evaluation and learning from mistakes in the right context. Tackling it is particularly appropriate in situations where poor planning or failure to monitor progress appears to be playing a role in a learner's difficulties (e.g. when questions are not being read correctly, leading to a lot of time being spent answering the wrong thing). Some possible strategies for facilitating metacognition in these scenarios include:

- allocating time to discussing how to answer a problem as a class or group, rather than starting to answer them straight away;
- rewarding appropriate processes, including self-evaluation, rather than just correct answers; and
- explicitly asking students to comment on their own thought processes as part of a post-task plenary, or for homework.

Inaccurate metacognitive beliefs about one's own learning can lead to inadequate revision for tests. Indeed, learners are generally poor at judging what they do and do not understand (Küpper-Tetzel, 2017). Feedback can be very useful for tackling this problem, but especially when learners attempt to retrieve information first and are then given corrective feedback (Rawson and Dunlosky, 2007). Similarly, marking can be tackled with metacognition in mind. To boost a learner's understanding of their own learning processes, marking could be conducted alongside a learner – at least on occasion – for them to more easily appreciate the thinking behind the feedback.

The benefits of metacognition are likely to be greater for older and more experienced learners as good habits become automatic, but misconceptions can also have a more damaging effect; after all, when learners study more independently, their beliefs – rather than those of the teacher or course designer – come to the fore (see Chapter 8).

A theory: Baddeley's working memory model

As discussed earlier, researchers have gradually developed a more sophisticated conception of working memory, which is now seen as a flexible and active system for processing incoming information and completing tasks in the here and now. Beginning in the 1970s, Baddeley and colleagues (e.g. Baddeley and Hitch, 1974) presented a theory that distinguished between verbal and visual processing systems

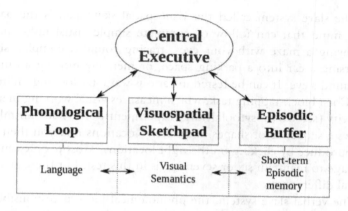

Figure 2.1 Baddeley's working memory model

(previous theories had seen short-term memory as a unitary system). Their model focused around a 'central executive', a component that is based on attention and is responsible for the executive functions described in the previous section. Baddeley and colleagues believe that the central executive controls the other, simpler functions of working memory. These other 'slave systems' can only process specific types of information (e.g. word sounds), and can hold small amounts of information in the here and now. Without the involvement of the central executive, they can only do tasks that are routine and relatively automatic. Figure 2.1 shows the most recent version of the model (Baddeley, 2000).

Using the slave systems

The key slave systems – at least those that are understood and described so far – are a verbal and a visual system, called the 'phonological loop' and the 'visuospatial sketchpad' respectively as well as the 'episodic buffer' which is responsible for linking sensory stimuli together into a coherent event.

The slave system called the visuospatial sketchpad is the part of your mind that can follow or complete simple visual tasks such as following a maze with your eyes, tracing round a complex shape, reversing a car into a parking space, or mentally moving around in the mind's eye. It can be tested in various ways; try looking online for the Corsi block-tapping task, which measures visual working memory capacity (see www.psytoolkit.org/experiment-library/corsi.html) – it shows a sequence of shapes in different locations that you then have to reproduce by clicking on the right locations. Most people can only manage to maintain six or seven items in this test, but there are individual differences.

The verbal slave system, the phonological loop, is responsible for all language-based processing, including both written language and spoken/heard words. It is important in most educational settings, due to the highly verbal nature of most lessons and exams. Although it probably plays a role in the passive learning of verbal information that occurs when speaking and reading (Baddeley, 2000), its primary role is to take in and hold items while we are using them, such as a string of numbers that we need to use in a puzzle, or a phrase that is heard and then written down in a student's notebook. Again, its capacity is small – most people would struggle to hold more verbal information than could be spoken in just under two seconds (Schweickert and Boruff, 1986).

The basic structures shown by the working memory model appear to be complete by age 6, after which they develop steadily in capacity without the need for any particular intervention (Gathercole et al., 2004). Individual differences could be very significant in terms of educational performance – a greater capacity of the phonological loop, for example, could affect a learner's ability to follow instructions, to process complex verbal tasks (such as parsing sentences or working out anagrams), and to take in new vocabulary. Such individuals will have a head start in education that will only increase over time, as their better verbal ability results in the development of superior vocabulary and factual knowledge.

Using the model

An important implication from a teacher's point of view is what this model tells us about multitasking. The slave systems can work simultaneously, meaning that people can complete, for example, a simple visual task at the same time as a simple verbal task without any major reduction in speed or accuracy. However, if either task were more complex, it would start to draw heavily on the limited attention available via the central executive. Attention is shown to be at the very heart of working memory, and anything that distracts learners will have a detrimental effect, at least when it comes to their performance on relatively novel (rather than automated) tasks. Our central executive deploys our limited attentional resources to make key decisions, plan processes and inhibit choices. Again, any concurrent task will reduce performance, but complex or creative tasks are especially intrusive.

The model helps to provide more detail to the concept of cognitive load, clarifying why some tasks overload learners and others do not. So, for example, a learner can listen to a verbal explanation while drawing a diagram without being overloaded, because an understanding of speech in our native language is largely automatic, and uses a different slave system (the phonological loop) from a drawing task (which requires the visuospatial sketchpad). And they could complete two routine tasks involving both verbal and visuospatial processing and still deploy their attention/executive functions for analysis, creativity or problem-solving. A body of research evidence has supported these assumptions of the model (e.g. people of all ages can perform routine dissimilar tasks to the maximum level of their ability and still perform at 80–85 per cent of the accuracy with which they would complete either task individually; Logie, 2016). An absolutely key consideration for the teacher, therefore, is to minimise the use of simultaneous tasks that draw on the same modality (e.g. two verbal tasks, such as note taking and listening).

Task

Try to link up the following learning tasks with the relevant concept:

1 Listening to dictation
2 Judging which area(s) they most need to revise
3 Cognitive ability essential for processing new information; harmed by distractions
4 Doing two or more tasks simultaneously
5 Paying attention to a lecture for 1–15 minutes
6 Putting together a jigsaw or other visual puzzle
7 Cognitive abilities, including planning and task switching
8 Thinking or daydreaming rather than focusing on a lesson
9 Finding reading increasingly fast and easy with age
10 Assuming that rereading is a good revision strategy
11 Harm done to learning due to the fact that too much mental effort was spent on irrelevant tasks

- Sustained attention
- Attention
- Beliefs about learning
- Mind-wandering
- Metacognition
- Cognitive load
- Multitasking
- Visuospatial sketchpad/ visual working memory
- Automation
- Phonological loop/ verbal working memory
- Executive functions

Using the principles of cognition

Thinking and attention play a role in many teaching decisions, particularly these concerned with how learners tackle tasks in the here-and-now.

Lesson planning

Due to the very limited nature of both attention and working memory, distractions of any kind can harm learning, and it is important to consider whether the tasks planned throughout the lesson, however engaging, are prompting learners to focus on the right things. Even when distractions are managed, learners tend to mind-wander regularly throughout the school day. As mind-wandering is more associated with routine activities, one way to minimise it is to manage the challenge level of planned tasks so they ramp up quickly in difficulty from a few introductory-level problems to more extended and creative activities, particularly where learners are motivated (e.g. via their own interests) and have been well prepared in advance for the more challenging work. It is also important to vary the pace of lessons, plan some tasks that are more active, and accept that in some tasks, such as reading or colouring in, a certain level of mind-wandering is inevitable and may have cognitive advantages.

An important but often misunderstood point made in Chapter 1 is that repetition of information is not enough to guarantee that it will enter LTM. Verbal repetition draws primarily on working memory, a system that is responsible for temporary storage and solving immediate problems. As discussed above, even the language acquisition process depends on experiencing vocabulary in multiple meaningful contexts rather than repeating the same ones. This is not to say that repetition is bad; clearly, more opportunities to learn will lead to better learning if other things are kept equal. It just doesn't guarantee learning, and is therefore an ineffective strategy.

The inevitable drop-off of attention levels during the day implies that evening is also not a great time for trying to take in new complex concepts – something that could be borne in mind when setting homework. The beginning of a lesson is likely to be associated with a good level of attention, while towards the end, pupils may be more easily distracted by other things – not least the anticipated school bell.

Materials design

One implication of managing cognitive load in the classroom is that the materials that we present to learners may need to be simplified at times, with more focus on the essential learning processes. The addition of extraneous quotes, pictures and cartoons might make a worksheet look better, but could harm its efficacy in the learning process! The visual noise of vivid and colourful wall displays, which are the norm in many classrooms, could be distracting, although this should be balanced against benefits such as their potential to motivate learners (by celebrating their work) and to reinforce key concepts from earlier in the year.

The working memory model, too, suggests that it is very difficult for learners to process two sets of verbal information at a time – and yet most teachers talk at the same time as presenting PowerPoint slide shows, essentially providing a stream of auditory verbal information at the same time as that written on the slides. The limited capacity of the phonological loop means that nobody is capable of listening to a sentence and reading a different sentence at the same time without a major drop in their ability to comprehend one or both. A possible solution could be to present mainly visual information on a screen when giving a verbal explanation. Anything that needs to be written – quotes, terminology, etc. – could be presented in relative silence to give learners time to think about it or take notes. This could be done as a follow-up to a verbal description, allowing meaningful consolidation. Alternatively (or in addition), verbal information on slides could be presented as a task (e.g. a gap-fill exercise) rather than simply shown and read out.

Note taking

Following on from the previous comments on PowerPoints, any kind of note taking could also be left until after information is presented, rather than copying off a slide or whiteboard or jotting down what a teacher is saying – all of which would occupy the phonological loop of working memory, but do not require serious meaningful engagement. This allows more attention to be focused during the task, while the meaningful and active retrieval of recently heard concepts will help to reduce forgetting.

The obvious downside of a retrieval-based approach to note taking is that information may be less accurate, especially when it comes to information such as formulae, names, dates or quotes. This is because the phonological loop operates on the basis of sound rather than meaning, and therefore is better equipped to retain sentences verbatim. However, the detail-focus of human working memory can be put to use in checking notes, looking for the inevitable mistakes in recall by comparing the student's work (or a classmate's) to the original version. Drawing attention to easily forgotten aspects of the information could have knock-on benefits for metacognition, too, prompting learners to take care over these details in future.

Some learners do not take clear and effectively organised notes for themselves, if given freedom to do so. One way around this could be to provide partial notes with gaps and spaces for the learner to complete, as is often done with workbooks for younger learners. Doing so could provide a form of scaffolding, helping the learner to see how good notes should appear, while ensuring that the essential terms and concepts are not skipped. This way, note-taking skills can be developed by gradually reducing the amount of pre-written notes and increasing the demand on learners as they get older and more experienced.

Cognition and behaviour

Discipline is a broad issue with relevance to several chapters of this book; here, the focus is on how discipline issues may interact with the cognitive processes of thinking and attention. The issue of distractions is discussed above as a major influence on learner attention levels, which are limited and easily consumed with superfluous tasks such as viewing mobile phones and other devices, or maintaining a constant awareness of the behaviour of others in the class. An uncontroversial conclusion is that such distractions should be minimised.

One piece of discipline advice that is typically given to new teachers is to avoid rather than manage discipline problems by keeping pupils occupied, and this makes a lot of cognitive sense; if learners are occupied with a task, the limited nature of working memory means that they lack the processing abilities to focus on irrelevant information or dream up distraction activities. Part of the success of such a strategy involves pitching learning tasks at the right level – too difficult and pupils may become frustrated and stop working, while things that are too easy may seem pointless or boring, meaning that their full attention is not engaged. To use Csikszentmihalyi's (1990) term, a learner can experience a sense of *flow* when a task is challenging but manageable, meaning that they become fully absorbed in the task and work at a high level of efficiency. Of course, this can be very difficult to achieve in a highly teacher-centred lesson due to individual differences between learners, and therefore may require some flexibility in how lessons are structured. It will often be necessary to provide challenging but worthwhile extension tasks for more advanced learners to move on to while their classmates are still practising more basic skills.

An additional consideration, on the basis of limited attention and/or cognitive load, is that it is quite demanding to understand and monitor one's own progress. If a pupil is engaged with a complex writing task such as reporting a historic event in journalistic style, metacognitive functions – such as checking their own progress or reflecting on their decisions – can be a distraction. Learners are likely to work and focus better when these demands are removed. For younger pupils, this could involve breaking complex tasks into a series of steps, perhaps supported with a visual flow chart, while more advanced learners (who may have automated at least some metacognitive monitoring) could be prompted to engage in reflective activities after rather than during a task.

The role of attention and cognitive function has a huge role to play in the messy set of constructs and behaviours that we term additional support needs. When it comes to attention, some learners find it easier to focus than others, and the diagnosis of attention deficit hyperactivity disorder (ADHD) is based on the idea that some children have an unusually poor ability to focus. Addressing specific special educational needs is beyond the scope of this chapter, but it would at least be worth raising the issue with an educational psychologist if a pupil seems to struggle with cognitive abilities in a way that differs notably from their peers. In some cases, minor adjustments could make a large difference. For example, a learner may have difficulties centred on metacognitive monitoring, and their ability to do the task(s) could be equivalent to their peers in other respects. In such situations, adjustments to the learning environment or to the structure of tasks could help them to engage fully, while failing to do so could see them begin to lag behind and develop negative beliefs about their own ability.

Conclusions

Noticing and taking in information is an essential part of the learning process, yet most teachers know relatively little about how the immediate processes of the cognitive system work – even though it is one of the most studied areas of psychology. Learners are constantly using their working memory abilities to register and combine information, while monitoring their own progress via a set of processes known as metacognition.

This chapter has also discussed ways of minimising mind-wandering when key information is being presented, while at the same time recognising that it is an inevitable and perhaps, at times, desirable process. Finally, we have seen how executive functions and metacognition develop throughout adolescence. As well as contradicting the traditional view that intelligence can meaningfully be tested at an early age, this area of psychology suggests strategies that could be applied in your context in order to support learning. However, as with other areas of cognition, both maturation and gradual automaticity of key skills will allow progress over time, suggesting the need to continually challenge learners.

We may appear to have made a major omission in not focusing on the concept of *intelligence* (i.e. a general cognitive ability as measured by IQ tests, often assumed to be innate). However, much of what is traditionally called intelligence depends on a combination of the cognitive processes described above; most IQ items require verbal and/or spatial reasoning, as well as maintaining and processing via attention – very much the functions of working memory; although IQ tests can be a useful approximation of these attributes in an individual (e.g. in research studies), the idea that they relate to a single intelligence factor is widely seen as over-simplistic. What's more, tests of working memory have been found to be a more accurate way of predicting academic success than IQ tests (Alloway and Alloway, 2010). In addition, the benefits of effective teaching and good evidence-based learning strategies, as well as the developmental factors in working memory discussed above, speak against the idea that educational potential is written in our DNA (issues surrounding intelligence, development and the academic self-concept are explored in Chapter 3).

As we have seen, the traditional conception of short-term memory is also vague and simplistic; modern psychological science suggests that what was previously considered a single system actually has several key components and is more relevant to active processing than memorising. Its limits can form a bottleneck for pupils' classroom task performance, and taking account of these in your planning and materials design is likely to make learning both more successful and less stressful for your pupils.

Further reading

Why Don't Students Like School? A Cognitive Scientist Answers Questions About How the Mind Works and What It Means for the Classroom by D. T. Willingham (Jossey-Bass, 2010)
An easy-to-read book by a cognitive psychologist, tackling practical classroom problems such as why students avoid having to think too hard!

Working Memory and Learning: A Practical Guide for Teachers by S. Gathercole and T. Packiam Alloway (Paul Chapman, 2008)
A useful overview of how working memory functions in classroom learning, with a particular focus on its role in the learning of younger children, and on learners with additional support needs.

Thinking, Fast and Slow by D. Kahneman (Penguin, 2012)
A fascinating account of the decades of research into thinking by Kahneman and colleagues, usefully highlighting the roles of both automatic and effortful processes.

Models of Working Memory: Mechanisms of Active Maintenance and Executive Control edited by A. Miyake and P. Shah (Cambridge University Press, 2009) A more in-depth look at Baddeley's working memory model, as well as several competing explanations. Ideal for anyone who wants to delve more deeply into the psychology of working memory.

The Psychology of Dyslexia: A Handbook for Teachers (2nd edn) by M. Thomson (John Wiley & Sons, 2009) This useful guide explains how cognitive psychology can help to explain learning in pupils with dyslexia, and discusses a broad range of evidence and its implications.

References

Alloway, T. P. and Alloway, R. G. (2010). Investigating the predictive roles of working memory and IQ in academic attainment. *Journal of Experimental Child Psychology*, 106(1), 20–29. doi: 10.1016/j.jecp.2009.11.003

Amass, H. (2017). TES talks to . . . Sarah-Jayne Blakemore. *TES Online*. Retrieved 19 March 2017 from www.tes.com/news/school-news/breaking-views/tes-talks-tosarah-jayne-blakemore

Ambady, N. and Rosenthal, R. (1992). Thin slices of expressive behavior as predictors of interpersonal consequences: a meta-analysis. *Psychological Bulletin*, 111(2), 256–274. doi: 10.1037/0033-2909.111.2.256

Andrade, J. (2010). What does doodling do? *Applied Cognitive Psychology*, 24(1), 100–106. doi: 10.1002/acp.1561

Arnsten, A. F., Wang, M. J. and Paspalas, C. D. (2012). Neuromodulation of thought: flexibilities and vulnerabilities in prefrontal cortical network synapses. *Neuron*, 76(1), 223–239. doi: 10.1016/j.neuron.2012.08.038

Atkinson, R. C. and Shiffrin, R. M. (1968). Human memory: a proposed system and its control processes. In K. W. Spence and J. T. Spence (eds), *The Psychology of Learning and Motivation* (pp. 89–195). New York: Academic Press.

Baddeley, A. D. (2000). The episodic buffer: a new component of working memory? *Trends in Cognitive Sciences*, 4(11), 417–423. doi: 10.1016/S1364-6613(00)01538-2

Baddeley, A. D. and Hitch, G. (1974). Working memory. In G. H. Bower (ed.), *The Psychology of Learning and Motivation: Vol 8* (pp. 47–89). London: Academic Press.

Baird, B., Smallwood, J., Mrazek, M. D., Kam, J. W., Franklin, M. S. and Schooler, J. W. (2012). Inspired by distraction mind wandering facilitates creative incubation. *Psychological Science*, 23(10), 1117–1122. doi: 10.1177/0956797612446024

Bargh, J. A. and Chartrand, T. L. (1999). The unbearable automaticity of being. *American Psychologist*, 54(7), 462. doi: 10.1037/0003-066X.54.7.462

Blakemore, S. J. and Choudhury, S. (2006). Development of the adolescent brain: implications for executive function and social cognition. *Journal of Child Psychology and Psychiatry*, 47(3–4), 296–312. doi: 10.1111/j.1469-7610.2006.01611.x

Blakemore, S. J. and Mills, K. L. (2014). Is adolescence a sensitive period for sociocultural processing? *Annual Review of Psychology*, 65, 187–207. doi: 10.1146/annurev-psych-010213-115202

Boothby, E. J., Clark, M. S. and Bargh, J. A. (2017). The invisibility cloak illusion: people (incorrectly) believe they observe others more than others observe them. *Journal of Personality and Social Psychology*, 112(4), 589–606. doi:10.1037/pspi0000082

Bransford, J. D., Brown, A. L. and Cocking, R. R. (2000). *How People Learn: Brain, Mind, Experience and School.* Washington, DC: National Academy Press.

Carlson, S. M. and Moses, L. J. (2001). Individual differences in inhibitory control and children's theory of mind. *Child Development*, 72(4), 1032–1053. doi: 10.1111/1467-8624.00333

Chang, A. M., Aeschbach, D., Duffy, J. F. and Czeisler, C. A. (2015). Evening use of light-emitting eReaders negatively affects sleep, circadian timing, and next-morning alertness. *PNAS*, 112(4), 1232–1237. doi: 10.1073/pnas.1418490112

Ching, B. H. H. (2017). Mathematics anxiety and working memory: longitudinal associations with mathematical performance in Chinese children. *Contemporary Educational Psychology*, 51, 99–113. doi: 10.1016/j.cedpsych.2017.06.006

Cohen, S., Glass, D. C. and Singer, J. E. (1973). Apartment noise, auditory discrimination, and reading ability in children. *Journal of Experimental Social Psychology*, 9(5), 407–422. doi: 10.1016/S0022-1031(73)80005-8

Csikszentmihalyi, M. (1990). *Flow: The Psychology of Optimal Experience.* New York: Harper & Row.

Dunbar, R. I. (1998). The social brain hypothesis. *Brain*, 9(10), 178–190. doi: 10.1002/(SICI)1520-6505(1998)6:5<178::AID-EVAN5>3.0.CO;2-8

Edmiston, R. W. and Braddock, R. W. (1941). A study of the effect of various teaching procedures upon observed group attention in the secondary school. *Journal of Educational Psychology*, 32(9), 665–672. doi: 10.1037/h0062749

Ericsson, K. A. (2008). Deliberate practice and acquisition of expert performance: a general overview. *Academic Emergency Medicine*, 15(11), 988–994. doi: 10.1111/j.1553-2712.2008.00227.x

Farrington, C. A., Roderick, M., Allensworth, E., Nagaoka, J., Keyes, T. S., Johnson, D. W., et al. (2012). *Teaching Adolescents to Become Learners: The Role of Noncognitive Factors in Shaping School Performance – A Critical*

Literature Review. Chicago, IL: University of Chicago Consortium on Chicago School Research.

Gathercole, S. E., Pickering, S. J., Ambridge, B. and Wearing, H. (2004). The structure of working memory from 4 to 15 years of age. *Developmental Psychology*, 40(2), 177. doi: 10.1037/0012-1649.40.2.177

Gladwell, M. (2006). *Blink: The Power of Thinking Without Thinking*. London: Penguin.

Glenberg, A. M. and Epstein, W. (1987). Inexpert calibration of comprehension. *Memory & Cognition*, 15(1), 84–93. doi: 10.3758/BF03197714

Gopnik, A. (2016). How babies think. *Scientific American*, 25, 4–9. doi: 10.1038/scientificamerickankids0616-4

Grier, R. A., Warm, J. S., Dember, W. N., Matthews, G., Galinsky, T. L., Szalma, J. L., et al. (2003). The vigilance decrement reflects limitations in effortful attention, not mindlessness. *Human Factors*, 45(3), 349–359. doi: 10.1518/hfes.45.3.349.27253

Gruber, M. J., Gelman, B. D. and Ranganath, C. (2014). States of curiosity modulate hippocampus-dependent learning via the dopaminergic circuit. *Neuron*, 84(2), 486–496.

Hassin, R. R., Bargh, J. A., Engell, A. D. and McCulloch, K. C. (2009). Implicit working memory. *Consciousness and Cognition*, 18(3), 665–678. doi: 10.1016/j.concog.2009.04.003

Hattie, J. (2012). *Visible Learning for Teachers: Maximizing Impact on Achievement*. Oxford: Routledge.

Krashen, S. (2009). Does intensive decoding instruction contribute to reading comprehension? *Knowledge Quest*, 37(4), 72–74.

Küpper-Tetzel, C. (2017). How to improve your metacognition and why it matters. *Learning Scientists Blog*. Retrieved 28 April 2017 from www.learning scientists.org/blog/2017/3/30-1

Landauer, T. K. (2011). Distributed learning and the size of memory: a 50-year spacing odyssey. In A. S. Benjamin (ed.), *Successful Remembering and Successful Forgetting: A Festschrift in Honor of Robert A. Bjork* (pp. 49–69). New York: Psychology Press.

Lee, H., Plass, J. L. and Homer, B. D. (2006). Optimizing cognitive load for learning from computer-based science simulations. *Journal of Educational Psychology*, 98(4), 902. doi: 10.1037/0022-0663.98.4.902

Logie, R. H. (2016) Retiring the central executive. *Quarterly Journal of Experimental Psychology*, 69(10), 2093–2109. doi: 10.1080/17470218.2015.1136657

McEwen, B. S. and Morrison, J. H. (2013). The brain on stress: vulnerability and plasticity of the prefrontal cortex over the life course. *Neuron*, 79(1), 16–29. doi: 10.1016/j.neuron.2013.06.028

Moss, B. (2008). The information text gap: the mismatch between non-narrative text types in basal readers and 2009 NAEP recommended guidelines. *Journal of Literacy Research*, 40(2), 201–219. doi: 10.1080/10862960802411927

Moss, B. and Hendershot, J. (2002). Exploring sixth graders' selection of non-fiction trade books. *The Reading Teacher*, 56, 6–17.

Naismith, L. M. and Cavalcanti, R. B. (2015). Validity of cognitive load measures in simulation-based training: a systematic review. *Academic Medicine*, 90(11), S24–S35. doi: 10.1097/ACM.0000000000000893

Nation, K. (2017). Nurturing a lexical legacy: reading experience is critical for the development of word reading skill. *npj Science of Learning*, 2(1), 3–5. doi:10.1038/s41539-017-0004-7

Pachai, A. A., Acai, A., LoGiudice, A. B. and Kim, J. A. (2016). The mind that wanders: challenges and potential benefits of mind wandering in education. *Scholarship of Teaching and Learning in Psychology*, 2(2), 134–146. doi: 10.1037/stl0000060

Ravizza, S. M., Hambrick, D. Z. and Fenn, K. M. (2014). Non-academic internet use in the classroom is negatively related to classroom learning regardless of intellectual ability. *Computers & Education*, 78, 109–114. doi: 10.1016/j.compedu.2014.05.007

Rawson, K. A. and Dunlosky, J. (2007). Improving students' self-evaluation of learning for key concepts in textbook materials. *European Journal of Cognitive Psychology*, 19, 559–579. doi: 10.1080/09541440701326022

Reyna, V. A. (2012). A new intuitionism: meaning, memory, and development in fuzzy-trace theory. *Judgment and Decision Making*, 7(3), 332–359.

Rinaldi, C. and Gardner, H. (2001). *Making Learning Visible*. Reggio Emilia, Italy: Reggio Children.

Risko, E. F., Anderson, N., Sarwal, A., Engelhardt, M. and Kingstone, A. (2012). Everyday attention: variation in mind wandering and memory in a lecture. *Applied Cognitive Psychology*, 26(2), 234–242. doi: 10.1002/ acp.1814

Romine, C. B. and Reynolds, C. R. (2005). A model of the development of frontal lobe functioning: findings from a meta-analysis. *Applied Neuropsychology*, 12(4), 190–201. doi: 10.1207/s15324826an1204_2

Saner, E. (2016). The secret to calm classrooms? Lose the shoes. *The Guardian*, 24 May. Retrieved 28 April 2017 from www.theguardian.com/education/shortcuts/2016/may/24/secret-to-calm-classrooms-lose-the-shoes-schools

Schweickert, R. and Boruff, B. (1986). Short-term memory capacity: magic number or magic spell? *Journal of Experimental Psychology: Learning, Memory, and Cognition*, 12(3), 419–425.

Simons, D. J., Boot, W. R., Charness, N., Gathercole, S. E., Chabris, C. F., Hambrick, D. Z., et al. (2016). Do 'brain-training' programs work? *Psychological Science in the Public Interest*, 17(3), 103–186. doi: 10.1177/1529100616661983

Smallwood, J., Fishman, D. J. and Schooler, J. W. (2007). Counting the cost of an absent mind: mind wandering as an underrecognized influence on educational performance. *Psychonomic Bulletin & Review*, 14(2), 230–236. doi: 10.3758/BF03194057

Stansfeld, S. A., Berglund, B., Clark, C., Lopez-Barrio, I., Fischer, P., Öhrström, E., et al. (2005). Aircraft and road traffic noise and children's cognition and health: a cross-national study. *The Lancet*, 365(9475), 1942–1949. doi: 10.1016/S0140-6736(05)66660-3

Steinberg, L. (2007). Risk taking in adolescence: new perspectives from brain and behavioral science. *Current Directions in Psychological Science*, 16(2), 55–59. doi: 10.1111/j.1467-8721.2007.00475.x

Sweller, J. (1994). Cognitive load theory, learning difficulty, and instructional design. *Learning and Instruction*, 4(4), 295–312. doi: 10.1016/0959-4752(94)90003-5

Sweller, J., Ayres, P. and Kalyuga, S. (2011). *Cognitive Load Theory*. New York: Springer.

Wilson, K. and Korn, J. H. (2007). Attention during lectures: beyond ten minutes. *Teaching of Psychology*, 34(2), 85–89. doi: 10.1080/00986280701291291

Xu, J. and Metcalfe, J. (2016). Studying in the region of proximal learning reduces mind wandering. *Memory & Cognition*, 44(5), 681–695. doi:10.3758/s13421-016-0589-8

3 | Self-theories

Our self-assessments can play a major role in our success and failure. How students see themselves as learners can impact learning in a number of hidden ways. This chapter argues that students' beliefs about themselves influence academic outcomes in both positive and negative ways:

- The types of theories and how they impact on learning.
- The relationship between self-esteem and other forms of self-concept.
- The difference between mastery and performance orientations.
- How views about intelligence impact learning outcomes.

'Self-theories' can be defined as people's beliefs about themselves. Although we can certainly explain learning in terms of cognitive functioning (see Chapter 2) and brain architecture, the self-reflective nature of the human species results in a more ambiguous and personal view of who we are in relation to others and in relation to our goals and desires.

These 'meaning systems', as Dweck (2000) describes them, pertain to people's beliefs about themselves and the way individuals create different psychological worlds that lead them to think, feel and act differently in identical situations. We can therefore think of self-theories as being a number of separate yet related constructs that help people to place themselves in the world, while at the same time building on what we can loosely describe as our identity. Such theories include (but are not confined to):

- theories of self-esteem;
- theories of academic self-concept;
- mastery and performance orientations; and
- implicit theories of intelligence (mindset).

These interrelated constructs are specific to education and learning apart from the global self-esteem construct. Self-esteem, however, does play a role in the formation of an academic specific self-concept (the way individuals perceive themselves in terms of ability in a specific academic domain). Dweck has perhaps done more than any other theorist in bringing self-theories into the wider public domain through her work in so-called 'growth mindset', an area examined later in this chapter.

Self-esteem in life and educational settings

We often use the term self-esteem in a rather non-specific and vague manner. We might view someone as having low self-esteem because their behaviour suggests to us that they have a rather low feeling of self-worth, lack confidence, and rarely engage in conversations or avoid social situations. At the other extreme, we might know someone who abounds in self-confidence, is always the life and soul of the party, and appears competent and comfortable in their own skin. Intuitively, people tend to relate self-esteem with success because common sense would suggest that a more positive view of yourself influences your confidence and feelings of control; after all, the self-made billionaire must feel good about themselves and their achievements.

One of the first attempts to define self-esteem was proposed by William James (1842–1910):

$$\text{self-esteem} = \text{success} / \text{pretentions}$$

In other words, the more success we achieve and the lower our expectations, the higher our self-esteem. In order to feel better about ourselves, we either need to succeed more in the world or downsize our hopes. Self-esteem, therefore, is an affective or emotional state, and good feelings are rooted in the world and emerge through the tension between feeling good and doing well.

The study of self-esteem fell out of fashion for many years while psychology concerned itself more with the forces that pulled or pushed individuals in certain directions. During this time, people were viewed as creatures at the mercy of invisible forces, and while the Freudians saw internal conflict as being responsible for pushing human behaviour, behaviourists saw positive reinforcements and punishments as being the key to human action. Others still viewed humans as being under the control of fixed action patterns governed by genes.

It wasn't until the 1960s that the whole area of self-esteem resurfaced through a more humanistic change in trajectory. Self-direction replaced unconscious and innate drives as an explanation of human behaviour; more specifically, the role of choice, control, personal preference, decision and will replaced elements that people couldn't control with those described as self-development techniques. Researchers such as Stanley Coopersmith and Morris Rosenberg (e.g. Coopersmith, 1967; Rosenberg, 1965) became interested in the way children developed and nurtured their sense of self in the form of self-esteem and self-image, and the components that led to increased well-being and feelings of self-worth.

Coopersmith was particularly interested in the feeling good side of self-esteem and people's personal judgements of worthiness. He defined self-esteem as 'a personal judgement of worthiness, that is expressed in the attitudes the individual holds towards himself' (Coopersmith, 1967, p. 5). Coopersmith assessed the child-rearing practices of parents with children who were rated as high in self-esteem, concluding that the clearer the rules and limits enforced by parents, the higher the self-esteem of that child. More freedom, suggested Coopersmith, resulted in lower levels of self-esteem.

However, self-esteem is dependent upon what you value, and this is often shaped by culture and upbringing.

According to Coopersmith, there are four dimensions of self-esteem – significance, competence, power and virtue:

- *Significance.* Significance concerns our feelings of being loved and cared about – the feeling that you matter to someone. Importantly, this feeling is a matter of personal choice; in other words, it is not something that can be instilled. Significance also assumes that the child is an active participant in the development of their sense of self, the act of which does not in itself determine self-esteem, but rather the way in which the individual reacts to or deal with certain events.

- *Competence.* Competence is dependent upon whether the child compares him or herself with someone perceived as more competent. This is a decision the child makes, although adults and other significant people can influence this by, for example, making comparisons or demanding perfection. If competence is particularly important to the child, then they might experience lower self-esteem, despite high levels of competence, due to feelings of not being competent enough. In other words, a discrepancy arises between what the child wants and where the child is, leading to a conclusion that the high standards set haven't been met.

- *Power.* People obtain a sense of power by: feeling that they have control over who they are; making things happen in the world; having an effect on people and events in life; and living life satisfactorily. If an individual feels that power is important, then having it leads to higher levels of self-esteem. Note, however, that power is not defined as having control over other people.

- *Virtue.* For some individuals, being good is important. Again, the importance here is the gap between how good we perceive ourselves to be and how good we want to or need to be.

Nathaniel Brandon expanded on this earlier work into self-esteem, retaining the 'feeling good' and 'doing well' aspects proposed by William James (Brandon, 1997). Brandon saw self-esteem as concerned with our confidence in our own abilities to think and to cope with the basic challenges of life (doing well), and the confidence in our own right to be happy. Being happy is related to our feelings of being worthy, deserving, the entitlement to assert our needs and wants, and our entitlement to enjoy the fruits of our efforts (feeling good).

Harter (1999) proposed the idea of domains of self-esteem, in that people might have higher or lower levels of self-esteem for different things. Harter suggests five different domains:

1 *Scholastic competence*: How able the child considers him or herself to be at school.

2 *Athletic competence*: How able the child considers him or herself to be at sports.

3 *Social acceptance*: Whether the child feels popular with peers.

4 *Physical appearance*: How good-looking the child feels he or she is.

5 *Behavioural conduct*: To what extent the child considers his or her general behaviour to be acceptable to others.

The measures on each domain are then combined to form a single assessment tool known as the Self-Perception Profile for Children (SPPC). This also includes a 'global self-worth scale' that asks how much children like themselves as people. Profiles can be consistently high, consistently low, or vary across domains.

Is high self-esteem always a good thing?

High levels of self-esteem can certainly lead to positive outcomes, but are far from a cure-all. Fiske argues that while the benefits are real, they can be taken too far and used as a panacea for all the ills that ail us (see Neff, 2011). Baumeister found that the most aggressive people tend towards high levels of self-esteem, suggesting that violence becomes more likely when other people and situations contradict a person's highly favourable view of themselves. Very high levels of self-esteem might also lead to arrogance and fragile self-concept. This results in such individuals being easily threatened and more likely to use violence in order to protect their fragile and inflated sense of self-worth. People high in self-esteem often have a mistaken impression of themselves, and are more likely to claim to be more likeable and attractive, to have better relationships, and to make better impressions on people than those with low self-esteem. Objective measures, however, appear to cast doubt on these beliefs, leading Baumeister to conclude that 'narcissists can be charming as first, but tend to alienate others eventually' (Baumeister et al., 2003).

There are certainly benefits to having high levels of self-esteem. Self-esteem is strongly correlated with happiness, although without a clearly established causation. What this means is that there is no way to confirm that high levels of self-esteem cause people to be happier. It could be that happy people develop higher levels of self-esteem, or that other factors indirectly lead to higher levels of happiness. It is clear, however, that low self-esteem is related to depression and stress, but the direction remains unclear. High levels of self-esteem have also been shown to foster experimentation among children, leading to an increase in risky behaviours such as smoking, drinking, drug taking and underage sex. However, high self-esteem does reduce the risk of bulimia in females (Baumeister et al., 2003).

Self-esteem and academic performance

While some studies have identified a link between high self-esteem and academic attainment, correlations have been modest at best. High self-esteem, therefore, appears to have little impact on academic outcomes, but findings do suggest that high levels of self-esteem emerge from good school performance. Furthermore, efforts to boost the self-esteem of school pupils have not resulted in improvements in academic performance, and in some cases have been found to be counterproductive. Similar results have been found in adults, in that job performance is sometimes related to self-esteem, but such correlations vary widely, and again direction of causality hasn't been reliably established. Certainly, high levels of occupational success may boost self-esteem.

It would appear, therefore, that while self-esteem is related to some positive outcomes, there is little to suggest that students with high self-esteem do any better academically than those with low self-esteem. This is not to say that schools should abandon such notions, but that interventions should be directed towards well-being rather than formal academic outcome. Additionally, because high self-esteem appears to emerge from academic success, concentrating on achievement will be of greater benefit academically than stand-alone self-esteem-boosting interventions.

As noted earlier, Harter (1999) suggests that scholastic competence can be seen as a specific type of self-esteem that might be better placed as a means of investigating the role of self-esteem and academic outcomes. A more developed concept similar to that proposed by Harter is that of 'academic self-concept'.

Academic self-concept and academic outcomes

Self-esteem, as already described, can be viewed as a global rather than specific construct, an umbrella term beneath which are found other components relating to target constructs. Global self-esteem, therefore, represents an overarching feeling of self-worth and competence in comparison to others. One such component is academic self-concept, itself a component of wider general self-concept. Shavelson et al. (1976) (see Marsh and Martin, 2011) describe self-concept as a person's self-perceptions formed though experience and the interpretations of one's environment.

Self-concept includes feeling of:

- self-confidence;
- self-worth;
- self-acceptance;
- competence; and
- ability.

A person's self-concept is influenced by a number of factors, including evaluations received by significant others, reinforcement, and the attributions we apply to our own behaviour. Furthermore, self-concept represents an important mediating variable that helps to explain other outcomes. One of the most important features of self-concept is its multifaceted and hierarchically organised structure, with perceptions of personal behaviour in specific situations at the base of the hierarchy, inference about the self in broader domains (e.g. social, physical and academic) at the middle of the hierarchy, and global self-concept (or self-esteem) at the apex (see Figure 3.1).

Academic self-concept represents our personal beliefs about academic ability and skills. Tiedemann (2000) has suggested that academic self-concept arises between the ages of 3 and 5, and is heavily influenced by both parents and early educators. By age 10 or 11, children are assessing their academic abilities by comparing themselves to their peers. Feedback represents an important factor in the development of a positive or negative academic self-concept and the way educators are able to successfully guide learners towards positive outcomes. Research indicates that prior academic attainment is certainly one determinant of academic self-concept but that causal relationships are generally less clear. The self-enhancement view postulates that academic self-concept is a determinant of academic achievement (i.e. the more positive

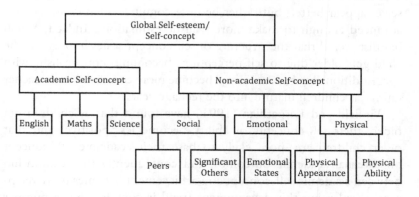

Figure 3.1 Hierarchy of self-esteem

a person's view of themselves as a learner in a specific domain, the higher their attainment in that domain). Alternatively, the skills development view suggests that positive academic self-concept arises through high academic achievement.

Marsh argues that both views are partly correct, but that these factors influence each other (Marsh and Martin, 2011). Marsh's reciprocal effects model of academic self-concept suggests that prior self-concept affects subsequent achievement, and that prior achievement also affects subsequent self-concept. Muijs (1997) concurs, concluding that academic achievement has a strong influence over academic self-concept, and that this relationship appears to be reciprocal. However, Muijs agrees with previous findings that self-esteem does not influence academic achievement. Self-concepts of very young children are very positive and not highly correlated with external indicators such as skills, accomplishments, achievement and significant others, but as children get older and their life experiences increase, specific self-concept domains become more differentiated and are more highly correlated with external indicators.

With younger children, self-descriptions typically represent an over-estimation of personal abilities (known as positive halo effects), but it is thought that such overestimations represent cognitive limitations rather than an attempt to deceive. Younger children will therefore over-inflate their abilities, not through any desire to make themselves appear better, but rather because cognitive abilities are not yet advanced enough to make more realistic estimations. Indeed, Marsh has discovered that the structure of self-concept scales improve as the child gets older due to self-perceptions becoming more realistic with age. Additionally, student ratings become more correlated with teacher ratings as children mature into the teenage years.

Wigfield and Karpathian (1991) have found that as children get older, their self-concepts of ability become less positive, and that older children are more likely to base their academic self-concept on external academic outcomes, and consequently the relationship between academic self-concept and achievement becomes more reciprocal. Explaining this development trend is complex, but a number of proposals link normal development processes and self-concept. Cognitive abilities grow with maturation so that older children have higher cognitive abilities than younger ones. These abilities improve coordination between self-representations that were previously considered to be opposite, and this leads to better agreement between self-concept ratings and external ratings offered by teachers and other significant others. The higher cognitive skills developed by older children allow them to use social comparison (they compare themselves to others), which in turn fosters a more balanced view of the self. Finally, older children have internalised evaluative standards of others, which leads to less egocentric (self-centred) evaluations of the self. Together, these three developmental processes lead to greater accuracy among older children, allowing researchers to predict change in academic outcome. Evidence has also discovered that boys, on average, have higher academic self-concept scores than girls in all school subjects other than English, and that the strategy of setting students by ability also impacts self-concept, but with a greater impact in English than in maths and science.

Certain common strategies used by schools can have both positive and negative impacts on academic self-concept. While Parsons and Hallam (2014) found that setting by ability benefits the more able pupils, Marks (2016) found that even very young children are aware of the consequences of being placed in lower ability sets. Children as young as 9 know what their placement means and build up a view of themselves and others based around setting. In one of the many interviews Marks conducted, 9-year-old Yolanda stated that some children are good at maths because 'their brains are bigger . . . it just happens. They are born like that. They are born clever'. Such research indicates that even very young children buy into these ability labels, which in turn impacts on how they see themselves as learners. Marks argues that this limits their ability to 'have a go', leading many to view ability as fixed now and in the future. These labels influence children's academic self-concept and make it difficult for them to psychologically and physically move from the bottom set. Researchers, including Carol Dweck, argue that such strategies create learners with 'entity' or 'fixed' mindsets.

Academic self-concept and self-efficacy

Schunk and Pajares have described self-efficacy as 'an individual's convictions that they can successfully perform given academic tasks at designated levels' (cited in Wigfield and Eccles, 2002). This might lead many to suggest that self-efficacy and academic self-concept are similar constructs, with no clear demarcation between the two. However, it is possible to identify specific conceptual and operational differences, not least in the manner in which such constructs are measured and assessed. Bong and Skaalvik (2003) have noted that academic self-concept is related to one's perceived ability within an academic area, while self-efficacy relates to one's self-perceived confidence in successfully performing a particular academic task. In terms of measurement, self-efficacy stresses the cognitive nature of self-efficacy beliefs, for example: 'How sure are you that you can solve the following mathematical problems?' Such items tap exclusively into the cognitive aspects of students' self-perceptions, while academic self-concept comprises both self-evaluative cognitive dimensions and affective-motivational dimensions, for example: 'I am proud of my mathematics ability', or: 'I hate mathematics'. However, Eccles et al. (1998) have suggested that self-evaluating one's ability might give rise to affective-emotional reactions that might not be thought of as part of a student's academic self-concept.

Self-efficacy and academic self-concept also differ in terms of specific judgements, in that academic self-efficacy is more often than not measured on a task-specific level while academic self-concept is more general. Such differences are particularly noticeable when both constructs are assessed in reference to a particular domain or subject area. Maths self-efficacy items such as 'How confident do you feel about solving an equation like . . .?' clearly measures self-perceived competence at a more task-specific level than self-concept maths items such as 'Compared with others of my age, I am good at maths'. Academic self-concept and self-efficacy are therefore measured using questionnaires that seek to quantify different learning perceptions. Most notably, academic self-concept relies heavily on social comparisons (i.e. how students rate their ability in comparison to others). Additionally, academic self-concept measures examine confidence based on past experiences of learning, while self-efficacy items emphasise the future (how you think you will perform on a specific task).

It is clear from the significant work undertaken on academic self-concept that how students feel about their own abilities in a specific subject area impacts heavily on future academic outcomes. Academic self-concept provides teachers with a more realistic view and possesses greater prediction qualities than more global constructs, specifically self-esteem. Self-concepts are also built upon histories and experiences of past successes, failures and struggles in specific subject areas. However, like any measure, there are also drawbacks. Reliance on self-completion measures can create problems because young people are often more concerned with giving the 'correct' answer, even when it has been stressed to them that there is none. Nevertheless, understanding students' beliefs about their own abilities can help teachers to identify those who feel less confident, allowing for appropriate targeted interventions.

Mastery and performance goal orientations

Many teachers are familiar with the work of Carol Dweck and the popularisation of her mindset theory. However, Dweck's earlier pre-mindset research allows us to see how the theory developed, and its connection with other areas such as emotion, helplessness and self-esteem. This research identified the specific motivational orientations that would form the basis of Dweck's later growth versus fixed mindset dichotomy.

Dweck has suggested that learners generally fall into one of two categories in terms of their learning orientation:

- *Performance orientation*: Learners are motivated by how well they do in comparison to others. The main aim is to achieve in order to enhance extrinsic self-esteem and to be seen as 'better' than their peers.
- *Mastery orientation*: These learners are motivated by a desire to become skilled at whatever it is they are learning. They are less interested in ranking themselves against peers, and more concerned with their own progress and the achievement of personal goals.

During the 1980s, Dweck, along with Carol Diener, carried out several studies using fifth- and sixth-grade children in the US. They divided the children into two groups based on the outcome of a questionnaire designed to identify those children who displayed helpless character- istics (see Dweck, 2000). The aim was to attempt to separate those children who showed persistence in the face of failure (most associ- ated with the mastery-oriented approach) from those who tended not to persist when presented with the possibility of failing. The children would then be presented with a number of tasks, ranging in difficulty, to see who would persist and who would give up. More importantly, Dweck and Diener also recorded the flow of the children's thoughts and feelings, as well as their performance.

This early research uncovered a number of fascinating behaviours related to learners and the learning process, and highlighted the dan- gers of helplessness:

- When children are comfortable with their learning and can com- plete tasks or problems successfully, they remain quite confident about their ability and intelligence – this is the case regardless of orientation.
- Setting goals too low may create a false sense of success because challenge is negligible; however, increasing the level of challenge will trigger helpless behaviour in certain learners and mastery behaviour in others.
- Pupils categorised as helpless begin to act in dysfunctional and damaging ways when things start to get harder, and success on the task becomes more elusive.

One of the first things these students begin to do is denigrate their own abilities and blame their intelligence (or rather their perceived lack of intelligence) on their inability to succeed. Dweck and Diener found that children made specific verbal attacks on their own ability such as 'I guess I'm not very intelligent' or 'I'm no good at things like this'. One-third of the helpless group spontaneously denigrated their own intellectual ability, while none of the mastery group resorted to such intense self-criticism.

These children had already had a string of successes, and it was only when they hit problems and began to fail that they began to lose faith in their own ability. Before they hit problems, their performance was indistinguishable from that of the mastery group; they had rapidly discarded these earlier successes and decided that they weren't clever enough, even though their earlier success should have made them feel more confident about their ability. When asked how many problems they had solved successfully, the helpless children recalled more unsuccessful attempts – they remembered their performance as poorer than it actually was.

In another study, students were presented with difficult problems first and solvable problems later. It was found that the helpless group were less likely to solve the later problems, even though they were easier, suggesting that the helpless orientation is a reaction to failure that carries negative implications for the self. Furthermore, it works to impair ability and results in less effective cognitive strategies.

We can get a better insight into how helpless-oriented students cope with failure by examining their ongoing verbal responses during the task. Dweck and Diener tracked the thoughts and feelings of the children as they solved the problems, in an attempt to gain insight into their thoughts and feelings. Change in attitude was rapid in the helpless group once the tasks got difficult and they started to fail. While the problems presented were solvable, the children appeared quite pleased with themselves, but when the problems became difficult they lost interest and complained of being bored.

The ways in which they coped with the rising anxiety and self-doubt that arose once they realised that they were having difficulties solving the problems often involved the children drawing attention to other non-task-related successes. In what appeared to be an attempt to counter the failure experienced in the experimental situation, some children would inform the researchers that they had been given an important part in the school play or had succeeded in some other activity unrelated to the task. Others would try to change the rules or give plausible explanations for giving the wrong answer. Even these young children were found to be making desperate attempts to safeguard their self-esteem; in other words, they were trying hard not to seem unintelligent. As a result, the helpless group displayed a significant deterioration in the strategies they used to solve the problems as they increased in difficulty. Interestingly, they didn't appear to objectively decide that the task was too hard for them, but increasingly condemned their own abilities.

Carol Dweck's early work investigated the different ways in which helpless and goal-oriented learners approached problems. Other psychologists working in the area of motivation and learning have identified two specific 'goal orientations' that appear to influence the way in which learners approach the goals set for or by them. The first is known as the 'performance goal' orientation (the 'helpless' group in the Dweck and Diener study), while the second has been labelled the 'mastery goal' orientation. The primary aim of the performance goal learner is, first and foremost, to demonstrate their competence or to avoid looking incompetent. Furthermore, performers tend to select activities that are easier, and therefore represent a higher chance of success. For performers, success is everything, even if that success comes about because they have chosen a task that is below their capabilities. Revising and preparing for exams might include constantly going over the same material because they already know it, rather than moving on to a topic they don't fully understand. In a similar way, given the choice between a task that requires little cognitive investment and one that takes a great deal of effort and thought, the performer would be more likely to choose the latter. The performer might claim that a particular task is pointless or stupid, or say that they just can't be bothered with it. Those displaying a mastery goal orientation, however, are more likely to choose more challenging tasks and persist at them; the primary aim here is to attain a new skill, one that requires dedication and persistence. So the child who constantly complains that it's pointless to become skilled at algebra because he is never going to use it again is more than likely anxious about others in the class viewing him as unintelligent because he struggles with algebra, whereas another child perseveres because she wishes to master the techniques of algebra regardless of how useful it will be in the future.

Elliot further developed the view of master and performance orientations, in part due to the inconsistency of the evidence linking performance goals to a number of other motivational constructs (Elliot and McGregor, 1999). Elliot proposes a trichotomous model that further differentiates between performance approach, performance-avoidance and mastery-goal orientations. It's important to understand that this separating out of the two performance goal orientations grew from the inconsistencies within the research involving the performance-only goal orientation; essentially, the original distinctions were unable to be explained in terms of research findings. Basically, performance-approach goal orientations represent the individual's attempts to demonstrate competence (through the strategies already discussed), while performance avoidance orientations represent attempts for the learner to avoid being seen as incompetent. Goal orientations funda-mentally alter the way learners view achievement situations, having a knock-on effect on the ways in which individuals approach learning situations, and ultimately achievement outcomes. While those students displaying performance goal orientations will continue to avoid chal-lenging tasks as a way of demonstrating competence, performance avoiders are more likely to disengage and withdraw from the learn-ing process altogether. The performance avoidance orientation has also been linked to a number of other outcomes, including shallow process-ing, poor retention of information, and performance decrements.

Mastery-goal learners, on the other hand, are expected to enhance their achievement though placing a greater value on improving their skills and developing competencies. Not only that, but, as both Elliot and Dweck discovered, they are also more likely to display greater levels of persistence and employ more advanced cognitive strategies that lead to the deeper processing of information. Furthermore, empirical evidence has discovered that those students who focus more on trying to develop competence are more resilient in the face of challenge, and are more likely to employ higher-level cognitive strategies such as elaboration, critical thinking and self-regulated learning. All this would suggest that a mastery-goal orientation is directly related to higher levels of achieve-ment; however, the evidence doesn't necessarily support this view.

Linnenbrink-Garcia analysed 74 correlational studies, finding that only about 40 per cent of them showed a positive relationship between mastery orientation and academic achievement, with 5 per cent showing a negative relationship (see Tyson et al., 2009). This would certainly suggest that there is some benefit to mastery-goal orientation, but in research terms the results are not deemed statistically significant; in other words, the effect is too small, so we can't be sure of any causal relationship. Frustratingly, there is also some concern over the relationship between performance approach goals and academic outcomes, with some studies showing a positive correlation between performance-approach goals and cognitive regulation, while other studies have found no significant relationship, or even a negative relationship.

These inconsistent findings don't necessarily indicate that the theory is flawed. It could be that the issues being investigated are more complex than originally proposed or that explanations are nuanced. The evidence would indicate that mastery and performance conflict with academic outcomes, that is, findings related to performance approach goals have been inconsistent with regards to persistence. These inconsistencies highlight the problems that can arise when academic research is applied to the classroom. As already described, students who displayed a performance approach orientation were less likely to persist once the task became more difficult; this observation is also supported by other research studies. However, even though much of the research found that performance approach students were more likely to withdraw or opt out of a task, other studies have found no significant relationship between performance approach orientation and effort. Indeed, Elliot and McGregor (1999) identified a positive relationship between approach goals, effort and persistence.

The main problem we face is that there appears to be no strong relationship between performance approach orientations and achievement. There is certainly an emotional component at play, and this could provide us with a way to reconcile these findings. It appears that while some learners are able to successfully regulate possible debilitating emotions, others are unable to do so, leading to less effort and persistence and the feeling that the task is somehow unworthy of their efforts. Mastery-goal-oriented learners are less likely to develop debilitating emotions because they view learning as a challenge and something to become skilled at – they view difficulty and challenge as a vital part of the learning process, rather than something that exists in order to trick them or to reveal their incompetence to the world. They also see failure as part of the route they must take in order to reach the goals they have set for themselves.

Implicit theories of intelligence (growth versus fixed mindset)

The term 'implicit theories of intelligence' refers to the unconscious views individuals hold about the nature of intelligence. Some people view intelligence as an absolute entity (i.e. intelligence is something fixed that cannot be increased through effort or other means). Others are more flexible with their ideas about intelligence, and see it as something that can be nurtured through effort and thoughtful care and attention. This has little to do with the actual 'truth' about intelligence, and doesn't represent a theory of it; rather, it concerns our beliefs about how people achieve and why some don't. According to Dweck (2000), children often worry about their level of intelligence, and can often obsess over it. This worry suggests a fixed view – the belief that we are all born with a fixed amount of intelligence and that there is nothing we can do to change it. On the other hand, some people hold an alternate view – the belief that intelligence can be developed and cultivated through effort. These beliefs led Dweck to propose that there are two implicit theories of intelligence, both of which impact on student motivation and attainment in different ways:

1 *Entity theory (fixed mindset)*: This is the view that intelligence is fixed. Students displaying a fixed orientation (or mindset) are more concerned with showing others that they are smart – in other words, they display a performance goal orientation.

2 *Incremental theory (growth mindset)*: The view that intelligence is malleable. Students displaying an incremental orientation (or growth mindset) are less concerned with how smart they are and more concerned with getting smarter through mastery.

Students therefore either display a need to validate or a desire to learn (although it is more of a continuum), and a number of studies over the years appear to support such a hypothesis.

For reasons of clarity, I shall refer to entity theories as 'fixed mindset' and incremental theories as 'growth mindset', even though these terms weren't used by Dweck until much later.

In one study, after completing a questionnaire to determine their implicit view of intelligence, students were given a number of tasks to choose from and were asked to pick the one they would like to work on. The tasks were described to the students in the follow ways. A task that was:

- 'easy enough so you won't make mistakes';
- 'something you're good at but hard enough to show you're smart'; and
- 'hard, new and different – you might get confused and make mistakes, but you might learn something new and useful'.

The first two statements describe a task aimed at performance goals, while the final statement relates to learning goals. Results showed a significant relationship between students' theories of intelligence and their goal choices. Specifically, fixed mindset students were more likely to choose performance goals, while growth mindset students were much more likely to choose learning goals.

In another study, it was found that 80 per cent of students holding entity theory beliefs (fixed mindset) chose performance goal tasks, with 50 per cent of those choosing the very easy task. This is compared with more than 60 per cent of incremental theorists (growth mindset) choosing learning goal tasks. The majority of the remaining incremental theorists chose the challenging performance task, with only a small number choosing the very easy task.

Mueller and Dweck (1998) tested their hypothesis on college students by presenting them with a number of statements and asking them to indicate how much they agreed. Fixed mindset students were more likely to agree with the statements 'Although I hate to admit it, I sometimes would rather do well in class than learn a lot' and 'If I knew I wasn't going to do well on a task, I probably wouldn't do it, even if I might learn a lot from it'. However, growth mindset students tended to agree more with the statement 'It's much more important for me to learn things in my classes than it is to get the best grades'.

Participants were also asked a fourth question where they were instructed to circle the statement that best represented their beliefs: 'If I could choose between getting a good grade and being challenged in class, I would choose . . . a good grade [or] being challenged'. Sixty-eight per cent of the growth mindset students circled 'being challenged', compared to 35 per cent of fixed mindset students.

So what does this research tell us about the views people hold about their own and others' intelligence? As self-theories propose, our internal views form the basis for our psychological worlds, so the way we think about things such as intelligence impact on 'the self' in a particular way. The belief that schooling is about ensuring that you are better than everyone else creates certain roadblocks because schooling becomes a performance task rather then a learning one. If we think of intelligence as being a fixed and immovable entity, we become more concerned with proving it than improving it.

From implicit theories to mindsets

Dweck's research has managed to reach a wide audience, mainly through the publication of her most influential book *Mindset*, published in 2012. By expanding on her earlier work with a number of collaborators, Dweck further categorised the master and performer orientations and the entity and incremental belief systems into 'fixed' and 'growth' mindset.

Fixed mindset

These individuals tend towards a more performance oriented style, primarily due to their belief that intelligence is fixed. They believe that people only have a certain amount of intelligence and that they need to prove to others how clever they are. They are more likely to choose easy tasks, resist challenge and give up when things get too difficult. Their main aim is to look intelligent at all costs, they are less likely to work hard or spend time practising, and when faced with failure and setbacks they are more likely to give up or conceal their deficiencies.

Growth mindset

These individuals are more concerned with mastery than with performance, and view intelligence as something that can be worked on and improved. Their main aim is learning rather than displaying their intelligence, and they tend not to measure themselves against others. They work with passion and dedication, accept new challenges, and keep going when things become difficult. They embrace mistakes, confront their deficiencies and work hard to overcome them.

In practice, few individuals display pure fixed or pure growth orientations, and are more likely to appear on a continuum based on their responses to a number of self-completion questionnaires.

The role of praise

An individual's particular orientation arises in different ways. Dweck suggests that environmental factors play a much greater role in their development than innate factors. Specifically, research has found that the way in which teachers and parents praise children helps to define their mindset, and that praising ability will lead to a fixed mindset while praising effort will lead to a growth mindset. Furthermore, it would appear that no matter the individual's original inclination or predisposition, the consistent use of the right kind of praise could foster a growth mindset.

Early research found that feedback and praise that measured a child's traits (such as their 'cleverness') led to often-significant problems later on when the child encountered setbacks. These children learned to measure themselves from their performance, and if they judged this performance to be poor or lacking, they reached negative conclusions about themselves. Conversely, praise that measured effort or the strategies the child used in order to complete a task (known as 'process praise') led to greater effort and persistence when things became difficult. Phrases such as 'You're really good at this' or 'Aren't you clever' therefore pinpoint certain innate and fixed traits – that 'cleverness' is a thing you have rather than something you work hard at; something you develop and nurture. On the other hand, phrases such as 'You've worked really hard on this' or 'Well done, all that hard work really paid off, didn't it?' emphasise effort over intelligence and help to develop a mastery orientation or growth mindset.

Research has found that a mother's level of process praise to a toddler predicts their growth mindset five years later (e.g. see Pomerantz and Kempner, 2013), suggesting that a growth mindset can be taught indirectly from a very young age. Furthermore, process praise has a number of advantages over praise that measures personal traits:

- It gives students a feeling of control over their own learning by emphasising the role of effort over ability.
- It conveys the message that children can develop their abilities and suggests ways in which they can accomplish this.
- It reinforces the view that children can get better at something through their own efforts and actions.
- It emphasises the view that failure and setbacks can be overcome. In other words, process praise encourages resilience and academic buoyancy – the ability to bounce back from daily disappointments (see Chapter 6).
- It makes it more likely that children will want to engage in challenging work and to persist when it becomes difficult.

Process praise therefore provides a simple way to foster a growth mindset, but shouldn't be used simply to make children feel better about themselves. Dweck (2000) suggests that praise:

- Should be focused on outcome and not used as an excuse for a lack of progress. If students do fail, praising the effort they put into the task is essential, but the student must then be helped to understand the reasons behind their lack of progress and be given advice on how to rectify it.

- Shouldn't just be used when students struggle. Struggling students are more likely to receive praise in an effort to raise their spirits and encourage them to keep going. However, it's also very important that all students should be praised for their accomplishments, particularly in respect of their effort and the strategies they have employed.

Criticisms

A substantial number of studies support the hypothesis that students with a growth mindset do better in school. However, many of these studies have involved small samples and have taken place within controlled environments. A 2015 randomised controlled trial carried out in the United Kingdom did find that a growth mindset intervention can add around two months additional progress in maths and English when compared with a control group. However, the results failed to reach the threshold required for the difference to be statistically significant, meaning that the researchers were unable to confirm that the difference was down to the interventions alone.

Understanding the reasons behind the results of the UK study provides some clues as to why a theory that has been supported in numerous studies fails when examined within the framework of a large trial. Dweck suggests that the problem arises at the school level and that the theory itself remains empirically robust. Nevertheless, a number of wider issues have been raised that might further explain why Dweck's work, despite its overwhelming popularity, is failing to make a significant impact.

Do educational systems conspire against the theory?

In an attempt to nurture the growth mindset, it is first necessary to convince students of varying ages that intelligence is malleable. However, many educational systems use a number of policies to identify limits to individual students' ability. These might include ability setting and streaming, and the use of predicted grades. This situation can cause dissonance between the strategy schools are attempting to employ (the view that we can increase our intelligence through effort) and what actually happens in the classroom and beyond. Target grades, for example, set limits on intelligence and ability, disrupting the view that intelligence can be nurtured.

Does the theory ignore the quality of the curriculum?

It could be argued that the theory assumes that students will thrive even when the curriculum is poor or badly thought out. Teaching and learning represents an interaction between student, teacher and subject content, yet mindset theory places the emphasis on the student rather than the environment.

Does the theory ignore pedagogy?

Like the curriculum, the quality of pedagogy can differ between schools and between teachers within schools. If achievement is simply about how learners view their intelligence, then does this downplay the importance of quality teaching? Both pedagogy and curriculum quality might lead to the suggestion that growth mindset theory places teachers into a situation where they are attempting to fix the students rather than fix a broken system.

Does the theory appeal to teachers because it seems so simple?

Taken at face value, Dweck's notion of growth and fixed mindset learners appears to be simple enough. However, as has been discussed here, the concepts that underpin the theory are more complex, as are the methods necessary to make it work. Some schools might initiate wide-ranging and effective strategies, while others will hold an assembly, describe the basic principles and send students away to ponder their target grades while sitting in their ability sets.

Does the theory simply label children?

Labels can be damaging and often arise through stereotyping. Research has found that teachers often unconsciously label their students, creating behaviour that is self-fulfilling. It can be argued that labelling students as fixed or growth mindset simply leads to the perpetuation of underachievement for some groups of learners. Rather than teachers explaining poor academic performance in terms of laziness, there arises the real possibility that the explanation becomes one of a fixed mindset.

Does the theory fit in with other aspects of learning and self-theories?

There are a number of other contributory factors related to academic achievement such as emotions and socialisation. There are also other self-theories at play, primarily the role of academic self-concept. Anxiety, for example, can be detrimental to a number of cognitive processes, including working memory and attention, while academic self-concept remains state- rather than trait-specific. Can students therefore hold a growth mindset in maths but not in English because their English academic self-concept is low?

Does the theory fit with what we already know about intelligence?

The idea behind the development of growth mindset assumes that how we think about intelligence impacts academic achievement. This means that if people adopt the position that intelligence is highly heritable (as some studies have concluded), it becomes more difficult to reconcile this view with the one that insists that intelligence is malleable. This is true at both the student level and the teacher level. The student might want to believe that they can develop a growth mindset, but remains mindful that academic success does not run in the family. This nurtures a belief that the student is limited by her or his genes, rather than effort and persistence. Similarly, some teachers might be reluctant to support the idea of malleable intelligence if they believe that it is highly heritable. This then creates dissonance between what is required and what is believed, leading to the development of a fixed mindset. This can be offset by placing more emphasis on how the brain learns new tasks, irrespective of ideas around intelligence.

Using the principles of self-theories

By integrating a number of strategies that both encourage a growth mindset and a positive academic self-concept, teachers can help students adopt a more positive attitude, progress more rapidly and feel confident in their learning. Some of these strategies are discussed below.

Educating students on how the brain learns

Dweck used specially designed audiovisual material and computer software to help children understand how the brain makes new connections each time we learn something new. Allowing children to see how the brain works in this way adds legitimacy to the theory; simply telling children that they can succeed through effort is rarely effective and misinterprets the research that underpins it.

Emphasise personal best goals

Overemphasising competition between peers can lead to performance-oriented approaches and reduce mastery. Pitting your previous success against your future success, however, places the emphasis on mastery and progress – doing better than the time before. Educational psychologist Andrew Martin describes these as 'personal best goals' (see Liem, 2012), and studies have found that their use can increase mastery, encourage a growth mindset, and result in more realistic and rapid progress.

Practise what you preach

Teachers who demonstrate their own growth mindset are more likely to see pupils buy into the theory. A whole-school approach leads to consistency, and this in turn strengthens its impact.

Reconceptualise failure

While some have emphasised the need to celebrate failure, the more realistic approach would be to alter the way in which failure is viewed. Investigating people from history, science and sport in terms of their struggles, rather than concentrating on their success, has been found to increase motivation and engagement (see Chapter 7) (Lin-Siegler et al., 2016).

By identifying how students describe themselves and their ability to progress, teachers create opportunities to aid students in reframing these academic self-concepts. Table 3.1 offers some examples of how teachers can rewrite these beliefs.

Table 3.1 Reframing maladaptive beliefs

Maladaptive self-appraisal	Adaptive self-appraisal
I'm stupid.	I've missed something. What is it?
This is so easy.	I've pretty much mastered this. What next?
This is too hard.	I need to put more effort in if I'm going to master this.
I can't do this.	How can I use the strategies I've learned to do this?
I'm no good at this.	If I put in more effort and/or ask for help, I can be good at this.
Why is she so smart?	What is she doing that I'm not?

Praising effort over intellect

Praise is a valuable tool for both motivation and for nurturing a growth mindset. How and when praise is used is also important:

- Use process praise rather than trait praise. Phrases such as 'Aren't you clever' impress on students the innate nature of intelligence (a fixed mindset), while phrases such as 'You've worked really hard on this' or 'You've made good progress through the effort and hard work you have displayed' place the emphasis on what the student has done rather than their inborn capabilities.

- Be strategic with praise. Never offer praise simply to make students feel good about themselves. Praise must be linked to both effort and progress.

- Praise teenagers in private if possible. Teenagers enjoy being praised but they often shy away if the praise is given in full view of the class. Written praise in books and on assignments and projects is preferable to public praise. Again, praise where effort and progress is evidential, not as a tool to raise self-esteem.

Table 3.2 Trait praise versus process praise

Trait praise	Process praise
Students view intelligence as unchangeable and as something that they have or don't have.	Students view intelligence as something that can be developed.
Examples	**Examples**
'You are so intelligent.' 'You're very bright.' 'Aren't you clever?'	'I can see you've worked very hard on this, well done.' 'You've made good progress today because of the effort you've put in.' 'You're a very hard worker.'
Leads to	**Leads to**
The need to be better than everyone else. The view that failure is indicative of low intelligence. Less effort after encountering setbacks.	The desire to do better than last time. The view that failure is necessary in order to progress. Higher levels of resilience.

Conclusions

While self-theories often relate to indirect influences on educational attainment, they can impact on more direct strategies such as behaviour management, engagement and conscientiousness. As we have seen, some views of the self (especially those concerned with self-image and self-esteem) have very little impact on academic achievement and appear somewhat counterintuitive. Others, however, have been found to impact considerably on academic attainment.

Self-theories such as growth mindset also rely heavily on context. Mindset theory isn't a theory of intelligence in itself, but rather attempts to change students' implicit views of the nature of their own intelligence. If early educational experiences have been negative, these in turn have damaged the student's view of him or herself as a learner (academic self-concept), and will most likely have resulted in a fixed mindset. This fixed mindset will then be more resistant to change due to these negative educational experiences. As time goes by, each negative experience reinforces both the negative view of the self and the belief that there is little the student can do to change the current state of affairs (the construct known as learned helplessness). Mindset theory therefore never operates in isolation, and is influenced by a number of other concepts related to psychological development of the learner.

There may be a tendency to downplay the role of such theories due to their indirect nature, seeing as schools often spend a great deal of time on behaviour management strategies that are often viewed as a better investment of time and money. Nevertheless, investigating the role of self-building and encouraging a more positive academic self-image is likely to complement these other strategies. Furthermore, the evidence base for much of these theories remains strong, unlike other popular strategies that lack experimental rigour and favourable empirical outcomes.

Further reading

Self-Theories: Their Role in Motivation, Personality, and Development by
    C. S. Dweck (Psychology Press, 2000)
Before *Mindsets*, there was *Self-Theories*. The extent of Dweck's research cannot always be appreciated from her later, less academic works.

References

Baumeister, R. F., Campbell, J. D., Krueger, J. I. and Vohs, K. D. (2003). Does high self-esteem cause better performance, interpersonal success, happiness, or healthier lifestyles? *Psychological Science in the Public Interest*, 4(1), 1–44. doi: 10.1111/1529-1006.01431

Bong, M. and Skaalvik, E. M. (2003). Academic self-concept and self-efficacy: how different are they really? *Educational Psychology Review*, 15(1), 1–40.

Brandon, N. (1997). *How to Raise Your Self-Esteem*. New York: Random House.

Coopersmith, S. (1967). *The Antecedents of Self-Esteem*. San Francisco, CA: W. H. Freeman.

Dweck, C. S. (2000). *Self-Theories: Their Role in Motivation, Personality, and Development*. Hove: Psychology Press.

Dweck, C. S. (2012). *Mindset: The New Psychology of Success*. New York: Robinson.

Eccles, J., Wigfield, A. and Schiefele, U. (1998). Motivation to succeed. In W. Damon and N. Eisenberg (eds), *Handbook of Child Psychology: Social, Emotional, and Personality Development* (pp. 1017–1095). New York: Wiley.

Elliot, A. J. and McGregor, H. A. (1999). Test anxiety and the hierarchical model of approach and avoidance achievement motivation. *Journal of Personality and Social Psychology*, 76(4), 628–644. doi: 10.1037/0022-3514.76.4.628

Harter, S. (1999). *The Construction of the Self: A Developmental Perspective*. New York: Guilford.

Liem, G. A. D., Ginns, P., Martin, A. J., Stone, B. and Herrett, M. (2012). Personal best goals and academic and social functioning: a longitudinal perspective. *Learning and Instruction*, 22(3), 222–230. doi: 10.1016/j.learninstruc.2011.11.003

Lin-Siegler, X., Ahn, J. N., Chen, J., Fang, F.-F. A. and Luna-Lucero, M. (2016). Even Einstein struggled: effects of learning about great scientists' struggles on high school students' motivation to learn science. *Journal of Educational Psychology*, 108 (3), 314–328. doi: 10.1037/edu0000092

Marks, R. (2016). Children put in the bottom maths group at primary believe they'll never be any good. *The Conversation*. Retrieved 31 October 2017 from https://theconversation.com/children-put-in-the-bottom-maths-group-at-primary-believe-theyll-never-be-any-good-54502

Marsh, H. W. and Martin, A. J. (2011). Academic self-concept and academic achievement: relations and causal ordering. *British Journal of Educational Psychology*, 81(1), 59–77. doi: 10.1348/000709910X503501

Mueller, C. M. and Dweck, C. S. (1998) Praise for intelligence can undermine children's motivation and performance. *Journal of Personality and Social Psychology*, 75(1), 33–52. doi: 10.1037//0022-3514.75.1.33

Muijs, R. D. (1997). Predictors of academic achievement and academic self-concept: a longitudinal perspective. *British Journal of Educational Psychology*, 67, 263–277.

Neff, K. D. (2011) Self-compassion, self-esteem, and well-being. *Social and Personality Psychology Compass*, 5(1), 1–12. doi: 10.1111/j.1751-9004. 2010.00330.x

Parsons, S. and Hallam, S. (2014) The impact of streaming on attainment at age seven: evidence from the Millennium Cohort Study. *Oxford Review of Education*, 40(5), 567–589.

Pomerantz, E. M. and Kempner, S. G. (2013). Mothers' daily person and process praise: implications for children's theory of intelligence and motivation. *Developmental Psychology*, 49(11), 2040–2046. doi: 0.1037/a0031840

Rosenberg, M. (1965). *Society and the Adolescent Self-Image*. Princeton, NJ: Princeton University Press.

Tiedemann, J. (2000). Parents' gender stereotypes and teachers' beliefs as predictors of children's concept of their mathematical ability in elementary school. *Journal of Educational Psychology*, 92(1), 144–151. doi: 10.1037/0022-0663.92.1.144

Tyson, D. F., Linnenbrink-Garcia, L. and Hill, N. E. (2009). Regulating debilitating emotions in the context of performance: achievement goal orientations, achievement-elicited emotions, and socialization contexts. *Human Development*, 52(6), 329–356.

Wigfield, A. and Eccles, J. (eds) (2002). *Development of Achievement Motivation*. San Diego, CA: Academic Press.

Wigfield, A. and Karpathian, M. (1991). Who am I and what can I do? Children's self concepts and motivation in achievement situations. *Educational Psychologist*, 26, 233–261. doi: 10.1080/00461520.1991. 9653134

4 | Creativity

What is the role of creativity in the classroom, and what can psychology tell us about the process of creative thinking? This chapter makes the case that creativity plays a role in all school subjects, not just those that are traditionally viewed as creative arts, and presents a view of creativity that is based on transferring knowledge and skills to new contexts. In particular, it covers:

- The breadth of creativity, from the great inventors and scientists to useful ideas in more everyday situations.
- The role of knowledge and expertise – the preparation element of creativity.
- The processes involved in creative thinking, including association and divergent thinking.
- Incubation – the potential benefits of delays and forgetting.
- The role of creative traits and motivation, and the argument that creativity is specific to domains of expertise.
- Lesson planning, covering activities from brainstorming through to extended writing.

Teachers are in a difficult position when it comes to creativity. On the one hand, it seems essential to develop it in our learners – we are frequently told that in a rapidly changing world, it is essential that young people should not only develop facts and skills, but also learn how to be flexible. They must have the cognitive abilities to apply what they have learned in new ways and to transfer their learning to novel contexts.

On the other hand, the education system as a whole does not always greatly favour creativity. Some elements of learning are very closely structured, with a limited range of acceptable responses to exams and coursework, and improving attainment in this context can conflict with allowing greater freedom of choice. However, an argument can be made that exams which test retention of content with little real-world application are not assessing the skills that people need to become successful in life (Sternberg, 2008). There is a risk in such circumstances that creativity becomes a covert, even subversive, activity for the teacher. In areas such as emotions and behaviour, too, there is a conflict between creativity and compliance, where pupils' motivation for creativity might involve figuring out how to bend or break the rules.

For these reasons, creativity is increasingly the subject of heated debate in education, with more traditionally minded educators accused of stifling it (Zhao, 2017), but more progressive educators often vague about what exactly it is or how best to develop it. From a psychological point of view, what exactly is creativity – and is it even a single trait or skill? Are we right to see it as being neglected in the current educational climate, and how can it productively combine with the essential aspects of the daily procedures of teaching and learning? This chapter will look at these questions from a research-informed point of view.

The creative individual

A traditional view of creativity is that some people are more creative than others – they have a particular 'gift' in this area. Is there such a thing as a creative individual, and if so what can we do to foster this in learners?

It might be assumed that people who produce great creative work are highly intelligent – after all, the word 'genius' is used in everyday speech to refer both to someone highly intelligent and to people who are unusually gifted in a field such as music. Great scientific breakthroughs such as the discovery of radiation or evolution spring to mind, as well as culture-defining giants of literature. Interestingly, though, the statistical link between high IQ scores and success in creative fields is quite weak: it helps to have an above-average IQ, but beyond this point it makes little difference (Jauk et al., 2013). Intelligence, is, in any case, an overly simplistic concept, and cognitive functions develop throughout adolescence (see Chapter 2).

Additionally, creative work can be viewed more as a process of learning skills than of realising an innate talent. Detailed investigations into the background of individuals from many fields who have made major creative contributions to society suggest that this pattern is relatively common – while these individuals vary in whether they had stellar early careers or not, what they have in common is that their creative work had a foundation of many years of work and learning. Csikszentmihalyi (1996) notes that the main factors that lead to major cultural advances or cultural breakthroughs are the development of deep expertise in a field, an unstinting hard work and focus on the area, attention to detail, and an insatiable curiosity.

The good news for the teacher, therefore, is that most of our students (perhaps all) are capable of creative thinking. The knowledge, curiosity and motivation to produce successful creative work is likely to vary from one individual to the next, but there are things that we can do as educators to influence these factors.

Creating things, great and small

So, what exactly is meant by creativity? To take the term literally, it means the ability to create something, ideally something that is useful or entertaining in some way. Typically, this is going to involve a rearrangement of existing parts or concepts (words, musical notes, mathematical notation, etc.), rather than making something completely new and unrecognisable. It is also the creation of something useful, rather than a random or pointless recombination of ideas. The term might be usefully defined, therefore, as novel and useful combinations of existing information (Kim and Zhong, 2017).

How broad is creativity, and what activities should we include in discussions of the term? Importantly, psychologists recognise that creativity plays a role in every school subject and a great many tasks, not just school activities that are traditionally viewed as creative, such as art or drama. Furthermore, these creative acts occur on a daily basis. It's not necessary to do a large project or diorama – creative thinking on a small scale occurs during problem-solving, decision-making or improvisation (Sawyer, 1992). Everyday examples of creative thinking include figuring out how to get from A to B by public transport, or make do without a missing piece of apparatus. As most school pupils are unlikely to be producing creative work of global significance, it is important to understand the role of these smaller-scale creative acts.

When researchers focus on a larger scale of creativity – the great ideas – this is sometimes nicknamed 'big C' creativity in contrast to the more everyday 'small c' creativity (also called historical and psychological creativity, respectively) (Boden, 2004). Big C therefore refers to the highly significant breakthroughs of artists, scientists and others. Of course, it remains difficult for researchers to define exactly what is accepted as a major creative idea and what is not. Csikszentmihalyi (1996) argues that to be considered creative, an idea or product has to make a major difference to a field, as acknowledged by experts in the field. However, this is very open to subjectivity and to the trends of a particular culture – it could be the case that certain new ideas challenge the establishment, and are therefore ignored. Overall, however, big C creativity refers to pieces of work that are of such cultural significance that they may significantly impact on the lives of others, and may be the product of years of work, including theories, compositions, novels and inventions.

As teachers, we probably don't require our learners to show big C creativity, nice though that would be. It is enough for them to be creative in more day-to-day 'small c' tasks. Thinking up an idea that saves them time in the morning, or drawing a mind map that helps with revision – such things may not be original, but do involve creating something new and personally useful, thereby fitting the definition suggested above. It is, of course, of some theoretical and practical interest to know whether there is a link between the two types of creativity, and how schools can contribute to 'big C' – after all, we do want to develop great scientists and artists of the future. At least some researchers (e.g. Sternberg, 2008) think that developing the skills and attributes associated with small c – such as playing with ideas and new combinations, curiosity about how things work, and being perceptive at noticing and seeing connections – is likely to pave the way towards greater creative work. And even it doesn't lead to their becoming the next Leonardo da Vinci, such traits will serve them well in life and the workplace.

While it's helpful to consider the longer-term implications of creativity for society, the focus in this chapter will remain particularly on processes that a teacher can control within the confines of a classroom, with pupils who are still of a young age, and within a time frame that tends to be limited to a few months. In the classroom, creative processes may often involve simulated rather than real problems, and/or aim to act as a vehicle to progress other learning. For example, learners may plan how to build a colony on Mars or discuss how to tackle global warming without the expectation of carrying these things out. By tackling a problem, learners are retrieving items from memory and considering how they can be put together in new ways. This can help to consolidate factual knowledge, and provides experience of processes that are required when thinking creatively in the real world.

Social and classroom context

If creativity involves creating something new and useful, then creative thinking is required when putting elements together to solve a problem, assembling facts into a coherent explanation when peer teaching, or when making links between different areas of content when evaluating a theory. The importance of factual knowledge is one area where teachers can start to reconcile the debate mentioned at the start of this chapter – the more our learners know, the better able they are to tackle creative problems. This means there needn't necessarily be a tension between exam-focused learning and the value of creativity. In fact, creative tasks can be an excellent vehicle for some of the retrieval-based activities discussed in Chapter 1, and will provide a meaningful context too.

Although the general assumption – reflected in the points discussed so far – is that creativity is largely based on an individual's skills and talents, teachers can also benefit from considering how groups interact. Creativity is at least in part a social process – groups provide both the context in which ideas develop and the fora in which contributions are evaluated (Cropley and Cropley, 2010). Although essential processes take place in one individual learner's mind, people share ideas and then build on them, meaning that creativity in a group is more than the sum of its parts (Sawyer, 2007). Group or cultural attitudes can also serve to either encourage or stifle creativity, impacting on whether people are motivated to be curious and to develop new ideas (Amabile, 1996; Moran, 2010). For the teacher, this can mean the immediate subculture of their own classroom – developing a space where curiosity and playfulness with new ideas is welcomed.

What are the key principles of creativity?

Preparation

As we have seen, creativity is less a matter of mysterious genius, and more down to developing knowledge and skills. In terms of 'big C' creativity, the most impactful ideas come not from random flashes of inspiration, but through having a solid foundation of facts and an expert understanding of the problem that needs to be solved. And although years are not required for 'small c' insights, they can likewise benefit from prior learning. For example, it is easier to solve a problem via analogy if you have learned about two or more previous examples of a principle than if you have only learned about one (Gick and Holyoak, 1983).

Ironically, then, the route towards creativity among our pupils does not just involve the creative activities themselves, but also teaching factual information (perhaps in a fairly traditional way) in order to develop a sound body of knowledge. Just as poets cannot create masterpieces without knowing the rule of grammar, other learners also need to learn the facts and rule systems in their fields – film students need to carefully study previous films if they are to create something novel, researchers need a thorough understanding of scientific methodology and of the area of study itself, and artists need to master basic techniques and understand the problems that past masters have tried to tackle.

Ultimately, creativity can't happen without factual and conceptual understanding, and therefore any criticisms which state that schools kill off creativity by focusing on teaching and testing facts should be considered in this light; that shouldn't be all that they do, but it also can't be neglected. This is perhaps most obviously the case in the realms of science and technology, but applies to any field. Many of the anecdotes popularly used to illustrate the 'flash of insight' view of creativity – such as Kekule's discovery of the benzene ring – actually reflect the culmination of years of work, and could not have happened if the individual hadn't put in the effort first (Cropley and Cropley, 2010). While a moment of luck or inspiration – perhaps stimulated by a chance association – might be necessary, the background is a process of building skills and expertise.

Creative activities can occur at all ages – it would be absurd to wait until their learners have full mastery of a discipline before any creative work can begin. It may therefore be best seen as a recursive process, with creative work helping to consolidate the factual learning and show how it can be applied, and also stimulating curiosity that aids later learning.

Creative tasks can help with consolidation, in that they often involve active retrieval from memory, and do so in more varied contexts than those in which they were originally learned. For example, when designing an experiment, the student often needs to draw on and integrate factual information about more than one topic, and to draw on what they have learned about research methodology as well. This integration of knowledge helps to build a sound foundation for future creative tasks.

Association

Amid the debate over which acts constitute creativity, some of the most useful contributions from psychology have focused on specific mental processes involved in coming up with creative ideas or solutions to problems. Much of our thinking involves making connections between different ideas, thoughts and memories – combining them in ways that are either routine or novel. Psychological views of creative thinking focus on the novel connections – putting together learned information in new ways. In this way, creativity can be seen to involve both retrieving stored information from memory and combining it in new ways.

One absolutely essential building block of this process is association – the mental linking of stimuli or ideas. The idea of associating two things in the world has been widely studied throughout the history of psychology, primarily in animals! Behaviourist psychologists have looked at everything from how rats associate places with rewards, to how dogs can generalise from one music tone to another. It is well established, for example, that animals which respond strongly to one stimulus such as a musical tone will still respond – but more weakly – to a changed version of the stimulus (Carlson, 1998).

People can also make associations between an idea and a stimulus, or even between two ideas. Whether an association is made will depend on how closely a problem resembles other ideas or stimuli, and therefore depends on each individual's past experience – similarities will make it easier for analogies to be drawn when formulating a solution to a problem (Dewey, 1910).

If memory is the foundation for creativity, creative thinking can also influence what we remember. Wilson (2016) presented people with objects to consider how they could be used in various scenarios such as a bank heist, moving house or being surrounded by dangerous animals. It was found that the scenarios that had the most potential for creative ideas (as measured by how many uses for the objects people could think of) were also those in which memory for objects was superior. The researcher concluded that creative thinking is a uniquely complex form of deep processing, leading to items being better recalled over the long term. This suggests that creative thinking can impact on the structures of LTM, developing the extent to which concepts and information are learned and interlinked in schema knowledge.

Surprisingly, sleep also appears to play a role in building or strengthening associations. Rasch and Born (2013) cite a study where priming before naps (i.e. giving people problems before they slept) resulted in better problem-solving, particularly when the naps included REM sleep, the type associated with dreaming. When given a problem to solve and then a time delay during which they either had a nap or did not, naps filled with REM sleep led to better creative answers compared with naps without REM or simply resting quietly. The researchers described the moments immediately after REM sleep as a 'hyper-associative state'. To look at this another way, the mind consolidates new memories and forms or strengthens new associations during sleep. Indeed, sleep researcher George William Domhoff (2005) likens the process of dreaming to that of daydreaming/mind-wandering, saying that it is what occurs when the conscious mind is switched off and our thoughts are allowed to flow freely (readers may remember that mind-wandering can have positive effects on creativity, as described in Chapter 2).

As creativity depends so fundamentally on both memory and association, teachers can take account of the well-understood factors that govern both of these processes – some of which have been described in previous chapters. For example, it is easier to make familiar associations than more novel ones, and they can be prompted by varied external stimulation (something that may be lacking in some learning environments). The active retrieval of information from memory is affected by a learner's limited attentional capacity, while associations often form automatically and sometimes without our being aware of them.

Creative tasks are often seen as an inefficient use of teaching time in contrast to traditional direct instruction (Zhao, 2017), but the evidence that there is an important link between creativity and memory implies that such tasks have potential to consolidate learning via the development of rich, meaningful associations (i.e. deep processing). This is a good argument for using tasks with elements of creative thinking to follow up on earlier work.

REM sleep may be essential for making associations, but this does not suggest a practical strategy for most classroom situations! It could be utilised during longer projects that require work outside class – coming up with creative ideas may be more successful first thing after a learner wakes up. Within school – assuming a nap is impractical – a learner could at least be given some 'downtime' away from the task, or reading/thinking time where some reflection and mind-wandering is possible.

The importance of forming new associations may appear to conflict with the value, discussed elsewhere, of fast and automated thinking that occurs when facts and processes are well learned. In other words, there could be a conflict between the importance of knowledge and the value of novelty. If facts and skills lead to automatic associations, little attention is being paid to the thinking process involved, and there may be a lack of curiosity about other possible responses. For example, if a learner is repeatedly taught that an essay should start with a definition of the topic, or a paragraph with a topic sentence, this may become an automatic approach for them (reducing cognitive load; see Chapter 2), making it less likely that they will experiment with different options. A teacher may wish to be mindful of building a curiosity to try out different forms and approaches in their subject matter. Presenting problems and questions for discussion and reflecting on the strengths or weaknesses of alternatives can stimulate learners to reflect on why things are done in a particular way, in contrast to the highly rule-based approach of a novice learner. A similar point could be made about artistic techniques, scientific methodology, or ways to put together an electronic circuit – it may be worthwhile for learners to consider alternatives, if only to find out why they don't work as well.

Divergent thinking

Forming an analogy by generalising a principle or procedure from one context to another is another key facet of the mental processes behind creativity. In doing so, learners take something known, and use it to create a new or alternative solution. Although often termed lateral thinking (or 'thinking outside the box') in everyday speech, researchers tend to call this 'divergent thinking' – the form of problem-solving meaning the ability to come up with many novel associations or solutions to a stimulus, such as to think of alternative uses for an object or how to improve a product (Torrance, 1966). This contrasts with convergent thinking, which is where people think through a well-defined problem such as a logic puzzle, where there is only one correct solution. Divergent thinking can therefore be helpful for finding alternative solutions to a problem where a more conventional approach is flawed or ineffective.

An early test of divergent thinking was developed by Guilford (1950), focusing on a task that asked people to think of as many alternative uses as they could for everyday objects, such as a brick or paper clip. A more elaborate later test developed by Torrance (1966) added considerably more categories, and both tests are still widely used today. Key elements that are tested include not only the ability to create solutions, but also the number of ideas thought of in a given time, and the unusualness of these solutions (measured by assessing their frequency in a bank of previous answers).

Divergent thinking could play an important role in problem-solving, but this will depend on the nature of the problem. Convergent thinking is involved in problems where the steps required are clear and the learner simply needs to follow them accurately, as may be the case in many maths tasks. In other situations, there simply isn't one way to solve the problem, and the most immediately obvious solution may not be the best one – for example, how should we best design an experiment? For this, it is important that a learner is able to both come up with many ideas (fluency) and to evaluate those ideas.

A curious recent finding is that scores on tests of creativity have fallen since 1990, particularly among younger pupils, even as IQ scores have gradually risen among school pupils (Kim, 2011). This could be because this kind of thinking is encouraged less than in the past; an experiment by Bonawitz et al. (2011) found that pupils explored a new object less and were less curious when they heard explicit instruction about how it worked, even if the instruction was directed at another pupil.

Divergent thinking is not the sum total of creativity, but does appear to be a reasonably valid way of predicting future creative actions. It can be prompted via tasks that are structured in such a way that more than one solution is possible (although it needn't be the case that all are equally worthwhile). It tends to occur more during discovery/exploration-based activities, which are often highly motivating (Ryan and Deci, 2017) but less efficient in terms of imparting content knowledge (Mayer, 2004; Zhao, 2017).

In order to tackle the efficiency problem, a teacher could design divergent thinking activities in such a way that they simultaneously link to evidence-based learning strategies, such as deep processing and retrieval practice, and use them towards the end of topics to develop more interconnected concept knowledge within a particular subject area. Based on the classic tests of divergent thinking, activities could include:

- *Fluency.* Thinking of multiple uses/problems based on a situation or stimulus. For example, health risks faced during a historic sea voyage that the learners have studied, and how to tackle them.
- *Originality.* Trying to think of an evaluation point that nobody else in the class has thought of.
- *Abstractness.* Thinking of an example use/application of a concept that is as different as possible from the example provided by the teacher.
- *Elaboration.* Developing an idea to its fullest extent. For example, when identifying a weakness of a theory or a piece of research, a student could be prompted with 'And that would be a problem because . . .?', leading to a (potentially) extensive cause and effect chain of thinking.

Curiously, movement may also be helpful in promoting divergent thinking; Oppezzo and Schwartz (2014) found that walking improved performance on a test of divergent thinking but mildly hurt performance on more traditional problem-solving tasks. This may, at least in part, relate to different viewpoints stimulating more associations in a learner's mind.

Motivation

Creativity could be seen to form part of our instinctive behaviour as a species – after all, children are spontaneously creative in their play and talk. Humanistic psychologists have suggested that the development of this drive and motivation is more to do with surroundings than innate talent – we are all inherently creative, they suggested, but prevented from fulfilling our creative potential by the life situations we find ourselves in (see Chapter 7).

This would make sense from an evolutionary perspective too. Genes that contribute to human creativity may have been selected during the evolution of our early human ancestors due to the advantages of being able to use an object in new ways, to make analogies that allow problem-solving in dangerous situations, or for the social benefits that creative thinking can afford.

One important area in this regard is a person's motivation to achieve. Amabile (1996) has looked at the interaction between motivation and learning, and found that intrinsic motivation – finding things interesting and valuable for their own sake – leads to more successful and sustained learning, particularly when tasks require creative and analytic thinking. Learners are also more likely to focus fully on such tasks, in contrast to ones that are motivated by external factors such as grades (see Chapter 7). At its most effective, this can lead to what Csikszentmihalyi (1996) calls 'flow' – where a skilled learner becomes deeply absorbed in a creative task, with little awareness of passing time and of the outside world. This is most likely to occur when both the challenge and the skill level is high, and is therefore difficult for beginners.

Empathy and communication in groups can also play a role in motivation. Just thinking about others can lead to more creative and useful ideas and increase motivation (Grant and Berry, 2011), and people often find it motivating to work on what other people find interesting, and to solve problems for and with others (Hidi and Harackiewicz, 2000).

Combining the research points above, it is clear that while creative thinking is a natural talent that young people have, it can easily be stifled by a badly structured task. Considerable attention should be paid to ensuring that the task inspires curiosity and playfulness. In order to achieve a 'flow' state, the learner must have expertise in the form of relevant prior knowledge and skills, and the task must be both challenging enough to keep them engaged while flexible and open enough to give them a sense of ownership in the process.

Creative learning tasks that allow for a degree of choice and freedom can be both motivating and effective, particularly if there are opportunities to pursue existing interests, and ones that fit with shared social priorities. This must, of course, be measured against the need for learners to complete tasks that meet the aims of the syllabus. Rather than allowing complete freedom, therefore, elements of choice between carefully selected options could be provided. Problem-solving and brainstorming (see below) could be designed with a genuine need to solve problems for and with others.

Incubation

Incubation is the idea that creative ideas need a period of latent time – after initially tackling the problem or task – before they are ready. It appears that in order to make creative connections, it can help to take a break from the problem. An early idea from the psychology of creativity was that this is one stage in a broader process, beginning with preparation/learning and ending with a final moment of insight (Wallas, 1926).

Incubation may also indicate the important effect of *forgetting* on performance. Inhibition is a key process in memory, allowing the mind to select the correct or relevant information rather than similar but unwanted items (Storm, 2011). Ironically, forgetting is often desirable! However, this can mean that when a learner retrieves the wrong item, other similar items are temporarily suppressed, making it harder to recall them instead. This is more likely to happen when the items are from the same category, and is also worse when the learner is making an effort (Storm et al., 2007). An everyday example is when trying to remember a person's name and a similar (but wrong) name sticks in your head. In such situations, a period of time away from a task can be helpful, and incubation may therefore help the creative process because it helps us to reduce the focus on incorrect solutions.

In a similar vein to this, Smith et al. (1993) looked at the 'conformity effect' in creativity – the tendency for creative thinking to be constrained by previous examples. When participants were shown example toys and asked to design their own, they tended to include features seen in the example. A period of incubation may help to reduce the extent to which the creative process is interfered with by such undesired contextual associations.

It is clear that a number of cognitive process are at work without conscious attention, including inhibition. During sleep, too, memories are consolidated, while the interfering effects of activating or learning a particular memory reduces overnight (Walker et al., 2003). There might really be something to be said for sleeping on a problem, therefore, as sleep provides time for incubation, and boosts the mind's ability to form and consolidate new associations.

For the teacher, the concept of incubation presents a challenge – we often have limited time on tasks. How can we foster creativity if learners may need to 'sleep on it' or forget about a task for a period of time? In addition, taking too much time away may lead to forgetting of the key details (especially for non-experts).

A useful assumption is that planning a break, even a short one, will be helpful. This could be a break between teaching periods, a traditional 'timeout', or dividing a task across more than one lesson within the week. Another simple strategy would be to set a problem towards the end of one day/lesson, with the intention of tackling it the following lesson (ideally early in the day) – although the time period might not be optimal, it would usually be preferable to no incubation at all, and more or less guarantees that a night of sleep will have taken place.

When a task must take place within a single session, allowing for incubation may involve interspersing focused work with group discussions and feedback, thus occupying their working memory and attention (which fits well with the idea of interleaving; see Chapter 1). Another possibility is to build a period of reflection into the task, and allow (or actively encourage) a degree of mind-wandering. Learners will spontaneously engage in this when working on tasks such as extended writing, and it's important to value this thinking time. This differs, of course, from time that is spent on distractions such as browsing the Internet or chatting, which are more likely to be procrastination strategies.

The concept of incubation and the importance of sleep also suggests that while processes such as brainstorming and focused knowledge/skill building are valuable, creative processes as a whole are best when not rushed. Combining ideas in new ways and synthesising facts into a more well-rounded understanding of a topic may involve numerous opportunities to stop and reflect, and ideas can later come quite spontaneously, perhaps when in the middle of another activity. To capture these ideas, a simple tool – used by poets and inventors alike – is to prompt the journalling of any and all ideas in a general-purpose notebook that is not 'marked' by the teacher, encouraging freedom of thinking. More broadly, it is best for teachers not to see creative tasks as a short extension at the end of a lesson. This may tick a box as far as educational authorities are concerned, but is unlikely to prompt the more authentic and valuable aspects of creative thinking.

Traits

As mentioned above, great creative work can be linked to attention to detail, persistence and curiosity. A major long-term challenge for educators is the development of these traits.

First, are these traits at all – or skills? If they are personality traits, that implies that they are relatively fixed in the individual, while a skill can be learned. A prominent current theory of personality – the *big five theory* – suggests that everyone's personality is composed of five main traits, the levels of which vary between individuals but stay relatively fixed across the lifespan. These include traditional concepts such as extroversion (see Chapter 6), but also two others that are particularly relevant to creative work:

- *Conscientiousness.* The tendency to pay close attention to detail, and to complete work rather than leaving things unfinished.

- *Openness to experience.* The tendency to welcome rather than avoid new experiences. This tends to include curiosity, and an enjoyment of toying with new and unusual ideas.

According to the theory, these will vary among learners in a classroom, and to some extent they can be observed via a person's habits. While some people are content to repeat patterns of behaviour, others have more of a tendency to explore, such as by reading new authors or listening to unfamiliar musical genres rather than sticking to their favourites. Conscientious pupils are usually well organised, and when they submit work it will tend to be carefully done and punctual rather than sloppy.

Personality is viewed as being relatively constant across the lifespan, and possibly based largely on a person's genes (e.g. McCrae et al., 2000) – or at least depending on a combination of genetics and early experience. It can therefore, rather like intelligence, appear to be a fairly unhelpful concept to the teacher – if we can't change it in our learners, then what use is it?

However, the effects of 'nurture' on personality should not be ignored, and context is also very important. For all that it may come more naturally to some people than others, all babies and children are pretty curious, and maintaining that curiosity as they grow older can depend a lot on educational experiences. The social context can depend on peers – learners, especially younger age groups, are often motivated by similar interests to their peers. As they grow older, it can be helpful to motivate them via their emerging adult identities, and sloppy work could be more to do with its failing to tap into their interests than to their personality. The power of the group remains strong both as a motivating influence and as a source of feedback and suggestions for older learners (Glyer, 2008), as can be seen through the many historic examples of creative groups.

Learners may enjoy doing a personality test based on the big five (see www.psytoolkit.org/survey-library/big5-bfi-s.html for a quick but accurate version), and this can help them to become aware of their strengths and weaknesses. However, for the teacher to focus on the cause of poorer-quality creative work as being primarily a matter of habits rather than ability can be motivating, helping to foster a growth mindset. Besides, as with other areas of learning, improvement is possible for all pupils regardless of their current level.

In terms of conscientiousness, some pupils may be capable of producing excellent creative work, but may fail to do so because they are disorganised with their notes, leave tasks until the last minute, and don't redraft or replan as often as their more conscientious peers. Identifying pupils who struggle in these areas and providing support such as reminders could help considerably, as could scheduling class time for reworking rather than setting it as a homework activity.

Curiosity can also be encouraged, even if it comes more naturally to some learners than others. From a psychological point of view, curiosity can be linked to the innate exploration behaviour seen in most species – and certainly in children. For learners, there can be an unpleasant feeling of not knowing, and a desire to 'open the box' to see what's inside. As a teacher, we can stimulate learning by generating the mild frustration of not knowing, rather than explaining every aspect of a process or providing very detailed steps to follow. This combines well with the idea of incubation – leaving a problem unfinished may encourage them to think it over and discuss it with their peers, especially if it is the last thing they do in school before the end of the day.

A theory: transfer of learning

The section above has highlighted some of the key concepts and psychological processes relevant to creativity. The following theory helps to show how some of the underlying cognitive processes work together when learners create new ideas from existing knowledge and skills.

The term 'transfer' means the application of a skill or idea to a different situation from that in which it was first learned (e.g. taking what has been learned about fractions at school and applying it when scaling down, or up, the required quantities of a recipe). Also, and perhaps more importantly, it relates to the ability to make analogies between reasoning in one situation and another. As Barnett and Ceci (2002, p. 613) have argued: 'much of the financial and human investment in education has been justified on the grounds that formal schooling helps inculcate general skills that transfer beyond the world of academia and thus help students become more productive members of society'.

Transfer can play a key role in the creative thinking behind new ideas. For example, Charles Darwin developed existing ideas from geology (gradual change over millions of years) and demographics (the principles of population growth) when formulating his theory of evolution by natural selection (Desmond and Moore, 1992). It can also lead to mistakes – if a young child learns that a rubber can be used to erase graphite pencil and then tries to erase a drawing done in coloured pencil, they are transferring the skill and underlying knowledge to a new context, but doing so unsuccessfully. Either way, an analogy or association is drawn between a previous learning experience and an unfamiliar problem.

In other words, transfer relates to some of the key nuts and bolts of creativity – of relating what has been learned into something new, and therefore making a restricted amount of learning apply to a potentially unlimited set of situations.

The theory

Barnett and Ceci (2002) have identified some factors affecting a learner's ability to transfer from one context to another. These include:

- *Location.* It is easier to transfer learning within the same location that it was first learned (e.g. the classroom or lab).
- *Time.* It is easier to transfer learning that has been recently learned. This is because some aspects of transfer involve retrieving information from LTM.
- *Domain.* It is easier to transfer within one domain (e.g. a school subject) than to another one (such as transferring a learned idea from history to a problem in economics).

More broadly, these dimensions have been described as near transfer and far transfer. A near transfer situation could involve applying a recently learned concept to a problem within the class. If any of the factors above are very different from the learning situation, then far transfer is involved; all of the above factors could combine, making transfer even more difficult.

Although near transfer is easier, it is essential to develop far transfer through classroom work. Just as a learner driver does not develop their skill by driving around the same block continually, so in school education it is important to develop a learner's ability to use skills and knowledge away from the routine learning situations, or those that only relate to familiar learning scenarios. Fortunately, this can be developed with practice; rather like the study of memory, it will be valuable to push the learner as far as they can towards far transfer while still retaining a high chance of success, because successful retrieval of information and ideas will help to consolidate the required associations in memory and make them more likely to occur in the future.

Task

Consider the following learning tasks. In what way do they involve creative thinking? How could the learning be transferred to other contexts? Some are more obvious than others. Try to think of at least one example for each.

Table 4.1 Connecting creative thinking to common classroom activities

	Underlying knowledge or skills	Transfer to another context
Drawing a picture of a rare animal		
Writing a short summary of a video clip		
Thinking of a real example from a concept definition		
Giving a strength and a weakness of a theory		
Retelling a story or anecdote		
Summarising a textbook chapter		
Engaging in a classroom discussion		
Peer teaching – helping a classmate who is struggling		

A key implication of viewing creativity in terms of transfer is that it implies a certain degree of domain-specificity, with transfer to unfamiliar topics or domains being much more difficult. Following this principle, Baer (2016) argues that creativity is not a universal process; people can be very creative in one field and not at all creative in another. People are likely to show the most creativity in areas where they have put in a lot of preparation and developed skills and concept knowledge.

While it may be possible to test creativity in a more general way, the type of creativity tested will be quite superficial (Sternberg, 1985). From a transfer point of view, the more dissimilar two tasks are, the less easily skills, ideas and strategies will transfer from one to the other. However, over time, a skill or item of conceptual knowledge can become so well-practised in multiple contexts that it becomes relatively unconstrained by domain – in a similar way to how most people can use language or maths skills in multiple domains rather than associating them with a given context, or how several specific life experiences can contribute to our generalised concept knowledge.

As discussed at the start of this chapter, a key defining aspect of creativity is not just forming new ideas, but doing so in a way that is useful to the individual or to society. It is worth emphasising again that it is not the domain (e.g. writing, drawing) that makes something creative, but whether it involves a process of creating something new and useful by retrieving knowledge and skills and applying them in a context that differs from how they were learned. A small child is doing this when they learn that paint changes the colour of one object (e.g. a piece of paper) and then use it to change the colour of another object (e.g. a desk, or their hands!), but likewise are creatively applying learning in domains such as maths and language if they use what they have learned in new contexts and when tackling new problems.

Supporting evidence

There is evidence that transferring learning or thinking outside of a familiar task is very difficult; Simons et al. (2016) reviewed the evidence for 'brain training' programmes, finding limited evidence that improvements on one task generalised to similar tasks, and almost no evidence that improvements transferred to more distantly related skills or to everyday life. This suggests that far transfer is difficult and rare, and helps to explain why people tend to specialise in particular areas; it is difficult to transfer expertise (e.g. as a sports coach) even to a superficially similar context (e.g. moving from football coaching to cricket coaching).

In a study that was similar in principle but more specific to creativity, Baer (1994) trained participants to show more divergent thinking when telling or writing stories, writing poems, writing mathematical word problems, and making collages. He found that while improvements were made in individual tasks, these didn't transfer to the different types of creative task. This suggests that divergent thinking (or creative thinking more broadly) should not be seen as a general trait, but instead as something that people will be able to do better in one situation than in another. People are better able to transfer the skills involved in a 'near' context (i.e. one that resembles the situation where skills were learned).

Creativity also plays a role in the teaching process itself, and research suggests that as teachers gain experience, the tendency is to plan less and improvise more – Sawyer (2004) notes more experienced teachers deliver lessons that are more like an improvised performance than a scripted performance, and are more open to spur-of-the-moment learning opportunities. This again speaks to the idea that, at least in part, creativity involves transfer of skills and knowledge to novel situations.

Using the theory

One helpful aspect of this theory for the educator who wants to increase creativity is that it focuses on the task and its context. Many things that learners do are domain-specific, and can be learned to a level that becomes more or less automatic (as discussed in Chapter 2). The theory of transfer helps to illustrate the need to develop key conceptual knowledge, which can then be used to attempt tasks that reflect situations that increasingly deviate from the original learning context. It can't be one teacher's responsibility to teach creativity as a whole (interestingly, a similar point can be made of skills such as literacy; being a good reader in one domain such as history doesn't mean that skills such as skim reading will transfer successfully to another domain such as reading an article about chemistry).

Kim and Zhong (2017) note that creative ideas can arise from chaos, and that too much structure can be counterproductive. In a task involving Lego bricks, having a predetermined structure led to solutions which were less creative among their participants. This fits with the idea that transfer can depend on learned structure and has automatic elements, caused by well-practised associations with prior learning, and may in part link to the conformity effect discussed above. A degree of randomness in a task or situation can help to promote new associations while counteracting more automatic associations, as patterns from prior learning will not be immediately apparent. From this point of view, structure can cause problems – but on the other hand, structure and order can aid memory, and similarity to prior learning leads to a simpler 'near transfer' situation. For the teacher, therefore, decreasing the level of structure provided to learners as they become secure in their factual learning can be one way to promote divergent thinking. Including surprising or random elements can make a task more difficult, but may better prepare pupils for the transfer of skills to authentic problems outside of education.

Using the principles of creativity

The concepts and processes involved in creativity can be applied to many situations where learners have to create solutions or solve problems. The following sections explain how teachers can use these concepts.

Lesson and task planning

As discussed above, thorough preparation via the learning of facts and skills increases the likelihood there is of a good result in a creative task – something that applies just as much to a student of a factual subject as to an artist or inventor. For example, if a group of pupils are asked to come up with a plan for how their school could tackle exam stress, their ideas will be better if they have previously studied the biology and psychology of stress and are familiar with major theories and therapy approaches relating to this issue.

This doesn't mean that young children and new learning should be prevented from engaging in creative tasks – far from it. It just means that the output of these tasks will be consonant with the level of their expertise, and expectations set accordingly. Even a 5-year-old with an age-restricted vocabulary and a very limited grasp of writing is able to produce a novel sentence. Given a set of cards with words on or a set of pictures, a child is able to put them together in various ways to make stories with different meanings, perhaps including combinations that the teacher didn't think of.

Success on a creative task requires a certain freedom to think without basic demands distracting the process – in other words, there must be sufficient capacity in terms of attention and working memory (see Chapter 2) for divergent thinking to take place. If the student's entire focus is on their spelling, then the creativity of their poetry or story will be very limited. Planning a creative task could involve minimising the effortful 'nuts and bolts' of the task. For example, very few children could spend time writing phrases on separate slips of paper first, get feedback to tackle any errors, then move these around during a composition phase (rather like fridge magnet poetry!).

One form of notes that has also – at times – been recommended for brainstorming and revision is the *mind map*. This is a diagram combining visual and verbal information, with a single concept or idea, such as 'The Crimean War', at the centre, and the student draws branches out from this. It is sometimes contrasted with a 'concept map' – a freer structure with no particular 'main' element, where ideas are presented as boxes or 'nodes', and relationships between these ideas are shown along lines.

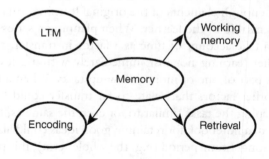

Figure 4.1 Mind map

What is the evidence that these actually work? Blunt and Karpicke (2014) asked learners to study a text, and then either draw a concept map or write a summary paragraph. Both groups did better than a restudy control group, indicating that mapping can be helpful when used for retrieval – but there was no difference between them. Importantly, this was true even when asked questions that involved making inferences, suggesting that concept or mind maps don't do much to promote creative associations beyond what would already happen when writing from memory. Their use as either review tasks or as notes to support creative thinking could therefore depend on preference, and must be balanced against the consideration that they are rather time-consuming to produce.

Finally, on the basis that more varied associations and the chance to walk appears to have a positive effect on coming up with creative ideas, brainstorming sessions could be done at least partially during drinks/toilet breaks – a form of multitasking that would not overtax working memory due to the different forms of processing required.

Course planning

As creative tasks will benefit from building on prior learning within a task or lesson, they could be located primarily towards the end of a topic or course and/or planned over several sessions, so that skills and knowledge can be developed first. This will also give opportunities for incubation.

Ideas are more likely to be successfully transferred to new contexts if they retain enough elements of the original learning situation to make them recognisable to the learner. When planning a series of lessons, a teacher can take account of time as a factor in transfer, requiring the use of earlier learning not just immediately within a lesson as practice, but as part of one or more follow-up tasks. When a long delay is involved, other factors that relate to far transfer could be minimised (e.g. by keeping the tasks similar to, or even the same as, the original).

The use of a notebook for retaining good ideas could also be continued over a longer time period (e.g. the whole term); this process could provide a free form of concept mapping, helping learners to see connections and draw analogies. Concepts that are written down can also help to reduce the demands on the working memory, making it easier for the learner to think through novel ideas and connections. For a major science project, for example, learners could jot down initial ideas early in the course, then refine these a month or so later into a detailed research proposal. This could again be put aside and edited after a period of time, and finally a detailed methodology could be worked out. The planning process could even be a short task that is scheduled weekly at the end of their final class of the week, prompting the learners to go away at the weekend and mull over options and obstacles.

Planning brainstorming

To put it simply, brainstorming means generating a large number of ideas in an uncritical environment. It is a creative task in itself, but more importantly can be used as the starting point for further creative work. For example, a writer might brainstorm ideas at the beginning of a chapter before starting to write, or a band could brainstorm ideas for a song.

There is a lot of psychology behind both how brainstorming works and how to do it best. In simple terms, it is a process of retrieval of information from memory and linking it (transferring it) to a new context. As early as the 1950s, Parnes and Meadow (1959) demonstrated brainstorming to be effective as a means of generating good-quality ideas. Recent work has focused on *how* to brainstorm in the optimal way; Deuja et al. (2014) found it beneficial when participants first brainstormed categories and then used those categories as prompts. For example, if learners in a history lesson were asked to think of problems that an invading army might have during a campaign, they could first brainstorm categories such as 'food, shelter, transport, etc.' and then use these as prompts. Each category constrains the process a little but also acts as a stimulus, prompting more associations. Compared to free brainstorming, prompts can extend the time that learners continue to produce useful ideas, and reduce the chance that learners will miss out some areas entirely.

Categories could be prepared in advance by the teacher or generated by a whole class ahead of brainstorming in small groups.

Although often done in groups, brainstorming can be done individually too, and there may be personal preferences – extravert personalities will probably be more comfortable when brainstorming in a group. Some learners may find group brainstorming to be an unpleasant process; although often the default for education, group activities can be stressful and unsuited to introverted learners – and indeed, there is an argument that some of the best thinkers and creators tended to work alone (Cain, 2013). One simple option to cater for different preferences would be to give some learners the option of brainstorming individually or in pairs rather than the standard group setting, or to find other ways to share ideas. Brainstorming can be done very effectively alone, while 'electronic brainstorming' via computers or smartphones is also effective (Baruah and Paulus, 2016).

A broad and varied list of ideas can help with the reduced structure and element of randomness that boosts divergent thinking (see above), but there is also the risk of a conformity effect within groups, whereby learners sharing their ideas (e.g. for a story or project) might harm others' ability to come up with original ideas. The teacher should therefore give some thought to whether brainstorming is appropriate. It is likely to work best in situations where having as many ideas as possible is beneficial (e.g. 'try to think of questions that could come up on the exam'), and group sharing of ideas makes it less likely that individual learners will miss something important. Following on from the points made earlier in the chapter, it should not necessarily be confined to the early stages of a task as it could benefit from learners' developing knowledge levels, and there could be benefits from building in a break to allow time for incubation/forgetting.

Planning for writing

Writing is a huge part of education, but often teachers are disappointed with the quality of what learners produce. This is slightly surprising, given that language is a unique human skill, founded on our evolutionary past (Pinker, 1995), constantly practised, and one where people are spontaneously creative; every day, people recombine their learned vocabulary to form novel and often unique utterances (Crystal, 2010).

Various factors could contribute to poor-quality writing in schools. Learners may lack the technical proficiency with the written forms required, and therefore more time may need to be spent making basic knowledge and skills more automatically accessible. As highlighted in the previous section, support notes to work from may help to free up working memory to focus on the demands of a task. A related problem would be insufficient planning (and brainstorming) time, and a lack of opportunities to develop work beyond a 'first draft' quality.

Another potential issue is that the sense that they are going to be judged or graded may cause pupils to play it safe – something that links to the concept of the fixed mindset. Grading is likely to be counterproductive for genuine creativity as it promotes compliance with predetermined standards – though constructive feedback can be very helpful.

One technological innovation that can help with both revision and feedback is the use of blogs, a form of writing that can boost collaborative learning due to a structure which promotes interaction and comments (Jimoyiannis and Angelaina, 2012). Peers are a different type of audience to teachers, and their feedback is qualitatively different (Rollinson, 2005); it is likely that a peer audience will encourage writing to be entertaining and to differ from the average, rather than focusing on being correct. If using peer feedback, teachers will need to consider how peers will be encouraged to be both positive and sufficiently detailed to prompt improvements, and also how responses/editing on the basis of feedback will be built into the process.

Conclusions

Creativity is not a random process – it depends upon careful preparation and the development of skills and knowledge. Although great creative achievements tend not to be produced by beginners in a subject, the process of broadening and developing knowledge and skills in specific domains is already a key aspect of the educational process, and creative tasks are well placed to develop knowledge by improving the associations between concepts and making them more general, potentially facilitating later transfer of skills. In addition, creativity has been shown to have a close link with motivation and to be boosted by curiosity.

Young learners today face an uncertain future, with great societal challenges ahead of them. Creative thinking is not a panacea, and nor is it something that should take precedence over factual learning. This chapter has shown how developing knowledge and skills is a key foundation to creative thinking, but that it is also vital that learned associations can be broadened to new contexts, and that tasks prompt learners to use the essential building blocks of creativity. The ability to think divergently and generate multiple ideas will help learners to develop their knowledge into new and useful forms.

Further reading

The Creative Mind: Myths and Mechanisms (2nd edn) by M. A. Boden (Routledge, 2003)
A fascinating discussion of the psychological processes behind having new ideas, looking at the issue via an analogy to computer processing.

Creativity: The Psychology of Discovery and Invention by M. Csikszentmihaly (Harper Perennial, 2013)
This book looks in depth at the links between expertise and creativity, via a study of highly successful inventors, scientists and artists.

Out of Our Minds: Learning to be Creative (2nd edn) by K. Robinson (Capstone, 2011)
A highly readable and thought-provoking look at the social value of creativity, and how it tends to be neglected in favour of more traditional models of academic success.

Unlocking Creativity: Teaching Across the Curriculum – A Teacher's Guide to Creativity Across the Curriculum edited by R. Fisher and M. Williams (Routledge, 2005)
Less psychological, but a useful guide that focuses on the thought processes and interactions involved in creativity, applied to many areas of the curriculum.

The Cambridge Handbook of Creativity edited by J. C. Kaufman and R. J. Sternberg (Cambridge University Press, 2010)
A more academic text, this book presents a series of short articles by creativity researchers, many of which have an applied focus and are highly relevant to teachers.

Creativity and Early Years Education: A Lifewide Foundation by A. Craft (Continuum Press, 2002)
A well-researched explanation, focusing on the 'small c' creativity of early childhood experience, and on the role of imagination in educating younger learners.

Creativity in Context by T. M. Amabile (Westview Press, 1996)
A classic on the social psychology of creativity, focusing on creative professionals as well as children and students. Emphasises the importance of motivation and the social context.

References

Amabile, T. M. (1996). *Creativity in Context*. New York: Westview Press.

Baer, J. (1994). Divergent thinking is not a general trait: a multidomain training experiment. *Creativity Research Journal*, 7(1), 35–46. doi: 10.1080/10400419409534507

Baer, J. (2016). Creativity doesn't develop in a vacuum. *New Directions for Child and Adolescent Development*, 151(1), 9–20. doi: 10.1002/cad.20151

Barnett, S. M. and Ceci, S. J. (2002). When and where do we apply what we learn? A taxonomy for far transfer. *Psychological Bulletin*, 128(4), 612–637. doi: 10.1037/0033-2909.128.4.612

Baruah, J. and Paulus, P. B. (2016). The role of time and category relatedness in electronic brainstorming. *Small Group Research*, 47(3), 333–342. doi: 10.1177/1046496416642296

Blunt, J. R. and Karpicke, J. D. (2014). Learning with retrieval-based concept mapping. *Journal of Educational Psychology*, 106(3), 849–858. doi: 10.1037/a0035934

Boden, M. A. (2004). *The Creative Mind: Myths and Mechanisms* (2nd edn). London: Routledge.

Bonawitz, E., Shafto, P., Gweon, H., Goodman, N. D., Spelke, E. and Schulz, L. (2011). The double-edged sword of pedagogy: instruction limits spontaneous exploration and discovery. *Cognition*, 120, 322–330. doi:10.1016/j.cognition.2010.10.001

Cain, S. (2013). *Quiet: The Power of Introverts in a World That Can't Stop Talking*. New York: Broadway Books.

Carlson, N. (1998). *Physiology of Behaviour* (5th edn). Boston, MA: Allyn & Bacon.

Cropley, A. J. and Cropley, D. (2010). Functional creativity: 'products' and the generation of effective novelty. In J. C. Kaufman and R. J. Sternberg (eds), *The Cambridge Handbook of Creativity* (pp. 301–317). Cambridge: Cambridge University Press.

Crystal, D. (2010). *The Cambridge Encyclopaedia of Language* (3rd edn). Cambridge: Cambridge University Press.

Csikszentmihalyi, M. (1996). *Creativity: Flow and the Psychology of Discovery and Invention*. New York: Harper Perennial.

Desmond, A. and Moore, J. R. (1992). *Darwin*. London: Penguin.

Deuja, A., Kohn, N. W., Paulus, P. B. and Korde, R. M. (2014). Taking a broad perspective before brainstorming. *Group Dynamics: Theory, Research, and Practice*, 18(3), 222–236. doi: 10.1037/gdn0000008

Dewey, J. (1910). *How We Think*. Boston, MA: D.C. Heath & Co.

Domhoff, G. W. (2011). Dreams are embodied simulations that dramatize conception and concerns: the continuity hypothesis in empirical, theoretical, and historical context. *International Journal of Dream Research*, 4, 50–62. doi: 10.11588/ijodr.2011.2.9137

Gick, M. L. and Holyoak, K. J. (1983). Schema induction and analogical transfer. *Cognitive Psychology*, 15, 1–38. doi: 10.1016/0010-0285(83)90002-6

Glyer, D. P. (2008). *The Company They Keep: C. S. Lewis and J. R. R. Tolkien as Writers in Community*. Kent, OH: Kent State University Press.

Grant, A. M. and Berry, J. W. (2011). The necessity of others is the mother of invention: intrinsic and prosocial motivations, perspective taking and creativity. *Academy of Management Journal*, 54(1), 73–96. doi: 10.5465/AMJ.2011.59215085

Guilford, J. P. (1950). Creativity. *American Psychologist*, 5, 444–454. doi: 10.1037/h0055400

Hidi, S. and Harackiewicz, J. M. (2000). Motivating the academically unmotivated: a critical issue for the 21st century. *Review of Educational Research*, 70(2), 151–179. doi: 10.3102/00346543070002151

Jauk, E., Benedek, M., Dunst, B. and Neubauer, A. C. (2013). The relationship between intelligence and creativity: new support for the threshold hypothesis by means of empirical breakpoint detection. *Intelligence*, 41(4), 212–221. doi: 10.1016/j.intell.2013.03.003

Jimoyiannis, A. and Angelaina, S. (2012). Towards an analysis framework for investigating students' engagement and learning in educational blogs. *Journal of Computer Assisted Learning*, 28(3), 222–234. doi: 10.1111/j.1365-2729.2011.00467.x

Kim, K. H. (2011). The creativity crisis: the decrease in creative thinking scores on the Torrance Tests of Creative Thinking. *Creativity Research Journal*, 23(4), 285–295. doi: 10.1080/10400419.2011.627805

Kim, Y. J. and Zhong, C. (2017). Ideas rise from chaos: information structure and creativity. *Organizational Behavior and Human Decision Processes*, 138, 15–27. doi: 10.1016/j.obhdp.2016.10.001

Mayer, R. E. (2004). Should there be a three-strikes rule against pure discovery learning? *American Psychologist*, 59(1), 14–19. doi: 10.1037/0003-066X.59.1.14

McCrae, R. R., Costa Jr, P. T., Ostendorf, F., Angleitner, A., Hřebíčková, M., Avia, M. D., et al. (2000). Nature over nurture: temperament, personality, and life span development. *Journal of Personality and Social Psychology*, 78(1), 173–186. doi: 10.1037/0022-3514.78.1.173

Moran, S. (2010). The roles of creativity in society. In J. C. Kaufman and R. J. Sternberg (eds), *The Cambridge Handbook of Creativity* (pp. 74–90). Cambridge: Cambridge University Press.

Oppezzo, M. and Schwartz, D. L. (2014). Give your ideas some legs: the positive effect of walking on creative thinking. *Journal of Experimental Psychology: Learning, Memory, and Cognition*, 40(4), 1142–1152. doi: 10.1037/a0036577

Parnes, S. J. and Meadow, A. (1959). Effects of 'brainstorming' instructions on creative problem solving by trained and untrained subjects. *Journal of Educational Psychology*, 50(4), 171–176. doi: 10.1037/h0047223

Pinker, S. (1995). *The Language Instinct*. London: Penguin.

Rasch, B. and Born, J. (2013). About sleep's role in memory. *Physiological Review*, 93, 681–766. doi: 10.1152/physrev.00032.2012

Rollinson, P. (2005). Using peer feedback in the ESL writing class. *ELT Journal*, 59(1), 23–30. doi: 10.1093/elt/cci003

Ryan, R. M. and Deci, E. (2017). *Self-Determination Theory: Basic Psychological Needs in Motivation, Development, and Wellness*. New York: Guilford Press.

Sawyer, R. K. (1992). Improvisational creativity: an analysis of jazz performance. *Creativity Research Journal*, 5(3), 253–263. doi: 10.1080/10400419209534439

Sawyer, R. K. (2004). Creative teaching: collaborative discussion as disciplined improvisation. *Educational Researcher*, 33(2), 12–20. doi: 10.3102/0013189X033002012

Sawyer, R. K. (2007). *Group Genius: The Creative Power of Collaboration*. New York: Basic Books.

Simons, D. J., Boot, W. R., Charness, N., Gathercole, S. E., Chabris, C. F., Hambrick, D. Z., et al. (2016). Do 'brain-training' programs work? *Psychological Science in the Public Interest*, 17(3), 103–186. doi: 10.1177/1529100616661983

Smith, S. M., Ward, T. B. and Schumacher, J. S. (1993). Constraining effects of examples in a creative generation task. *Memory & Cognition*, 21(6), 837–845. doi: 10.3758/BF03202751

Sternberg, R. J. (1985). *Beyond IQ: A Triarchic Theory of Human Intelligence*. Cambridge: Cambridge University Press.

Sternberg, R. J. (2008). Assessing what matters. *Educational Leadership*, 65(4), 20–26.

Storm, B. C. (2011). Retrieval-induced forgetting and the resolution of competition. In A. S. Benjamin (ed.), *Successful Remembering and Successful Forgetting: A Festschrift in Honor of Robert A. Bjork* (pp. 89–105). New York: Psychology Press.

Storm, B. C., Bjork, E. L. and Bjork, R. A. (2007). When intended remembering leads to unintended forgetting. *The Quarterly Journal of Experimental Psychology*, 60(7), 909–915. doi: 10.1080/17470210701288706

Torrance, E. P. (1966). *Torrance Tests of Creative Thinking: Norms-Technical Manual (Research Edition)*. Princeton, NJ: Personnel Press.

Walker, M. P., Brakefield, T., Hobson, J. A. and Stickgold, R. (2003). Dissociable stages of human memory consolidation and reconsolidation. *Nature*, 425(6958), 616–620. doi: 10.1038/nature01930

Wallas, G. (1926). *The Art of Thought*. New York: Harcourt & Brace.

Wilson, S. (2016). Divergent thinking in the grasslands: thinking about object function in the context of a grassland survival scenario elicits more alternate uses than control scenarios. *Journal of Cognitive Psychology*, 28(5), 618–630. doi: 10.1080/20445911.2016.1154860

Zhao, Y. (2017). What works may hurt: side effects in education. *Journal of Educational Change*, 18(1), 1–19. doi: 10.1007/s10833-016-9294-4

5 | Emotions

Studies often emphasise the cognitive mechanisms involved in learning, and ignore the social and emotional dimension. This chapter investigates the ways emotions can both help and hinder the learning process, without neglecting the important role played by the social and the cognitive:

- How emotions become part of the learning process.
- The relationship between emotions and achievement goal.
- The consequences of poor emotional regulation.
- The impact of positive and negative emotions on learning.
- How interest, curiosity and boredom impact learning.

Learning is often thought of as a wholly cognitive process (see Chapter 1), and yet other aspects of the internal and external workings of the individual also play a major role. Learning represents the combination of cognitive, social and emotional components; just as learning can't take place without the relevant cognitive architecture in place, neither can it take place in a vacuum. Schools are social institutions with a variety of relationships being forged, nurtured and broken. Emotions play a major role in both the cognitive and social aspects of learning, often overtly, as in the role of anxiety, where high levels can lead to working memory impairment (for a discussion of working memory, see Chapter 2), and covertly, in terms of the subtle aspects of positive and negative emotional states.

While some emotions can be thought of as detrimental to learning, others appear to enhance it, and though the distinction between positive and negative emotions appears straightforward, the reality is that some negative emotional states can actually enhance learning and some positive emotional states can hinder it. Furthermore, cognition and emotion are intricately connected both in terms of theoretical constructs and neurology. Nowhere is this interaction clearer than in the way memories are stored, processed and retrieved. For example, certain memories leave an indelible trace because of their emotional footprint (so-called 'flashbulb memories'), while damage to the pathways connecting certain memory centres of the brain to the more emotional areas can lead to situations whereby we might believe a loved one has been substituted for an imposter because the emotions we normally associate with that person cannot be accessed (a condition known as Capgras syndrome). Other emotions such as boredom and curiosity can both enhance and reduce learning, but it would be dependent upon the context in which the emotion is experienced.

During the early days of psychology, there was a great deal of interest in emotions, but serious study waned due to its reliance on introspection (asking people how they felt when they experienced a particular emotion). For many years, emotions were not seen as a particularly suitable area of research, in part due to their subjective nature. They are also quite difficult to quantify in any meaningful way because we can never really be sure that the emotion one person feels is the same as the one another person feels in the same situation. People react differently in different situations, and our behaviour can, at times, run counter to social norms, especially in traumatic situations. With the advent of new technologies and diagnostic tools, research is returning to the study of emotions and their role in people's lives. A growing number of scientists are now investigating the link between emotion and cognitive function (aspects related to memory, learning and attention), and this new field of investigation is beginning to inform us about the way emotions affect how we think and learn, as well as how emotions arise in the first place. Others are investigating how emotions impact on future success and failure in work and sport, and are asking questions about how factors such as emotional regulation influence our future goals.

Defining emotion

The main problem with discussing emotions in education is understanding what is meant by the term itself. Furthermore, there is the problem of deciding what does and does not represent an emotion. Emotions are certainly subjective, and often we (and especially young children) have difficulty in identifying a feeling in terms of a specific emotion (which is why psychologists often refer to 'affect' rather than emotion). Nevertheless, emotions can be seen as three separate yet interrelated constructs:

- *Affective tendencies.* The 'lens' through which we view our relationship with the world or how we view the world and our place within it. For example, if we see the world as a frightening and threatening place, then our behaviours and action become based on fear. A child whose experiences of school have been negative might become fearful and anxious of the school environment. This view of the world can also develop through a number of pathways, such as socialisation, individual beliefs, approach avoidance motives, and personality.
- *Core affect.* How we feel at any particular point in time. Researchers measure core affect through a combination of valence (a continuum from pleasant to unpleasant) and arousal (the range of activation measured from low to high). For example, we might measure the experience of a formal exam as unpleasant (valence) but high in arousal (raised heart rate, increased adrenaline secretion, etc.).
- *Emotional experiences.* Socially constructed and personally acted ways of being. These are formed through conscious and unconscious judgements about our perceived success at attaining goals or maintaining our standards and beliefs. If we view our goals as the

difference between where we are and where we want to be, then our core affect will tend to become our emotional experience via our appraisals and attributions about what is happening during a particular episode.

What are the key principles of emotion, mood and affect?

These three terms are often used interchangeably, not only in everyday conversation, but also in research. There are, however, subtle differences between them. There is some consensus when it comes to defining an emotion, and there is general agreement that emotions represent coherent clusters of components based around a number of features. Just how many of these features should be present for these clusters to be termed an emotion is open to some debate. There certainly seems to be a consensus that there are at least five, including:

- distinctive facial expressions;
- distinctive vocal expressions;
- distinctive physiology;
- rapid onset; and
- brief duration.

Emotions, then, can be seen in others as well as experienced by the individual – if we are sad, then we might cry; if we are angry, we might screw up our faces. So for an emotion to be an emotion, it must include the above features – if it doesn't, then it's something else. Mood, on the other hand, tends to be of longer duration and be more global in nature. There is rarely a particular target of a mood experience, and we might find ourselves in a bad mood for no good reason. Affect is the subjective experience of a particular emotional state. Being anxious (the emotion), for example, creates an experience personal to the individual (the affect), and might not present itself in a universal way. One student, for example, might not experience anxiety in the same way as another student – the emotion is the same, but the affect is different.

How many emotions?

As far as emotion researchers are concerned, there is no real consensus. Some say that there are six (anger, disgust, fear, happiness, sadness and surprise), with others claiming that there are eight (the previous six plus joy and anticipation), with all other emotions being a combination of these core emotions. We know when we experience an emotion, even if we can't give the particular emotion a name. The feeling is subjective, it's unique to our experience, and labelling it as, say, anger or sadness isn't always necessary. One might experience an emotion without being able to label it as such. Emotions are as much about having the language to describe them as having an objectively based label for them. American psychologist Robert Plutchik (2001) proposed eight basic emotions that he grouped in pairs of opposites. According to the Plutchik model, the eight basic emotions can be blended, just like colours, in order to produce a large number of related yet distinct emotions. This then widens our possibilities, allowing us to include more emotions that are relevant to teaching and learning. These might include states that aren't generally thought of as emotional but nevertheless fulfil the relevant criteria, such as curiosity and boredom.

Maladaptive behaviours

Younger people especially often use maladaptive strategies in order to cope with emotions, and because appropriate emotion regulation has been linked to higher levels of personal well-being and academic success, understanding and being able to identify these strategies can prove insightful.

Maladaptive strategies include:

- *Distraction.* Trying not to think about what is causing the distress.
- *Rumination.* Continually going over the problem in our mind and revisiting the distress it causes us.
- *Worry.* Focusing on the negative aspects of the problem.
- *Thought suppression.* Redirecting our attention away from the problem and focusing on other content. Thought suppression often leads to a greater focus on the distressing emotion.

Emotional regulation

Emotion regulation is the process by which individuals influence which emotions they have, when they have them, and how they experience and express them. Emotional regulation therefore pertains to the ability to think constructively about how to cope with feelings and not be overwhelmed by them. Poor emotion regulation can lead to a propensity to give up when things become too challenging, becoming distracted or reacting inappropriately in specific situations (e.g. becoming overly aggressive or tearful when learning becomes difficult). This regulation of emotions is a skill that develops with age and becomes more effective as we get older. The study of emotional regulation and its practical uses has been popularised in the form of emotional intelligence (or EI); however, due to competing models and the methodological problems often associated with EI, this chapter refers to emotional regulation rather than emotional intelligence.

Students who are able to employ adaptive strategies are said to display greater emotion regulation, and consequently function in a more positive way. This includes being able to resist acting on impulse and resisting temptation when presented with changing situations and adverse conditions. These might include coping with a change of teacher or being moved into a different class, but might also include less dramatic changes such as beginning a new topic or having to cooperate with a different group of people. For efficient learning to take place, students need to be able to control impulsive behaviour and inhibit emotional reactions to events. A series of studies that offer insights into how young children do (and do not do) this was conducted by Walter Mischel during the late 1960s and early 1970s (see Mischel, 2015).

Mischel and his team tested the ability of 4-year-old children to delay gratification of a desired object. The child was seated next to a table upon which had been placed a marshmallow. The experimenter told the child that they had to leave the room for a few moments and that the child must not eat the marshmallow. The child was also told that if they didn't eat the marshmallow, they would be allowed to eat two marshmallows on the experimenter's return. Results proved enlightening. It was discovered that the children were able to wait longer if they could distract themselves from the marshmallow or if they thought about the marshmallow's more abstract qualities (size and shape rather than taste). Some of the children would even distract themselves by turning away from it, sitting on their hands or even talking to it; most, however, gave in to temptation. Blakemore and Frith (2005) explain this behaviour in terms of brain development, in particular the frontal lobes. The brain at this age still has a long way to go before it is fully developed, and the frontal lobes (the part that helps us to control our impulses and resist temptation) are no exception.

Another, and perhaps most interesting, finding was that when the children who displayed the greatest level of restraint grew into teenagers, they were found to be more successful at school when compared to the more impulsive children. They scored better on tests of perseverance, concentration and on cognitive logic tests, suggesting that emotional regulation and impulse control play an important role in later academic success (for a more in-depth discussion, see Mischel, 2015).

Being able to control and express emotions in acceptable ways impacts heavily on the ability to learn; those students who are able to learn how to self-regulate are better equipped to succeed. Additionally, the ability to delay gratification by, for example, completing assignments and homework before engaging in activities unrelated to school places students at a more advantageous position. Recent research (Rybanska et al., 2017) has found that certain classroom rituals (specifically 'circle time') can improve self-regulation in young children, essentially eliminating the marshmallow effect.

The function of emotions

Emotions exist because they serve an evolutionary purpose; they have some kind of adaptive value. Emotions help us deal with life tasks and help our species survive; this is the reason why they share certain characteristics and common elements despite individual and cultural differences (i.e. even in the most diverse of cultures, emotions will display certain similarities that can't be explained through socialisation or learning that takes place within that specific society or culture). If emotions are evolutionary, we should also be able to detect them in other primates, even though certain emotions might be unique to humans. First and foremost, emotions are a biological response to a situation (be it good or bad), and the speed at which our biological system reacts can often be mesmerising. Our biology reacts by setting in motion a set of involuntary changes in both our expression and our physiology, so our facial expression might change even before we are aware of our response (as can often be seen with an emotion such as disgust). In relation to learning, a student might be struck dumb or freeze when asked a question in class, and while some might interpret this as defiance or ignorance, the student might not be fully aware of their response. In this case, the experience of an emotion (anxiety) is seen as happening to them rather than something chosen by them.

Psychologist James Averill (1980) agrees that emotions fulfil vital biological functions for the survival of the species. According to Averill, basic emotions should be universal – they should be seen in non-human primates and heritable. The problem here is that there is little consensus across cultures of what these basic emotions are; not only do they vary between cultures, but they also vary within cultures over time. While it's clear that emotions are evolutionary, exactly what constitutes a basic emotion can be thought of as socially constructed. Furthermore, the most basic of basic emotions are likely to be psychological in nature, in that they have a transformative capacity in terms of our sense of self.

This is important to the learning process as it suggests that constructs such as self-esteem and self-worth are guided by emotions and the ability to enhance and transform the way in which we see ourselves, as well as our beliefs about how others see us.

Let's take the example of the anxious student being asked a question in class:

- The teacher says the student's name and asks a question.
- The first component of any emotion is subjective – the personal experience of being singled out and quizzed.
- The second component is physiological (raised heart rate, increased perspiration, raised blood pressure, etc.).

The final component is a behavioural one, and for our over-anxious student this might manifest itself in silence, fidgeting or even crying. To the teacher asking the question, this might seem like a highly irrational response to a simple question, but to the student a complex set of variables are being played out, based on a number of largely psychological factors. The student has become overwhelmed by their emotional response to the situation – anxiety has been 'done to them', it is not a course of action they have chosen.

Positive and negative emotions

Common sense would suggest that positive emotions are beneficial while negative emotions are detrimental, and a great deal of research has centred on this vey assumption. Barbara Fredrickson was one of the first researchers to attempt a theoretical model of how and why positive emotions lead to improved emotional well-being and a greater capacity to bounce back from adversity. Drawing on findings from positive psychology, Fredrickson (2004) explains the relationship with a framework she calls 'broaden and build'. Emotions appear to have an evolutionary function related to survival. Emotions such as fear acted as a survival mechanism; this allowed early humans to escape potentially life-threatening situations, while anxiety kept them alert and constantly on the lookout for danger. When such danger presented itself, the stress response would activate, setting in motion the fight or flight response and summoning up stores of adrenaline and cortisol, while dampening down unnecessary functions in order to divert resources to those parts of the body needed to attack or to run. An emotion such as fear therefore narrows our responses to any given situation, essentially providing us with just two options – higher functions are less important in these kinds of situations.

What is being suggested here is that negative emotions such as fear and anger narrow our choices (what Fredrickson calls our 'thought-action repertoire'), while positive emotions such as joy, curiosity and interest broaden them. As they broaden, so they build, leading to the accumulation of further psychological repertoires. In other words, positive emotions lead to positive adaptations and the storing of more blueprints that can be activated should an appropriate situation arise in the future. We can therefore think of these repertoires as a type of psychological capital. In the same way that we can accumulate monetary or cultural capital, so we can also accumulate positive psychological ways to deal with specific situations. Employing positive emotions regularly to cope with different situations allows us to add to the resources available, ready for use in the future when we encounter the same or similar situation. Fredrickson also suggests that positive emotions can undo negative ones due to our inability to experience two conflicting emotions simultaneously. A student who, for example, is particularly interested in a subject and finds the experience of learning joyful cannot experience fear, stress or anxiety over his or her studies. Furthermore, a student who is plagued by anxiety and fear is less likely to view setbacks as productive, and is likely to see them as a direct attack on self-esteem and self-worth. Consequently, positive emotions feed resilience and the determination to overcome obstacles, which ultimately increases the chances of success (for an in-depth discussion on resilience, see Chapter 6).

The indication here is that positive emotions aid learning and negative emotions hinder it. In all probability, the situation is likely to be more nuanced. Not all negative emotions are maladaptive; indeed, many are likely to help us in a number of ways. Emotions such as anxiety and fear exist for our survival, raising our levels of adrenaline and transporting essential sugars to the muscles that are used for a quick getaway. Chronic anxiety can become debilitating, and humans can become ill if levels of adrenaline and cortisol remain high for too long. Nevertheless, an optimum amount of anxiety quickens our responses, heightens our awareness and fuels our cognitive processes, but when anxiety levels pass that optimum threshold, our cognitive functions become impaired.

Positive emotions and attainment

Unfortunately, the answer to this question is far from straightforward. A happy mood is certainly desirable, but happiness isn't always a good thing. This might seem counterintuitive seeing as we all want to be happy and engage in behaviours that will (to a certain degree) lead us in the right direction. One of the problems with such an endeavour brings us back to the idea that emotions are based on the pursuit of goals, the assumption being that positive affect is in some way preferable in this pursuit. The problem arises when we realise that positive emotions can actually interfere with long-term success because the emphasis is often placed on short-term goals.

Another problem is that happy people display a tendency towards lazy thinking. This revelation doesn't fit well with Fredrickson's view that positive emotions broaden and build psychological capacity. According to this alternative view, happy people tend to rely on superficial strategies in order to collect information from the outside world and are more likely to employ stereotypes than their unhappy counterparts. In fact, some negative emotions may actually enhance certain types of learning, as Sandi Mann of the University of Central Lancashire discovered when she found that boring activities could enhance creativity (Mann and Cadman, 2014). Research conducted by Elizabeth Kensinger (Kensinger and Corkin, 2003) discovered that negative life events are remembered better than positive ones, suggesting that negative affect actually enhances memory. Furthermore, laboratory studies have found that items thought to be negative (e.g. a poisonous snake) are more likely to be remembered than neutral items (e.g. a picture of a door) or positive items (e.g. an ice cream), as well as negative emotions leading to fewer errors in recall.

Unfortunately, studies have also found that happy people are much more likely to resort to stereotypes when evaluating situations. Christian Unkelbach conducted an experiment using a 'shoot 'em up' computer game where participants were told to shoot characters carrying guns. Some of the characters were wearing turbans (displaying the stereo-typical image of Muslims). Happy people were more likely to shoot the characters wearing turbans (even if they were unarmed) than less happy individuals (Unkelbach et al., 2008). The so-called 'turban effect' also suggests that people who display higher levels of positive affect are less likely to judge the situation in any real depth, unconsciously choosing instead to activate stereotypes stored in LTM and fuelled by current events and media representations.

If happiness can interfere with cognition and learning, can sadness enhance it? When we talk of sadness, we don't mean the debilitating depression that ruins the lives of so many people each year. Depression, as we have seen in a discussion on learned helplessness, impairs cognitive function, reduces motivation and leaves us feeling drained. Sadness, on the other hand, is a mood state that fluctuates quite rapidly, often within the same day. We're going to use the term 'negative affect' here just so we can be sure about what we mean. Negative affect is rarely thought of in favourable terms, and often we wish to 'snap out' of those inexplicable bouts of low mood. We often attempt to help our friends and loved ones to raise their spirits if they seem down because we rarely view such a state as adaptive or useful. In classrooms, we quite rightly identify pupils who might be upset or showing signs of low mood, the symptoms of which could suggest a deeper psychological problem. Most bouts of low affect, however, lift rapidly, and the child who seems sad in the morning will be laughing and joking with his or her friends by lunchtime. But could these occasional episodes of negative affect actually enhance learning?

It has been found that low affect can lead to positive consequences, certainly in terms of cognitive processes. Joseph Forgas, a psychologist at the University of New South Wales, has conducted a number of fascinating studies into the impact of negative affect on a number of cognitive and social psychological behaviours (Forgas, 2013). In one study, people were asked to recall items they had seen in a shop. In the first condition, the task was carried out on a grey rainy day in order to induce a negative mood state. In the second condition, and in an identical situation, the task was carried out on a bright day. Forgas found that the rainy day condition resulted in a larger recall tally and that memories for items were in much greater detail than the same task carried out on a sunny day. The suggestion is that while positive mood impairs memory, negative affect somehow enhances it. Though interesting, this study isn't as convincing as it might appear. Perhaps the participants in the second condition were just eager to get out into the sun and enjoy the good weather, impairing their attention and making them impatient?

In a second study, participants were shown a photograph of either a car crash or a wedding. Later on, the same participants were asked to recall either a happy memory or a sad memory from their past in order to shift their mood into either negative or positive affect. They were then asked a series of questions about the photographs, including some misleading information (e.g. asking about an object that didn't appear in the photograph). The use of misleading information is common in studies that test the accuracy of eyewitness testimony, and research conducted over the past 30 years or so has found that most people are highly susceptible to misleading information. Whereas studies of this kind tend to focus on interview techniques, Forgas was interested in how negative or positive mood would impact on recall. It was discovered that those participants who had recalled a negative memory from their past (the negative-affect group) were better able to recall the original details and were much less likely to be influenced by the misleading information. Participants in the positive-affect group, on the other hand, were much more likely to recall details that had been contaminated with the false information. Psychologists have known for some time that our memory of the past can be altered by false information given later on. However, Forgas managed to support the claim that our mood can either make us more or less susceptible and that negative mood appears to protect against the formation of false memories. Studies such as this would also support the view that happy people are lazy thinkers, because the susceptibility to false information indicates that happy people are paying less attention and are less focused when processing information.

It's not just memory that is influenced by emotion; negative affect can also make us better at judging other people's motives, and also turns us into more efficient lie detectors. In another study, participants were asked to detect deception in videotaped accounts of people accused of theft. Those participants displaying negative affect were not only more likely to reach a guilty judgement; they were also better at detecting lies and other deceptions than those in a more positive mood. In yet another study, participants were given 25 true and 25 false trivia statements and asked to rate the likely authenticity of each statement. After they had made their judgements, all participants were given the right answers. Two weeks later, only those participants with low mood were able to distinguish between the previously seen true/false statements. Positive mood participants displayed a greater tendency to rate all their previously seen statements as true. The study indicates that negative affect decreases the tendency to believe that what is familiar is also true, while positive affect appears to increase it.

Negative affect also makes people less susceptible to certain judgemental or cognitive biases such as the fundamental attribution error (the tendency to attribute behaviour to an individual rather than circumstances). It also makes us less likely to relate certain positive attributes (such a being smartly dressed) with other factors (being intelligent). The so-called 'halo effect' can certainly have detrimental consequences in the classroom, such as associating the scruffy boy at the back of the class with low levels of achievement. Finally, negative affect can reduce primary effects caused when people place too much information on early information and ignore later details.

Negative affect can also lead to a more detailed and attentive thinking style. Not only is low mood better for memory processing and recall, but it also protects us from stereotyping and bias. It can also make people more motivated because happy people are less likely to risk their happiness by engaging in something that might make them less happy; happiness makes us too comfortable and we lose the desire to strive. Becoming settled in the status quo reduces motivation because moving on might lead to less happiness. For example, a student who is happy and contented in a mid-range maths class might withhold effort for fear of losing the positive feelings that come with being in a class where they feel happy. Sad people, on the other hand, have something to strive for and aim towards, such as that small but personally significant achievement that lifts the spirits. Happy people have no real need to deal with challenge in their environment, while those with a more negative mood are more motivated to challenge themselves and push for change in order to lift their mood.

While well-being in schools should be nurtured wherever possible, doing so simply as a means of raising academic achievement might do more harm than good. Additionally, it's often necessary for students to feel uncomfortable if they are going to progress; supporting students through challenging situations is more important than making sure that they are happy.

Moving beyond positive and negative

Psychologist Reinhard Pekrun rejects the view that we must approach emotions as either positive or negative (Pekrun et al., 2007). He suggests that it's the circumstances in which the emotion arises that are important rather than any positive or negative label we choose to give them. Pekrun states that emotions are either activating or deactivating, regardless of the positive or negative categorisation. In certain circumstances, both negative and positive emotion can either activate or deactivate our motivational responses. Emotions such as joy, hope and pride can strengthen motivational processes (in line with the 'broaden and build' theory); they are 'activating positive' emotions. On the other hand, deactivating negative emotions such as hopelessness and boredom can undermine motivation. In other circumstances and with other emotions, the interaction is more complex. Positive emotions such as relief and relaxation deactivate motivational responses, and these responses have both long-term and short-term consequences. For example, a student might experience relaxed contentment after having taken an important test, reducing immediate short-term motivation and a reluctance to re-engage with schoolwork. However, this same emotion may well motivate the student to engage at a later time. Teachers are probably familiar with the difficult task of motivating pupils after they have completed a high-stakes test; their relief at putting the test behind them has led to a feeling of relaxation.

The power of negative emotions

In the same way that positive deactivating emotions can hamper motivation, some negative emotions can strengthen extrinsic motivation. Anxiety, as we have seen, can negatively impact on academic achievement; however, it can also motivate if the expectation of the outcome is likely to be a positive one. Fear of failure can therefore motivate because there is a very real chance of success, and not achieving the anticipated success would be viewed as a personal attack on intelligence and self-esteem. While intrinsic motivation remains the preferred motivational state, we must also accept that at times, only extrinsic methods will do. This view argues that emotions react in different ways with regard to different types of motivation. Intrinsic motivators in learning (a personal desire to engage with activities because of individual interest or the joy it brings) tend to be preferable due to their resilience and long-term sustainability, while extrinsic motivators (the desire to succeed based on a reward for doing so) are often short-lived and can backfire when incentives are withdrawn.

The research underpinning the view that anxiety can enhance extrinsic motivation has produced variable results, perhaps due to the subjectivity of the evaluation of possible success. Of course, if the student feels that success is less likely, then anxiety is assumed to lead to a lower level of activation, or worse still deactivation, because of the feeling that failure is inevitable.

Theories of learner boredom and interest

Boredom is perhaps one of the most relevant emotions when it comes to teaching and learning, but definitions vary. Organisational psychologist Cynthia Fisher emphasises the often-unpleasant nature of boredom as 'an unpleasant, transient affective state in which the individual feels a persuasive lack of interest and difficulty concentrating on the current activity' (Fisher, 1993). Psychologist Mark Leary offers a more concise overtly clinical definition: 'an affective experience associated with cognitive attentional processes' (Leary et al., 1986).

These definitions, as accurate as they are, suggest little in the way of the motivational aspects of boredom. Often when we are bored, we feel a desire to escape our feelings of boredom, with such feelings that often cause us a tangible pain. In an example of the lengths people are willing to go to relieve boredom, Chantal Nederkoorn and her colleagues found that people would even inflict painful electric shocks on themselves as a means of escaping the psychological pain of boredom (Nederkoorn et al., 2016). This highlights the often-tangible nature of boredom and the unpleasantness boredom can cause us.

Pekrun defines boredom slightly differently as 'an affective state composed of unpleasant feelings, lack of stimulation and low physiological arousal' (Pekrun et al., 2010). Pekrun's interest in boredom is specific to classroom settings, so his definition might be more pertinent. Because boredom, and people's propensity towards it, has been linked to academic underachievement, this makes boredom a particularly relevant emotion, especially as it has also been linked to other non-academic behaviours such as depression, anger, impulsivity, and even pathological gambling and bad driving. Eric Dahlen of the University of Mississippi suggests that boredom predicts a propensity to experience anger, and also to display maladaptive anger expression, aggression and deficits in anger control (Dahlen et al., 2004). This suggests that boredom could lead to some behaviours teachers witness in the classroom, especially from those students who display higher levels of aggression and poor emotional regulation.

Boredom is not the same as being uninterested

Thomas Goetz of the University of Konstanz, Germany, suggests that a lack of interest is neutral, in that it doesn't cause any emotional pain or discomfort, whereas boredom can be emotionally distressing. They also have different motivational consequences; a student who lacks interest neither wishes to engage in an activity, nor do they wish to avoid it, whereas, a bored student will feel compelled to escape the situation, perhaps by acting out or disrupting others (Goetz et al., 2014). The behaviours arising from boredom, such as restlessness, agitation and emotional upset, motivate the individual to escape, perhaps by misbehaving, falling asleep or daydreaming. Because the classroom represents a closed system (there is no physical escape), boredom can result in many undesirable behaviours.

Do teachers know why students get bored?

There is an expectation that teachers have a good idea about why their students might become bored; however, research doesn't necessarily support such a view. Elena Daschmann et al. (2014) carried out a study in an attempt to discover if there is a relationship between teacher and student views on why students get bored. The researchers gave open-ended questionnaires to 111 ninth-grade students and conducted semi-structured interviews with 117 ninth-grade teachers in German schools about what led to students' boredom. Results overlapped somewhat (e.g. the relevance of the subject or the content of the specific topic). Some students directed the cause of their boredom to other students (e.g. others in the class being 'too loud'), while teachers suggested the size of the class had an impact. Some were unrelated to school ('I was in a bad mood because of a boy' was one response), so perhaps we need to acknowledge that students bring their own baggage with them and that this can impact behaviour inside the classroom. The main reason for boredom cited by students was the continual monotony of the scheme, the going over of content everyday. Teachers, however, thought that boredom arose when pupils were over-challenged with 'a nut that they can't crack' or under-challenged because the teacher was going over material the students felt they already knew. However, the most startling difference was that while students identified the teacher as a source of boredom, the teachers themselves never did ('When the teacher is as boring as a sleeping pill' was one comment). Teachers therefore might have a reasonably good idea of the specific things that make their students bored, even though they don't appear to see themselves as a source of the boredom.

Findings such as these are quite specific; however, more general models of boredom have been proposed.

Fisher's model

Cynthia Fisher (1993) has proposed a three-pronged model based on aspects outside and within the individual, and the fit between the two. Certain antecedents of boredom, suggests Fisher, lie outside the person (e.g. the task or the environmental conditions), while others inhabit the person. Aspects within the person are perhaps more complex, but would certainly include personality. Genetic components unrelated to personality also play a role, specifically those related to academic achievement such as intelligence (as measured in terms of IQ). The third antecedent involves the fit between the external component and the internal component. The fit is important because you need to gauge the complexity of the task with the ability of the individual to complete it – if the task is too hard, then the student will feel overwhelmed; too easy, and they will feel under-challenged.

Control-value theory

Pekrun's control-value theory also relates to both subjective and environmental factors (Pekrun, 2006). Boredom arises through the interplay between certain external determinants (such as quality of teaching) and individual internal appraisals. Learning environments are approached through aspects of personal control and subjective evaluation. For example, if teaching quality is poor and the students feel that they have little personal control of the situation, plus the student feels the task has little value, is meaningless or irrelevant to their needs, the likelihood that they will be bored is increased. On the other hand, if the quality of teaching is high and the instructions are clear (the students have some kind of control), then whether or not the students become bored will be the result of perceived value and meaning of the task. In the study described above, one comment from a student was, 'I think German is the most pointless subject in general', meaning that even if instruction and teaching were excellent, the perceived value of the subject was low, and this was the antecedent of the boredom the student experienced. Unfortunately, this would imply that some subjects, or topics within subjects, would always be boring to some students, no matter how much cabaret teachers try to stage.

So far, we have only thought of boredom as being a negative emotion, but are there any benefits to being bored? It's highly likely that boredom pushes us to find meaning in our lives, but this might not relate to the classroom environment. However, can boredom serve an educational function, or, more specifically, can boredom benefit learning? Certainly, boredom could act as an alarm bell for teachers. Boredom, as we have already discussed, is not the same as not being interested; the emotions underlying boredom are screaming out for stimulation, and while it's far beyond the realms of possibility to engage all students all of the time, if a teacher looks out on to the classroom and sees the majority of the class nodding off, it's pretty clear the game needs to change. But this doesn't mean that boredom itself is inherently activating.

Boredom and creativity

There is some evidence indicating that even boredom can be viewed as an activating emotion in certain circumstances. Sandi Mann at the University of Central Lancashire wondered if boredom could actually make people more creative. Mann conducted a number of studies where participants were given either a boring or a control activity followed by a creative task, such as coming up with as many creative uses for an everyday object as possible. Those given the boring task were able to offer a greater number of uses than the control group, leading Mann to suggest that the boring activity allowed participants to let their mind wander and activate deeper levels of creativity (Mann and Cadman, 2014). Studies such as these are beginning to change the way in which we view boredom and related activities that are seen as serving little purpose (see also Chapter 4).

How do students cope with boredom?

Students roughly fall into one of three categories – reappraisers, criticisers and evaders:

- *Reappraisers.* This is the most effective coping activity, whereby students respond to boring tasks by increasing their focus on the potential value of the task or activity. These students find the task boring but are able to find some kind of value in it, such as a particular topic in a history lesson being able to provide a better understanding of a separate, more interesting topic.

- *Criticisers.* These students attempt to actively change the situation by expressing their frustration towards the teacher and asking for an alternative activity. Criticisers might complain that the task is 'stupid' or 'pointless' and suggest more interesting topics or activities.

- *Evaders.* The most destructive of the three strategists, evaders will employ a number of avoidant strategies in order to relieve the boredom. Younger students might chat to their classmates, while older ones might resort to using phones and other electronic devices.

So, from a teaching perspective, allowing students to find value in what they are learning creates a more productive learning environment than attempting to make lessons fun.

Interest and curiosity

If boredom represents a negative emotion, then interest and curiosity can be thought of as positive emotions. Although interest and curiosity differ slightly, the assumption here is that because they serve the same or similar purpose in the classroom, we can use the terms interchangeably.

Carol Sansone and Dustin Thoman at the University of Utah found that interest not only enhances motivation and performance, but it also triggers strategies to try to make boring activities more interesting (Sansone and Thoman, 2005). We can therefore think of interest as an activating positive emotion because of its ability to motivate and engage. Interest also has a positive impact on views of failure and, more importantly, the fear of failure. A teenager, for example, obsessed with playing the guitar is more likely to work through difficulties and setbacks in order to play along with his favourite band. Similarly, a student might attend early morning football training to master ball control in an effort to be selected for her local team. Academic interest is, of course, much more complicated, as students will view some subjects and topics within subjects as being more or less interesting than others. They will also view some subjects and topics as being more or less relevant to their wider needs, goals and conflicting interests.

Interest consists of two distinct components – 'situational' and 'individual' interest:

- *Situational interest.* This tends to be spontaneous and transitory; it's that 'hook' that many teachers use to catch the attention of young minds. Its transitory nature means that it can disappear as quickly as it appeared if interest isn't maintained. A science teacher, for example, might start off a lesson with a dazzling display of explosions and grabbing her students' interest, but once the whizz-bang excitement of the demonstration is over, interest begins to wane as the class get down to the complex nature of the chemical reaction.

- *Individual interest.* This kind of interest is much less spontaneous; it lasts longer because of its personal value (it's the child who can tell you all about the vast range of Pokémon, their strengths, weaknesses and evolutions). Individual interest is activated internally with close ties to intrinsic motivation (it's the student with an interest in chemistry that witnesses the whizz-bang of the demonstration and goes home to Google it in greater depth). Situational interest is important because it has the ability to facilitate individual interest, so we can think of situational interest as the 'catch' and individual interest as the 'hold'.

Situational and individual interest both enhance learning in different ways, and neither is considered more superior to the other. Situational interest is effective in increasing learning when the task or the information to be learned is novel or when the information is specifically relevant to the task or learning outcome. Individual interest, on the other hand, positively impacts learning through increased engagement, the acquisition of expert knowledge, and by making seemingly mundane tasks more challenging. Furthermore, Suzanne Hidi and her colleague Ann Renninger have discovered that individual interest mediates the relationship between situational interest, as well as long-term mastery and learning within a specific domain (Hidi and Renninger, 2006). Both types of interest therefore work together in order to transform short-term and long-terms resources into viable learning outcomes.

Interest can enhance motivation, and this in turn leads to higher achievement outcomes. There is also strong evidence suggesting that individual interest plays a facilitating role in academic self-regulation (e.g. being self-directed rather than having to be led or told what to do). Woogul Lee, Myung-Jin Lee and Mimi Bong found that individual interest played a role in the prevalence of self-regulation in Korean students, and suggested that self-regulation could be encouraged through the promotion of individual interest (Lee et al., 2014). The assumption is that students who are intrinsically interested in a particular subject or topic are better at regulating their own learning. This is a promising yet problematic suggestion. Some students are more adept at self-directed learning, but even these students could find it difficult to self-direct if they fail to be interested in or to see the value in what they are doing. There is also a greater emphasis placed on extrinsic motivators than intrinsic ones; what is taught and what is studied must have some kind of outcome reward, so many students might feel unmotivated even if they are interested in a topic that 'won't be in the exam'. This is the point made by psychologists Paul O'Keefe and Lisa Linnenbrink-Garcia, where they stress that self-regulatory behaviours can only provide optimal benefit if the task provides the student with a feeling of personal significance (O'Keefe and Linnenbrink-Garcia, 2014).

Emotions also impact on cognitive processes, and individual interest appears to help hold this relationship together. Interest therefore enhances cognitive ability and encourages the efficient processing of information. People remember the facts about things that interest them and often fail to recall facts about things that don't, suggesting that memory is at least in part related to relevance. Indeed, the relationship between interest (as well as relevance) and increased memory recall has been seen in a number of studies. Although some research has found that interest is more strongly associated with better memory in older people, there remains a general consensus that the effects remain relatively stable across the lifespan. This is certainly the case for text-based material, with research finding that subjectively interesting text is more accurately recalled than text deemed to be less personally interesting. Even more interesting perhaps is that in some studies, participants have been able to predict the information they will recall better based on subjective judgements of interest and relevance.

One study found that not only do curiosity and interest boost memory and learning; they also make it easier to remember unrelated information presented at the same time. Matthias Gruber, Bernard Gelman and Charan Ranganath asked participants how curious they were to find out the answer to a number of trivia questions. Participants were then placed into fMRI scanners and shown the trivia questions with the answers, followed by the image of a person's face. After this, participants were given a surprise test on both the trivia questions and tested on their ability to recognise the faces. Gruber and his colleagues were interested in two things: Would people who displayed higher levels of curiosity recall the answers to the trivia questions more accurately (and what would be the impact of the unrelated faces), and what parts of the brain were displaying the greatest activation during the task? Results showed that curiosity really did increase memory recall, even after 24 hours had passed. Curiosity also enhanced the recall of the unrelated material, suggesting that curiosity actively makes the brain more engaged and that interest to learn is better overall. Furthermore, when curiosity is stimulated, there is an increased activity in the hippocampus (the region of the brain associated with memory) and increased activation in brain regions associated with reward (Gruber et al., 2014). Although relying upon evidence from brain scans can be problematic, there remains a strong suggestion here that interest can enhance neurological function.

Using the principles of emotions

Evidence in support of the influence of emotions in learning isn't as straightforward as that for cognition. However, there is enough research evidence for us to begin to piece together a strategy for more emotionally aware or emotionally positive classrooms. Specifically, there are a number of interrelated components that can help to support all students emotionally.

Emotionally positive classrooms are:

- *Caring*. Relationships are strong and students feel safe, trusted and valued. Teachers are nurturing, supportive and sensitive to the needs of their students.
- *Prosocial*. Teachers and other students are supportive and accepting of diversity. Students care for and support each other, and encourage their classmates when learning becomes difficult.
- *Learning-focused*. Students share a common purpose and common values. Students and teachers are goal-oriented and everyone is clear about the goals they are working towards.

In addition, there are a number of focused solutions grouped into five broad areas:

- *Adaptability.* This is our capacity to respond to and manage new, challenging and uncertain situations. More broadly, adaptability allows us to recognise or accept when certain behaviours aren't working for us and critically assess how these behaviours can be altered to produce more suitable outcomes. Psychologist Tim O'Brien (2016) explains this by using the concept of 'inner stories' (i.e. the way we see ourselves in terms of an internal narrative). Changing behaviour is a matter of changing our story.

- *Mastery.* A mastery orientation drives our desire to become skilled in a particular area. This is in comparison to a performance orientation that involves the desire to be more successful than those around us. Because emotions and goals are linked, encouraging a mastery goal orientation allows students to better regulate maladaptive emotional responses to setbacks.

- *Relationships.* While there is precious little research available on the impact of teacher–pupil relationships, the evidence that is available strongly indicates that positive relationships promote positive academic outcomes. Longitudinal studies have found that students (and particularly those students faced with greater levels of adversity) tend to rely heavily on teachers and those in the wider community to assist them in coping with issues that can often damage both academic success and general well-being.

- *Support and feedback.* Support and feedback are useful for curtailing maladaptive emotional responses and promoting adaptive ones. Linking feedback to goals reduces anxiety and increases motivation. Anxiety can arise because students are unaware of where they are going and, more importantly, how they are going to get there.

- *Regulation.* Encouraging emotional regulation and steering students away from maladaptive behaviours (e.g. distraction, rumination, worry and thought suppression). This can be accomplished through rituals. Certain rituals, such as 'circle time', where children sit in a circle and closely follow the actions of the teacher, have been found to improve self-control and delay gratification. In other words, such rituals can help counter the 'marshmallow effect' discussed earlier in this chapter. However, while regular circle time can be beneficial for young children, it's not yet known if similar interventions would work with adolescents.

Finally, there are a number of skills that can be practised that allow students to adopt a more adaptive cognitive outlook:

- *Reappraisal.* By stepping back and attempting to see the bigger picture, students are able to adapt their behaviour and become more goal-oriented. For example, adopting a 'what's the worst that could happen?' approach allows students to think more rationally about their fears and what they mean in terms of the pursuit of longer-term goals.

- *Distancing.* By adopting an independent third-person perspective, students are more able to evaluate emotionally charged situations. One way this can be achieved is by asking students to adopt the position of 'good friend'. Ask them, 'If your friend came to you with this problem, what advice would you give them?'

- *Humour.* Humour might seem rather basic, but it can be effective. Humour also has the ability to relieve stress and anxiety because smiling and laughing leads to the release of certain hormones related to happiness and well-being.

Conclusions

While current understanding of the role emotions play in learning lags behind more cognitive-based approaches, research is beginning to increase significantly in this area. It's understandable that more cognitively inclined researchers might play down the role of emotions in the learning process seeing as cognitive psychology has a longer and more refined research history to select from. Emotion researchers are therefore often forced to negotiate their way through other research in order to identify those areas pertinent to their work on emotion and affect. Furthermore, by their very nature, emotions are more difficult to study, even though teachers see the impact they make in the classroom on a daily basis.

Further reading

The Marshmallow Test: Understanding Self-Control and How to Master It by W. Mischel (Corgi, 2015)
Mischel's work has been highly influential, and this book combines more than four decades of his research. Accessible and highly entertaining.

Inner Story: Understand Your Mind, Change Your World by T. O'Brien (CreateSpace Independent Publishing Platform, 2016)
Not so much about education, and more about understanding why we are the way we are and how we can change maladaptive life narratives. Tim is a psychologist who has worked with elite athletes, global businesses and high-profile public figures.

References

Averill, J. R. (1980) A constructivist view of emotion. In P. Plutchik and R. Harré (eds), *Emotion: Theory, Research and Experience* (pp. 305–339). New York: Academic Press.

Blakemore, S. and Frith, U. (2005). *The Learning Brain*. Oxford: Blackwell.

Dahlen, E. R., Martin, R. C., Ragan, K. and Kuhlman, M. M. (2004). Boredom proneness in anger and aggression: effects of impulsiveness and sensation seeking. *Personality and Individual Differences*, 37(8), 1615–1627. doi: 10.1016/j.paid.2004.02.016

Daschmann, E. C., Goetz, T. and Stupnisky, R. H. (2014). Exploring the antecedents of boredom: do teachers know why students are bored? *Teaching and Teacher Education*, 39, 22–30. doi: 10.1016/j.tate.2013.11.009

Fisher, C. D. (1993). Boredom at work: a neglected concept. *Human Relations*, 46, 395–417. doi: 10.1177/001872679304600305

Forgas, J. P. (2013). Don't worry, be sad! On the cognitive, motivational, and interpersonal benefits of negative mood. *Current Directions in Psychological Science*, 22, 225–232. doi: 10.1177/0963721412474458

Fredrickson, B. L. (2004). The broaden-and-build theory of positive emotions. *Philosophical Transactions of the Royal Society of London. Series B, Biological Sciences*, 359(1449), 1367–1378. doi: 10.1098/rstb.2004.1512

Goetz, T., Frenzel, A. C., Hall, N. C., Nett, U. E., Pekrun, R. and Lipnevich, A. A. (2014). Types of boredom: an experience sampling approach. *Motivation and Emotion*, 38(3), 401–419. doi: 10.1007/s11031-013-9385-y

Gruber, M. J., Gelman, B. D. and Ranganath, C. (2014). States of curiosity modulate hippocampus-dependent learning via the dopaminergic circuit. *Neuron*, 84, 486–496. doi: 10.1016/j.neuron.2014.08.060

Hidi, S. and Renninger, K. A. (2006). The four-phase model of interest development. *Educational Psychologist*, 41(2), 111–127. doi: 10.1207/ s15326985ep4102_4

Kensinger, E. A. and Corkin, S. (2003). Effect of negative emotional content on working memory and long-term memory. *Emotion*, 3(4), 378–393. doi: 10.1037/1528-3542.3.4.378

Leary, M. R., Rogers, P. A., Canfield, R. W. and Coe, C. (1986). Boredom in interpersonal encounters: antecedents and social implications. *Journal of Personality and Social Psychology*, 51(5), 968–975. doi: 10.1037/0022-3514.51.5.968

Lee, W., Lee, M.-J. and Bong, M. (2014). Testing interest and self-efficacy as predictors of academic self-regulation and achievement. *Contemporary Educational Psychology*, 39(2), 86–99. doi: 10.1016/j.cedpsych.2014.02.002

Mann, S. and Cadman, R. (2014). Does being bored make us more creative? *Creativity Research Journal*, 26(2), 165–173. doi: 10.1080/10400419. 2014.901073

Mischel, W. (2015) *The Marshmallow Test: Understanding Self-Control and How to Master It*. London: Corgi.

Nederkoorn, C., Vancleef, L., Wilkenhoner, A., Claes, L. and Havermans, R. C. (2016). Self-inflicted pain out of boredom. *Psychiatry Research*, 237, 127–132.

O'Brien, T. (2016). *Inner Story: Understand Your Mind, Change Your World*. CreateSpace Independent Publishing Platform.

O'Keefe, P. A. and Linnenbrink-Garcia, L. (2014). The role of interest in optimizing performance and self-regulation. *Journal of Experimental Social Psychology*, 53, 70–78. doi: 10.1016/j.jesp.2014.02.004

Pekrun, R. (2006). The control-value theory of achievement emotions: assumptions, corollaries, and implications for educational research and practice. *Educational Psychology Review*, 18(4), 315–341. doi: 10.1007/ s10648-006-9029-9

Pekrun, R., Frenzel, A. C., Goetz, T. and Perry, R. P. (2007). *The Control-Value Theory of Achievement Emotions: An Integrative Approach to Emotions in Education*. Amsterdam: Academic Press, pp. 13–36.

Pekrun, R., Goetz, T., Daniels, L. M., Stupnisky, R. H. and Perry, R. P. (2010). Boredom in achievement settings: exploring control-value antecedents and performance outcomes of a neglected emotion. *Journal of Educational Psychology*, 102(3), 531–549. doi: 10.1037/a0019243

Plutchik, R. (2001). The nature of emotions: human emotions have deep evolutionary roots, a fact that may explain their complexity and provide tools for clinical practice. *American Scientist*, 89(4), 344–350.

Rybanska, V., McKay, R., Jong, J. and Whitehouse, H. (2017). Rituals improve children's ability to delay gratification. *Child Development*, 18 February.

Sansone, C. and Thoman, D. B. (2005). Interest as the missing motivator in self-regulation. *European Psychologist*, 10(3), 175–186. doi: 10.1027/1016-9040.10.3.175

Unkelbach, C. Forgas, J. P. and Denson, T. F. (2008) The turban effect: the influence of Muslim headgear and the induced affect of aggressive responses in the shooter bias paradigm. *Journal of Experimental and Social Psychology*, 44(5), 1409–1413. doi: 10.1016/j.jesp.2008.04.003

Resilience, buoyancy and grit

Resilience is often used as an umbrella term to explain a number of different constructs, some more useful in the classroom than others. This chapter attempts to simplify the research on resilience by identifying those components of particular relevance to schools:

- Definitions of resilience.
- The difference between academic buoyancy and resilience.
- Definition and explanations of 'grit'.

Academic achievement occurs through a complex set of actions, behaviours and dispositions that are both intrinsic to the individual and affected by the wider external environment. Although cognition forms the backbone of learning, other processes such as motivation, perseverance and emotional regulation play important roles in academic achievement. Unfortunately, many of these other processes cannot be quantified through the same methods as those used to test more cognitive aspects of learning (e.g. memory retention can be measured through formal testing, and cognition through psychometric methods or experiments). For this reason, such attributes are often referred to as 'non-cognitive', even though they too involve complex cognitive processes such as the interplay between thought, action and emotion.

An important non-cognitive skill is the ability to bounce back from setbacks and cope with major assaults on self-confidence and self-esteem. We can use the umbrella term 'resilience' to describe this complex and wide-ranging set of personal attributes, beneath which other skills play out their intricate roles, dependent upon the type and severity of the situation. Although the term 'resilience' is often used as a catch-all to describe the ability to bounce back, more than three decades of research has discovered that the ability to cope with setbacks is conceptually different and dependent upon the perception and subjective or personal assessment of any situation. Furthermore, other skills such as persistence and optimism become influential at different stages of the process.

When we think about resilience, different circumstances might spring to mind. For example, what do we visualise as we consider a child, raised in poverty, whose life chances appear limited due to poor housing, health and educational outcomes? If this child grows up to be well educated, psychologically stable and financially solvent, do we then describe this person as resilient? What of the child who loses a parent in early childhood but goes on to form strong sensitive bonds with others despite the heartache of this early loss? There are many examples we could draw on: street children in the developing world who, despite the odds, survive into adulthood and thrive, or children thought to be at risk of mental health problems due to neglect and poor parenting, all are situations that require a degree of mental strength. All these situations have been examined by resilience researchers over the past three decades, but don't always spring to mind when we think of the term within its current and most popular context.

Perhaps we're considering a different kind of resilience? Perhaps the child who struggles at school but doesn't let a bad grade divert her from her mission to academically achieve, no matter what the day may throw at her, or the child who, despite his fear of maths, fights on to understand those complex equations that make his head spin? All of these individuals are displaying resilience, but the resilience we imagine differs significantly in terms of degree and outcome. What, then, do we really mean when we say that students should be more resilient?

What are the key principles of resilience?

Resilience is a complex subject, often made more complex due to the contradictory nature of a large proportion of the research. Definitions can vary, and are often dependent on the nature of the research itself and the group of people the research sets out to investigate. Generally speaking, there are currently three main theories relating to resilience, all with competing definitions: resilience as trait, resilience as outcome-oriented and resilience as process-oriented.

Resilience as a personality trait

The study of personality has a long history in psychology, and it would be difficult to discuss resilience and other non-cognitive skills without at least referring to it. Gordon Allport (1897–1967) is credited as being one of the founding fathers of personality psychology, identifying around 4,500 individual words he thought could describe a person. From this, Allport identified certain traits or habitual patterns of behaviour, thought and emotion, which he then divided into common and individual traits. These traits appear to have a genetic basis and remain stable over time; nevertheless, it's difficult to say with conviction that they are definitely inherited, or indeed stable.

Common traits are described as basic modes of adjustment that are applicable to all members of a particular cultural, ethnic or linguistic background. By this we mean that individuals adapt their behaviours to suit the prevailing acceptable and unacceptable levels within any specific society or culture. A good example is aggression, a trait that is necessary for interaction within competitive cultures but remains dependent upon appropriate levels that might differ between cultural groups. Individual traits, on the other hand, represent a unique set of personal dispositions and ways of organising the world. Individual traits are based on life experiences and cannot be applied to all people or measured by standardised tests. Individual traits are more about what makes us unique (the so-called idiographic approach) in contrast to the attempt to establish general rules (the nomothetic approach).

Trait resilience is therefore a habitual behaviour that remains relatively stable over time but differs across individuals. In some cases, it isn't necessarily a matter of being resilient or not, but rather your position on a continuum (such as introversion and extroversion – you might not display the classic behaviours of either extreme, but fall somewhere in between). It is thought that trait resilience operates by inoculating individuals against the impact of adversity and traumatic events. If we accept the view that resilience constitutes a trait, then the idea that we can teach resilience becomes problematic because of the suggestion that resilience is somehow part of our personality. Allport didn't necessarily claim that we are born with our personality, but rather the creation of that personality begins at the moment of birth.

More recent investigations into personality have identified five broad dimensions known as the big five (or the five-factor model). The five-factor model is generally regarded as an empirically valid means of assessing personality. According to the model, our personalities can be measured against five specific traits:

- openness;
- conscientiousness;
- extroversion;
- agreeableness; and
- neuroticism.

Studies investigating the relationship between these five factors and resilience have found that resilient individual have a tendency to score high on extroversion, openness, conscientiousness and agreeableness, and low in neuroticism (i.e. high on emotional stability). Of these, emotional stability is perhaps the most important from a clinical perspective, as those displaying low levels of emotional stability (high levels of neuroticism) have a tendency to suffer from more negative affect and lower self-esteem, and display more symptoms related to depression and anxiety. However, those individuals classified as resilient display higher levels of behaviours related to extroversion, such as good social skills, the ability to thrive in social contexts and higher self-esteem.

There is certainly considerable evidence to suggest that resilience is at least trait-like and an integral part of our personality. There is also an indication here that individuals who don't score so highly on certain factors are doomed to struggle with adversity and be more susceptible to mental illness and academic underachievement. Adopting the trait theory of resilience, however, leads to a very problematic situation when it comes to designing and delivering interventions, in that traits cannot be taught or nurtured if they are components of personality. Fortunately, the trait theory of resilience is only one of several possibilities, and other theories are less deterministic.

Resilience as outcome-oriented

Outcome-orientated approaches to resilience view it as a function or behavioural outcome that can help individuals recover from adversity. Researchers in this area see resilience as much more than just the ability to bounce back from adversity, but rather the ability to move forward with greater focus than before the challenge occurred. Furthermore, the outcome-oriented approach would suggest that resilience includes the capacity to turn setbacks into opportunities.

Resilience as process-oriented

Process-orientated approaches view resilience as a dynamic process where individuals adapt to changing circumstances in order to help them cope and rapidly recover from major adversities.

Some of these definitions would imply that resilience is teachable, while others (e.g. trait theory) would argue that you either have it or you don't. This distinction is obviously important when considering any intervention aimed at improving levels of resilience. Psychologists such as Dr Tim O'Brien have suggested that rather than resilience being specifically taught, we should really think about resilience as being effectively nurtured (O'Brien, 2016). This is certainly strongly implied by resilience research conducted over the past 30 years or so, which is where we now turn our attention.

Resilience and positive psychology

Positive psychology represents the latest attempt to move psychology into a slightly different orbit. It is mainly associated with the work of Martin Seligman, whose early research offered valuable insights into the role of cognitive and behavioural factors that lead to and sustain depressive illnesses. Rather than concentrating on the negative side of the human condition (such as mental illness), positive psychology attempts to identify the components of human existence that represent the 'good life'. This is why positive psychology is often (erroneously, some would say) described as the study of happiness. Resilience is viewed primarily from the viewpoint of positive emotions such as joy and optimism, and how they help people to cope in times of adversity through the extension of what are known as 'thought-action repertoires'.

The origins of positive psychology's understanding of resilience dates back to 1967 and Seligman's highly influential research into learned helplessness (e.g. Seligman, 1975). Seligman and his colleagues were investigating the use of behavioural conditioning in dogs (an extension of early research that has its genesis in the work of Ivan Pavlov). Like Pavlov, Seligman and his colleagues were attempting to pair a signal with a response (in Seligman's case, an electric shock) to see if the signal, such as the ringing of a bell, would allow the animal to anticipate the coming pain of the shock. The dogs reacted to the signal in the same way they reacted to the electric shock, by displaying distress even before the shock had been administered. The dogs were then placed into a 'shuttle box', a large crate divided by a low fence (low enough for the dog to jump over). The floor on one side of the box was electrified, and it was assumed that when the dog experienced the pain of the live floor, it would jump over the low fence to the safety of the other side. The dogs, however, made no attempt to escape the shocks, and simply lay down, whimpered and accepted their fate. When Seligman tried this second part of the experiment again, but this time with a set of dogs that hadn't received the initial shocks, he found that they quickly leaped over the partition in order to escape the pain. What this study indicates is that because the first part of the experiment involved inescapable pain, all later shocks were treated in the same way. Even when the researchers gave the dogs a way out, they didn't take it – they had learned that they had no control over the situation they had found themselves in and had become helpless. In the same manner, claimed Seligman, people who feel as if bad things happen to them all of the time begin to accept that they have little control over their own actions, and depression not only sets in, but is sustained by this negative life view.

Luckily for dogs, Seligman moved on to the study of more enlightening human significance, including the role of positive emotions and their influence on qualities such as resilience. Seligman also developed the Penn Resilience Program at the University of Pennsylvania, which has been adapted to be used in schools across the world, and formed the basis for the UK Resilience Programme. Another influential positive psychologist, Barbara Fredrickson, has proposed that positive emotions enhance problem-focused coping and positive reappraisal as part of the 'broaden and build framework'. According to Fredrickson, while negative emotions narrow our ability to think creatively and weigh up different options, positive emotions work in the opposite direction by broadening our ability and adding to what Fredrickson (2004) calls our 'thought-action repertoire'. In this way, positive emotions help to enhance resilience by providing the positive emotional state for individuals to work through setbacks and cope with potential failure.

Positive psychology has been highly criticised on methodological grounds; nevertheless, the criticisms don't entirely discount its usefulness with regard to resilience. One of the main concerns related to the view is that positive emotions always help while negative ones always hinder (e.g. fear is one negative emotion that can have detrimental impact on behaviour, but can also be a source of motivation – even happiness itself has been found to encourage lazy thinking). It's much more likely that positive and negative emotions operate on a case-by-case basis, an area discussed in more depth in Chapter 5.

Early research into resilience

Early research into resilience often concentrated on those individuals at risk of factors such as mental illness and susceptibility to addiction, and the way in which high-risk groups adapted to their situations. Later research moved on to other groups such as children who were at risk of school failure and possible non-completion. Resilience therefore becomes concerned with reactions to severe adversity that pose a major threat to future trajectories. Ann Masten (2001) has defined resilience as 'good outcomes in spite of serious threats to adaptation or development', and suggests that it arises as part of the normal human process of adaptation. This contradicts earlier assumptions that those individuals who thrive in spite of adversity are in some way special, and instead suggests that they are resilient for the very reason that they have experienced it.

The first thing we need to consider about resilience is the suggestion that it is a quality contained within the individual. As already mentioned, this trait view assumes that resilience represents a 'born with' quality, rather than a mechanism that evolves over time. Resilience is therefore seen as some kind of superpower trait bestowed on lucky individuals that makes them seemingly invulnerable. This was the general opinion during the early days of resilience research, and one that gained momentum, certainly within the psychoanalytic community. One particular proponent of this invulnerability hypothesis was the British child psychotherapist and psychiatrist James Anthony. Anthony studied for a time under the watchful gaze of the eminent Swiss developmental psychologist Jean Piaget, and throughout his highly successful and very long career (he died in 2014 and was still practising at the age of 90) collaborated with the likes of Anna Freud, Erik Erikson and John Bowlby. The psychoanalytic tradition, developed by Anna's father Sigmund Freud, was still very much in evidence at the time, despite the expansion and burgeoning influence of the behaviourists and growing relevance of cognitive psychology.

Anthony used what is known as the 'three dolls metaphor' to explain the tendency of some people to be able to overcome extreme adversity (Anthony and Cohler, 1987). Imagine I have three dolls; one is made of glass, one of plastic and one of steel. If I take a hammer and strike the doll made of glass, it will shatter into a multitude of tiny pieces. The plastic doll, however, will fare slightly better. It will certainly emerge battered and bruised, but it won't have suffered the same violent fate as its glass companion. The steel doll, however, will emerge unscathed, its impenetrable armour protecting it from the heavy blow of the hammer. Anthony suggests that we can think of children in the same way, and that those children born of steel will survive unscathed from any number of blows dealt by life. In his later work, Anthony would acknowledge the role of environmental factors in resilience; however, the three dolls metaphor gives us some indication about the way many researchers at the time viewed some people as invulnerable due to this specific aspect of their personality.

Many of these early research studies often employed retrospective methods to analyse the backgrounds of those individuals who went on to develop conditions such as alcoholism and schizophrenia. The problem often arises that looking back on an individual's life experiences to establish the cause of a condition often leads to a correlation in the absence of causation. In other words, personal histories might include risk factors (such as abuse or trauma) that appear positively correlated with later onset of mental illness, or other negative outcomes, but that one thing led to another cannot be conclusively established. For this reason, early research led to the erroneous conclusion that poor outcomes were inevitable. Longitudinal studies (those that identify high-risk groups and follow their progress for several months or even years), however, are better suited to establishing causation, and have discovered that the situation is far more complex than first thought. For example, Norman Garmezy, who conducted some of the most important research into the nature of risk and resilience at the University of Minnesota, found that less than half of vulnerable children went on to repeat the patterns of their caregivers in adult life, suggesting that at-risk children are able employ resilience strategies that are potentially part of the normal human adaptation system (Garmezy, 1991).

Garmezy's work represents one of the most important contributions to the study of resilience. He was highly influenced by earlier work undertaken by Swiss psychiatrist Manfred Bleuler, who studied children raised by schizophrenic mothers. Bleuler (1978) found that of the 184 offspring he studied, only 9 per cent became schizophrenic themselves, suggesting that there was something about the conditions in which they were raised that somehow protected them from developing the illness. It is widely believed that schizophrenia is an illness with significant genetic component but that the environment plays a secondary role in the development of the condition. In addition to those offspring who never went on to develop schizophrenia, the majority went on to lead successful personal and private lives, including achieving a higher social status than their parents. Within the resilient group, Bleuler found certain potent protective factors such as the opportunity to be exposed to at least some good parenting from either the afflicted or healthy parent, or the opportunity to connect with a parent substitute. It was also important for the child to have a sense of purpose such as jobs to engage in around the home, or to care for a sick child or parent (Rutter, 2012).

Garmezy recognised that there must be more to resilience than genetic factors or personality traits, as not all children raised by schizophrenic mothers went on to display symptoms themselves, while the very fact of being raised by a mother suffering from the disorder could itself lead to a chaotic and dysfunctional home life. Unlike Bleuler, Garmezy wanted to study stress resistance in groups from disadvantaged backgrounds. His systematic and scientific approach allowed him to try to understand how these protective strategies actually worked; furthermore, by relying on longitudinal studies rather than retrospective ones, he was able to trace the lives and experiences of children from at-risk groups in order to gain a fuller understanding of the mechanisms involved. Garmezy concluded that resilience wasn't just about personality traits, but also about gene-environment interdependence and the multiple causal factors that lead to some individuals being seemingly inoculated against the negative consequences of severe adversity. This would mean, of course, that there is no universal answer to why some thrive and others don't; it would also suggest that resilience is an interactive emergent concept, one that cannot be measured directly, but merely inferred (i.e. it is not a fixed attribute of an individual). It would also imply that it could be nurtured and encouraged, given favourable environmental and social conditions.

From this, we can suggest that any research into resilience must therefore include:

- the role of positive personality dispositions;
- the role of a nurturing family environment; and
- the role of external societal support mechanisms.

Garmezy stressed the importance of longitudinal studies as a means of rigorously investigating resilience. One highly influential longitudinal study was the 40-year Kauai study, led by Emmy Werner, that traced the lives of all 698 children born on the Hawaiian island of Kauai in 1955. Werner's team consisted of mental health workers, paediatricians, social workers and public health workers who monitored the development of all the children on the island at ages 1, 2, 10, 32 and 40, representing critical points in the life cycle in terms of the development of trust, autonomy, industry, identity, intimacy and generativity (the concern and nurture for those from older and younger generation than ourselves). Around 30 per cent of the sample had been born and raised in poverty, as well as displaying other risk factors such as divorce and parental psychopathology, or were raised by mothers with low levels of formal education. Two-thirds of the children who had experienced four or more risk factors by the age of 2 went on to develop learning or behavioural problems by the age of 10 or mental health problems by the age of 18 (Werner, 2005).

The most significant result from a resilience perspective, however, was that one-third of the high-risk group grew up to be competent, confident and caring adults. There was no evidence of behavioural or learning problems during childhood or adolescence, they succeeded in school, and managed home and social life well. By the time they had reached 40, all were employed and none had been in trouble with the law. Instances of divorce in this group were lower than their peers, as were their mortality rates.

What was it, therefore, that protected this group and not the other? Werner believes that there were a number of protective factors that acted to inoculate children from the negative consequences of early adversity. These were grouped into factors that were within the individual, within the family and in the community:

- *Factors within the individual.* As infants, the resilient children were more likely to display certain character traits that elicited positive responses from their parents and other caregivers. By the time the children had reached the age of 1, their mothers were describing them using positive language, utilising terms such as active, affectionate and good-natured in order to categorise their dispositions. At age 2, independent observers were describing the resilient toddlers in terms of agreeableness and cheerfulness. These children were also more advanced in their language and motor development, as well as in self-help skills. Other children who did not display these characteristics were more likely to develop problems later in life. By the age of 10, the more resilient children were scoring higher on tests of practical problem-solving and were better readers than those who developed learning or behavioural problems. These children were also said to have developed a special talent that gave them a sense of pride and they were more willing than the other children to help those in need. In late adolescence, the resilient teenagers had developed a strong belief in their own effectiveness and a view that the problems they encountered could be overcome by their own actions. They also had more realistic plans pertaining to future professional trajectories than did their less resilient peers.

- *Factors within the family.* Those children in the study who displayed resilience were able to establish close bonds with caregivers who were sensitive to their needs early on. These individuals were often substitute caregivers such as grandparents, older siblings, uncles and aunts. Interestingly, the resilient children appeared to be very skilled in recruiting these surrogate parents. Resilient girls were more likely to come from households where the family combined an emphasis on independence with the support of a female caregiver, while resilient boys came from households with structured rules and a male who served as a positive role model. Interestingly, the ability to safely express emotions also played a protective role for these boys. The families of the resilient children also tended to hold religious beliefs that appeared to provide some stability and meaning in their lives.

- *Factors in the community.* Community appeared to play an important role in the lives of the resilient youngsters. They tended to rely more on elders and peers in their community for emotional support, and many of these young people had a favourite teacher to act as a positive role model. Caring neighbours, elder mentors, youth leaders, ministers and members of the church, as well as parents of friends, provided guidance and support for many of these children.

The Kauai study highlights a number of interesting factors. Internally, there was something about the individuals' personality that seemed to inoculate them from the negative consequences to which they were exposed. This would support the view that resilience is indeed a personality trait, with protective qualities. However, the study also highlights the vital importance of social factors such as strong support mechanisms, both within the family and externally from the local community. It also rejects earlier assumptions that resilient children are somehow special or extraordinary, and that, on the contrary, resilience arises from what Masten describes as the normative functions of the human adaptational system.

Research such as the Kauai longitudinal study better helps us to understand the lives of resilient individuals and the ways in which multiple factors interact. It also helps us to reconcile some of the problems around trait and process-/outcome-oriented definitions of resilience. It is clear that resilient children possess that 'something' that helps them to thrive, even with challenging life histories, yet it is equally clear that external factors interact with intrinsic predispositions. Nowhere is this more obvious than in the role played by the school environment and teachers.

The role of the school environment

Resilient children like school, and a substantial amount of research supports this claim. Even resilient children who aren't seen as academically able like school and put their abilities (however limited) to good use. Furthermore, children raised in at-risk environments perceive school as a home from home, a refuge from the chaos and upset of a disordered household. The resilient children in Kauai had a favourite teacher, someone who provided them with a positive role model; this was especially true for young children. Michael Rutter's work in London schools during the 1970s further highlights the important role played by schools in nurturing resilient young people, finding that positive experiences in the classroom mitigate the stress often suffered by high-risk children at home. Some schools were found to be better than others at getting the most from pupils from vulnerable backgrounds and difficult home lives (Rutter et al., 1979).

The most successful schools:

- maintain appropriately high academic standards;
- use effective incentives and rewards;
- give effective feedback, along with adequate praise from teachers; and
- ensure that all pupils are given the opportunity to be awarded positions of trust and responsibility.

Children who attended schools displaying these characteristics were much less likely to develop emotional and behavioural problems, despite severe deprivation and discord at home. A similarity was also found between the characteristics of both home and school environments that were associated with greater resilience in children of divorced parents. Characteristics such as a responsive atmosphere, and organised and predictable environment, as well as clearly defined and consistently reinforced standards, rules and responsibilities, appeared to be common within the school and home lives of resilient children. For boys, the most important factors were likely to be structure and control, while for girls the most important factors were nurturing and assumption of responsibility.

More recent research (Sanders et al., 2015) tracked a cohort of 605 vulnerable young people in New Zealand and the factors that helped them to stay on track with their education. It was found that the ability to stay within a mainstream school was the strongest factor identified as a means to stay on track. Relational resources such as friends, family and community were also cited as important in the ability for these vulnerable youngsters to stay out of trouble and remain in school. Furthermore, other studies have reached similar conclusions regarding supporting mechanisms. Family support, school responsiveness to students' needs, student involvement in school, and involvement in school activities were all shown to be good predictors in the ability to recover from low grades. Again, resilience appears to be a culmination of several factors, including familial and community support. Nevertheless, its trait-like quality further suggests an interaction between personality and support mechanisms, or an indirect influencing factor between the adversity and successful coping and future personal growth.

Even though there remain significant individual differences in regard to specific protective factors developed by individuals, it does appear that such factors develop over time. However, outcomes are also dependent on the timing of any specific negative event. The younger a child is (e.g. in the event of a parental death), the greater the protective outcomes against negative separation experiences. Adaptational resources vary but appear to be more prevalent at certain times, particularly in very young children.

Despite some evidence of consensus in early resilience research, there remained problems in several areas. Operationalisation and measurement of key constructs varied, leading to issues surrounding definitions, as well as disagreements in the conceptualization of resilience being a personal trait or a dynamic process. Furthermore, the use of certain terms (e.g. 'protective', 'vulnerability') continued to be used in varied and inconsistent ways. For example, Garmezy and Rutter use the term 'protective' to refer to a particular attribute within certain individuals that appears to protect them from adversity, while Werner describes 'protective' as a variable that distinguishes high-functioning children at risk from those who go on to develop serious problems.

Despite problems with definitions, researchers have generally agreed on a number specific points, most notably the possible negative consequences of displaying low levels of resilience. While those individuals displaying high levels of resilience are able to successfully deal with major adversity and significant setbacks, low levels of resilience are associated with a number of negative outcomes, including:

- chronic underachievement;
- being overwhelmed and incapacitated;
- debilitation in the face of chronic failure and anxiety;
- clinical affect such as anxiety and depression;
- disaffection and truancy from school; and
- comprehensive and consistent alienation from school or opposition to teachers.

These negative outcomes represent a severe failure to cope with difficult situations, but don't necessarily represent the typical daily lives of students. While a small number of students might display such severe symptoms, most students find that their days are punctuated more by relatively minor setbacks, which might nevertheless be seen as subjectively significant. The overarching resilient construct therefore appears to be ill-suited to the purpose of raising achievement among students due to its emphasis on chronic adversity.

From resilience to buoyancy

If we think of resilience as an umbrella beneath which other concepts stand, we open up the opportunity to think of the ability to bounce back in slightly different ways. The bulk of the research into resilience has focused on how young people bounce back from extreme adversity, rather than specific school-based problems. More recently, research has begun to investigate the day-to-day problems that students are presented with – a term that has become known as 'academic buoyancy'.

Through extensive research, psychologist Andrew Martin discovered that the ability of students to cope and thrive within an environment beset by daily setbacks was conceptually different, but related to, the traditional resilience construct. While resilience research concerned itself with cases of extreme adversity, Martin was more concerned with the low-level setbacks experienced by students. The issues that interested Martin were not those of individuals at risk of psychopathology nor of complete school failure, but rather the underachievement experienced due to the inability to cope with situations such as a bad mark on a test, competing homework deadlines, or anxiety induced by exams and other high-stakes assessments. Rather than resilience, Martin (along with psychologist Herbert Marsh) proposed that the ability to cope with these types of daily setback be reconceptualised as 'academic buoyancy' as a means of distinguishing it from the traditional view of resilience and overcoming many of conceptual issues that have plagued resiliency research (Martin, 2013).

Academic buoyancy is therefore associated with the following factors:

- the process of dealing with isolated poor grades;
- the process of dealing with patches of poor performance;
- typical stress levels and daily pressure;
- threats to confidence due to poor grades;
- low-level stress and confidence;
- dips in motivation and engagement; and
- the process of dealing with negative feedback.

These factors are much more relevant to school settings than those investigated by research into resilience, and while a reciprocal relationship between resilience and academic buoyancy has been found, the two concepts remain connected but conceptually different. It has also been discovered that those high in resilience also score high on measures of academic buoyancy, suggesting that the differences between the two constructs relate to differences of degree (e.g. threats to confidence) and differences of kind (e.g. dips in motivation). In an attempt to establish that resilience and buoyancy are actually different constructs, Martin asked 918 Australian high school students to complete two questionnaires, one to measure risk and resilience (the so-called Academic Risk and Resilience Scale, or ARRS) and the other to measure academic buoyancy (the Academic Buoyancy Scale, or ABS). The ABS comprises four items rated on scale of 1–7, consisting of:

1   I am good at dealing with setbacks (e.g. bad marks, negative feedback on my work).
2   I don't let study stress get on top of me.
3   I think I'm good at dealing with schoolwork pressures.
4   I don't let a bad mark affect my confidence.

Statistical analysis of the results of the questionnaires confirmed that buoyancy is indeed different to resilience, but that the constructs overlap to a certain extent. Academic buoyancy appears to be more salient in predicting the impact of low-level negative outcomes, while resilience is better at predicting major negative outcomes. The important point here is that tests used to measure resilience won't tell us very much about how individuals are coping with low-level problems in their daily lives, so shouldn't be used as measure of minor academic adversity and the ability of students to bounce back from it. Of course, measures differ in their accuracy, reliability and relevance, with problems arising when we try to combine or identify patterns across schools and across interventions. Indeed, a review of school-based resilience interventions conducted by Angie Hart and Becky Heaver of the Centre for Health Research, University of Brighton, UK, found that the terms, definitions and interventions varied to such an extent that it was difficult to work out what they were measuring at all (Hart and Heaver, 2013).

Buoyancy and psychological risk

Psychological risk factors can be thought of as those things about ourselves that have the potential to make us vulnerable. In terms of learning, we can divide these risks into academic and non-academic, but just because the non-academic ones don't directly involve learning, it doesn't mean they can't still impact on the learning process. Academic risk factors include fear of failure, academic anxiety and uncertain control, while non-academic factors include emotional instability, self-concept and neuroticism. A higher proportion of academic risk factors have been associated with higher levels of disengagement, lower levels of class participation, lower educational aspirations and lower levels of school enjoyment. They obviously impact quite highly on academic achievement and also on levels of academic buoyancy, so it's worth looking at some of them in greater detail.

Fear of failure and the role of self-handicapping

Fear of failure (sometimes described as 'failure avoidance') is a motivational disposition where individuals experience shame upon failure and overgeneralize it. Failure is imbued with negative connotations, and some view failure as a personal attack on themselves rather than an integral part of the learning process. Despite what we might think of our students, many of them aren't as confident as they would like us all to believe, certainly when it comes to academic success. As a way of protecting themselves from failure, many students will actively attempt to avoid the whole failure experience altogether. Many will do this by 'self-handicapping' (sometimes referred to as 'self-sabotage'). This is a way of attempting to safeguard self-esteem by placing obstacles in the way of success – it's a way of saying 'I didn't fail because I'm stupid, I failed because I was ill', or 'I failed because I have a very bad memory', or any other number of reasons.

Needless to say, the more of these self-handicapping phrases that students use, the more likely they are to underachieve, and studies have found that self-handicapping is indeed negatively correlated with academic grades (e.g Urdan and Midgley, 2001). Unfortunately, academic self-handicapping is perhaps a symptom of the test-obsessed culture in which we live. It allows us to defend ourselves against setbacks by externalising the reasons for them and often leads to self-fulfilling failure. It's easier for many people (especially adolescents who have been sheltered from the realities of failure) to handicap themselves academically, so that if failure is encountered they can reply with 'Well, I did tell you I couldn't do exams' or 'Well, I was very ill on the day of the exam and that's why I didn't do very well'. They may also feign excuses, such as claiming that they are too tired when they are not; this allows them to fall back on the 'tired' reason for underachieving in an exam, keeping their academic self-esteem intact – and self-esteem is the important factor here.

It's also easier to say 'I failed because I didn't revise' as this doesn't reflect negatively on them in terms of their intelligence or 'cleverness', and this is what many young people are desperate to safeguard. They may of course claim that they didn't revise, when in fact they spent hours preparing for their exam. A common-sense assumption would be that self-handicapping is linked to poor self-esteem; however, research into this relationship appears very mixed, with studies showing no relationship, positive relationship and negative relationship (dependent on which study you consult). It is perhaps better to investigate self-handicapping on the basis of self-concept (and its consistency and stability – known as self-clarity) rather than looking for answers within the globalisation of self-esteem generally.

If self-handicapping isn't related to self-esteem, then this creates all sorts of issues for educators trying to get the most from learners. High self-esteem might even encourage self-handicapping in some learners in an attempt to safeguard their status (and we have seen as many learners underachieve through arrogance than through low self-esteem).

Praising effort over intelligence might be one way that educators can improve academic self-concept without impacting on self-esteem. Fear of failure represents a failure of academic buoyancy because it creates a situation where the ability to bounce back is impaired. Another way of identifying students who struggle with academic buoyancy is through their unrealistic expectations of success and failure.

Defensive pessimism: when students aim too low

Students will often hold unrealistically low expectations of themselves, especially in circumstances when they are being assessed in some kind of formal way, such as an exam or a piece of homework. Holding low expectations of ourselves allows people to cushion themselves against anxiety because of the way in which people create unrealistic targets for themselves. After all, if we set our expectations low, it's not as far to fall. It also means that we can feel better about ourselves when we meet or exceed our expectations. By doing this, we turn failure into a success, at least in our own minds. The crucial thing about defensive pessimism is that expectations aren't based on the evidence of past experience, which may well indicate high academic achievement, so a student might convince themselves that they will fail the test, despite past experiences of test taking being very positive in their outcomes. This might seem like a reasonable strategy to adopt; however, there is a real danger that such thinking will reduce motivation and engagement because the student convinces themselves that failure is the most likely outcome, despite a past history of success. This way of thinking can quickly develop into a self-fulfilling prophecy, whereby a student, convinced that they will fail, sees little point in working hard or revising for an important exam because of the expectation of inevitable failure.

Defensive optimism: when students aim too high

Defensive optimists set unrealistically high expectations for themselves even when past experience suggest that they are unlikely to reach these levels. Students who are predicted Cs and Ds might set their sights on As and Bs, even though past results on tests and other assessments don't support this view. While teachers want to encourage students to do well, unrealistic expectations are also damaging – optimism is good, as long as it remains realistic.

Defensive optimists often display a number of characteristics that identify their behaviour as potentially damaging. These include:

- striving towards an A grade when previous assessments have placed them closer to a D;
- choosing books, texts or other information that are far beyond their capabilities in terms of their previous attainment; and
- applying to the top universities, even though they are highly unlikely to obtain the required entry grades.

The main problem with this strategy is that it encourages students to concentrate on short-term goals. Defensive optimism removes the fear of failure by discounting even the possibility of it, and ignoring the evidence that implies failure is a real possibility. Like the defensive pessimist, the defensive optimist lacks motivation and buoyancy, and convinces themselves that success is inevitable, even without the hard work.

Successful learners see failure differently

Successful students often see failure in different ways to those who might be more vulnerable to self-handicapping and defensive strategies, and rather than viewing failure as a direct attack on self-esteem, they are more likely to see it as an opportunity to improve. Successful students don't tend to self-handicap or over/underestimate their chances of success, not because they have very high self-esteem, but rather because they don't worry too much about what others will think if they do underachieve – they tend not to compare themselves to their classmates (they hold mastery learning orientation). From a psychological viewpoint, comparisons don't necessarily lead to greater success and higher marks. Comparisons invariably lead to greater anxiety and increase in the possibility that students will self-handicap. Research indicates that the most successful students don't actually care that much about how they measure up against the others in their class, school or nationally.

Academic anxiety

Academic anxiety (or test anxiety) is a specific form of anxiety in which students perceive any test situation as threatening. Test anxiety is related to a number of negative academic outcomes, including threats to personal well-being and stronger tendencies towards self-handicapping. David Putwain, a psychologist at Edge Hill University in the UK, suggested that buoyant individuals may not view academic failure as threatening to either personal aspirations or self-worth due to their belief in their ability to bounce back from failure. Because of this belief, they are less likely to suffer high levels of anxiety during test situations because of the belief in their own ability to cope with failure (not necessarily their ability to succeed). Indeed, Putwain and other researchers have found that buoyant students are much less like to fret over exams than those students displaying lower levels of buoyancy (Putwain et al., 2013).

A further consideration around buoyancy is the probability of an emotional component, in that anxiety represents an emotional response to a perceived threat. Although a discussion of emotions is beyond the scope of this chapter (see Chapter 5 for an in-depth analysis of emotions in learning), there is substantial evidence to indicate that emotions have a key role to play in the learning process, and resilience and buoyancy specifically. While some have suggested that this is a simple case of positive emotions are good and negative emotions are bad, it's unlikely that the situation is that simple, and more likely that both positive and negative emotions can be both activating and deactivating. For example, anxiety is generally considered to impede learning (and there is plenty of evidence linking anxiety to working memory malfunction); however, anxiety can also motivate, and it might be more prudent to consider the level of anxiety rather than anxiety in itself.

Uncertain control

Students like to know that they have some control over their own learning; they need to know how they can succeed and do well, and they also want to understand why they might not be doing quite so well as they hoped. If they lack a clear idea about how to progress and how they can improve, then their control over this situation can be said to be uncertain. Uncertain control is related to another psychological construct, self-efficacy, which concerns the extent to which we feel we have control over a situation. A person who doesn't feel as if they know how to do well and how not to fail has very little subjective control over the situation, and therefore loses faith in their own ability. With high levels of uncertain control, students will have little confidence in their ability to cope with even the slightest setback.

Personality and buoyancy

Is there anything about our personality that makes us more likely to bounce back? We can predict academic buoyancy by aligning it with several motivational factors (or facets of our personality). In their wide-ranging investigations into academic buoyancy, Martin and Marsh identified five components of personality that appear to be common in those individuals displaying high levels of academic buoyancy. For the sake of simplicity, Martin and Marsh labelled these components the five Cs: confidence, coordination, control, composure and commitment (Martin et al., 2010):

- *Confidence (self-efficacy)*: The belief in our ability to control our own learning outcomes.
- *Coordination*: The ability to plan for academic success and have some kind of idea about the desired outcomes.
- *Control*: To know how we are doing, how we can improve, and what to do when we encounter some kind of roadblock.

- *Composure*: The propensity to cope with anxiety in a positive way.
- *Commitment*: The ability to persist when the going gets tough.

The five Cs have been found to correlate positively with academic buoyancy; in other words, students who display high levels of these components appear much better equipped to bounce back from daily setbacks. Furthermore, earlier work predating the identification of the academic buoyancy construct had found that resilience can be predicted by the prevalence of the following factors:

- enjoyment of school (a school-related cognitive-affective measure);
- class participation (a behavioural measure); and
- self-esteem (a global-affective measure).

The term 'affective' in psychology refers to our experience of emotion and is often seen as synonymous with emotion. You may recall that in the Kauai island study, it was found that the more resilient children enjoyed being at school and liked their teachers (or had at least one teacher they felt they could turn to). There is also a motivational element here – enjoying school and seeing the relevance in it increases levels of motivation and participation, which in turn can lead to higher self-esteem. We can therefore think of behaviours as being adaptive and maladaptive (e.g. anxiety is – usually – maladaptive because it impacts self-esteem, confidence and cognitive functions, such as working memory capacity). Adaptive functions, however, such as persistence and school enjoyment, can be seen as adaptive (as can certain emotions) because they increase motivation and raise our levels of buoyancy.

The role of academic self-concept

When we talk of self-esteem, we are usually referring to global self-esteem, a broad view of how confident we are with ourselves. Global self-esteem is relatively stable in that it persists in different circumstances;

in other words, it's more trait-like than state-like. However, beneath this broad view can be found a construct known as academic-self concept. Rather than being a global measure, academic self-concept is specific to different states. This is important for teachers and students because it suggests that while we view ourselves positively in some circumstances (e.g. a maths classroom), we may be less sure of ourselves in other circumstances (e.g. an English classroom). Furthermore, we might have high global self-esteem but still display low academic self-concept in certain academic subjects (for a more comprehensive discussion of academic self-concept, see Chapter 4).

As one would expect, academic buoyancy and academic self-concept are related. It is also highly likely that they have a reciprocal effect, and because academic self-concept is built up through previous experience, those displaying low levels of self-concept are more likely to display a lower ability to bounce back when the going gets tough. What we see here is a complex interaction between several components that predict academic achievement, and this highlights the complex nature of the process and how concentrating our efforts in a single area won't result in the impact we desire. A more recent component added to the mix in the past few years has been labelled 'grit'.

The role of grit in resilience and buoyancy

Like resilience, grit had become a highly prized educational attribute since its conceptualisation by Angela Duckworth, professor of psychology at the University of Pennsylvania. Grit shares many of its attributes with both resilience and buoyancy, including the tendency for influential individuals to misinterpret underlying concepts and to misattribute academic outcomes to the power of grit. According to Duckworth, grit represents perseverance and passion for long-term goals as well as the ability to maintain effort over years, despite failure, adversity and plateaus in progress.

This description would certainly suggest that grit belongs beneath the umbrella of resilience and that we can also suggest a reciprocal relationship. Part of what it means to be 'gritty' is the ability to be resilient in the face of failure and adversity, but you also need other traits to be gritty. Grit correlates positively with conscientiousness (one of the big five personality traits), but not with IQ, so intelligent people won't necessarily be gritty people. In fact, Duckworth believes that achievement arises from a combination of talent and sustained focus, and application of talent over time. The gritty individual doesn't think of short-term gains – they're in it for the long haul; achievement to the gritty ones is a marathon, not a sprint. Additionally, talented people have a tendency to set themselves goals, and once they reach that goal they stop. If a person is talented and displays high levels of grit, they propel themselves beyond an arbitrary threshold (Perkins-Gough, 2013).

One of Duckworth's earliest studies into grit involved the study of a group of cadets at the elite West Point Military Academy (Duckworth et al., 2007). Around 25 per cent of all officers in the US Army are graduates of West Point, and so arduous is the training that around 1 in 20 cadets will drop out during the summer of training that takes place before the first academic year. Admission to West Point is based on a 'whole candidate score', comprising SAT scores, class rank, demonstrated leadership ability and physical aptitude. The researchers were interested in how levels of grit were predictive of who would drop out of training before the end of the summer. To this end, they administered a short grit questionnaire in addition to the usual West Point psychological tests. They found that grit was a greater predictor of who dropped out than the whole candidate score, supporting the view that grit was able to predict success due to consistent and sustained perseverance. In a later study involving participants in a 'spelling bee' competition, Duckworth found that grit enabled spellers to persist with practice activities that were less intrinsically rewarding but more effective than other types of preparation (Duckworth et al., 2011).

Gritty learners are certainly buoyant learners; they're not affected by setbacks, disappointment or boredom. Gritty learners don't just bounce back; they come back fighting and can sustain this effort over very long periods of time (we're talking years rather than months). But is grit just a new name for an old concept? Certainly, 'persistence' fulfils the same criteria, as does the concept of 'mental toughness' (originally used to explain how athletes keep going despite failure, but more recently being applied to areas such an education). And what about conscientiousness – one of the big five personality traits?

The problem with much of the supporting evidence is that it involved highly specialised samples. West Point cadets are all high achievers in many different disciplines and spelling bee contestants are highly skilled at what they do for a reason – they work very hard at it. These participants don't equate to a representative sample; what researchers really need to do is test grit on ordinary people in ordinary situations. This is exactly what Kaili Rimfeld and colleagues from Kings College London did (Rimfeld et al., 2016). They recruited a sample of 4,500 16-year-old twins who were already part of the Twins Early Development Study, a longitudinal study run from Kings College that began in 1994. The researchers wanted to know if grit had any real impact on exam (GCSE) success, as well as its heritability (the extent to which genes contribute to differences between people in their levels of grit). They asked the twins to complete a questionnaire known as the Grit-S measure to test their consistency of interest. Participants were rated on the extent to which they agreed with statements that included 'Setbacks don't discourage me' (a measure of persistence) and 'I have difficulty maintaining my focus on projects that take me more than a few months to complete' (a measure of consistency of interest). Participants were also asked to complete the big five personality questionnaire to identify their personal traits.

Rimfeld and her colleagues found that aspects of personality predicted around 6 per cent of the differences between GCSE results, but when grit was measured alone it only predicted around 0.5 per cent of the difference between GCSE results. Furthermore, heritability for grit was pretty much the same for all other personality traits (around one-third). It would appear, therefore, that grit might not have the impact on academic achievement that had been previously predicted, and while this doesn't completely discount the relevance of grit, or indeed suggest that it doesn't represent a useful quality, it does throw up many questions surrounding the benefits of investing time, money and resources in strategies and interventions. These results would also cast doubts on the relevance of grit to buoyancy and resilience, especially if we can't identify grit as a distinct trait significantly dissimilar from conscientiousness.

Using the principles of resilience

The ability to bounce back from adversity and the propensity to continue in the face of setbacks are key components of academic achievement. Often, however, attempts to promote such qualities are problematic because the language used to describe these qualities is inconsistent.

However we label such qualities (e.g. resilience, academic buoyancy or grit), there are number of non-cognitive attributes that do relate to academic achievement. These are:

- the ability to cope and learn from mistakes and failures;
- the ability to bounce back when things don't go according to plan;
- the ability to keep going despite challenges and dips in motivation; and
- the ability to handle competing deadlines and to plan effectively.

Taken together, we can broadly assign the label resilience to these main points, even though they combine resilience, academic buoyancy and conscientiousness (or 'grit'). Attempting to teach or train students in such skills remains problematic, and there is as yet little evidence from research that would suggest that interventions of this kind have any long-term benefits. The most successful programmes embed structures within the school culture that help to nurture a resilient mindset.

We can identify a number of interrelated strategies that can support students in this way at all stages of their education.

Autonomy

While autonomous supportive classroom have been found to increase motivation, there is also evidence to support the hypothesis that autonomy can also help nurture resilience. Autonomy also positively affects *confidence* (one of the five Cs of academic buoyancy) by nurturing students' beliefs in their ability to control their own learning.

Autonomy needn't mean offering students a choice of how they learn (indeed, students at all stages of learning often draw erroneous conclusions when asked how they learn best), but rather including students in the process of their own learning and, more specifically, goal achievement. Choice can help in many circumstances, so long as choice is offered within strict parameters and each choice is equally challenging.

Clear guidelines

Ambiguity erodes resilience and increases anxiety. Instructions for classroom tasks, homework and further progression must be clear and not open to interpretation. Teachers can model what is expected, offer tick lists at each stage of a task or have students model the answers. Many students will view not understanding instruction as in indictment of their own ability rather than the clarity of task instructions.

Personal progress (personal bests)

Resilient learners display a mastery rather than performance orientation. They are less concerned with how they compare to other students, and tend to compare their current progress to their own previous progress.

Psychologist Andrew Martin has suggested the adoption of a 'personal best' approach to progress, finding it to be more effective than class rankings and less anxiety-producing (Martin, 2013). Students are encouraged to examine their current level of progress and to work with the teacher to produce a plan of how they work towards the next level. Progress is time-bound (perhaps twice a term) and a date for the next review is agreed. Personal bests also increase feelings of autonomy by placing progress partly in the hands of the student.

Personal bests nurture *coordination* (another of the five Cs of academic buoyancy) because they encourage the student to think ahead and plan their next steps. In addition, when students have a clear idea of how to reach the next stage (to exceed their previous personal best), they are more *committed* to the task.

Reconceptualising failure

The negative aspects of failure are deeply embedded into our culture, including school culture. Academic systems reinforce these aspects in a number of ways, including:

- Whole schools can be seen as 'failing' based on certain criteria.
- The assumption that if a school is failing, the teachers and students within the school are failures.
- The use of target grades and other such data reinforce the view that some students will be 'failing to reach' this standard. Many students will then attribute this situation to their inability to succeed.
- Setting and streaming is often associated with success (the students in the higher sets) and failure (the students in the lower sets). Students with a tendency towards performance orientation compare themselves to others (e.g. those student in the higher sets).

Fear of failure is more common within students adopting a performance orientation (or fixed mindset). This encourages them to employ a number of strategies in order to avoid failure (such as self-handicapping) and reduces their ability to cope in difficult situations. Fear of failure also nurtures learned helplessness.

Fear of failure is a difficult habit to break because elements of the system conspire against any attempt to alter students' perceptions. There are, however, a number of strategies that can yield positive results, including:

- Emphasising the non-linear nature of progress. Ensuring that pupils are aware that even the most successful learners rarely progress in a linear fashion can help students to come to terms with their own dips in performance. When employing a personal best approach, many students will find that they haven't managed to beat their last performance, but analysing the reasons for this and offering insights for future success can be used to reinforce the often-erratic nature of learning.

- Students will often view isolated failure as indicative of learning in general. This can lead to defensive pessimism and other similar strategies. Encouraging a more global-oriented perspective by looking at learning as a whole, rather than isolated grades, helps students to focus as much on their successes as their failures. This would include the correction of faulty attributions such as 'I failed because I'm not intelligent enough'.

- Using examples of successful people who failed as a way of emphasising the importance of setbacks. For example, discussing the role of failure in scientific discovery with reference to figures such as Einstein, or in business in reference to successful entrepreneurs such as Richard Branson.

- The normalisation of failure. Emphasising the more general view that success and failure exist together, and that failure is part of life and the emphasis should be placed on bouncing back.

Relationships

Relationships based on trust help to support resilience and nurture more positive learning environments. Early research into resilience found that those young people who felt supported by teachers and had at least one teacher they felt they could turn to in times of need were better able to cope with setbacks. Years after leaving education, many people are able to identify the teacher who 'made a difference'. What is important to note, however, is that being popular isn't always the same as being influential, and the emphasis must be placed on positive relationships rather than pseudo-friendships.

Strong positive relationships also help to support *composure*. Students feel less anxious when they are part of a nurturing environment and where they are confident of receiving positive support from teachers and peers. The use of nurture groups has also been found to increase levels of academic achievement, as well as improve problem behaviours, especially with children with social, emotional and behavioural difficulties.

Conclusions

Like many psychological constructs, resilience has been approached from a number of different positions. This makes applying it to school settings highly problematic because it's necessary to ensure that outcomes are linked to intentions. If resilience is viewed as a personal trait, then this creates problems in terms of explicitly teaching the skills necessary to be resilient. Traits are fixed and consistent over time; changing them is incredibly difficult. If, on the other hand, it is accepted that resilience is a dynamic emerging process with trait-like qualities, we also accept the view that resilience can be taught and nurtured. If we adopt this position, it is necessary to then clarify the purpose of any intervention and what the expected outcome will look like. Higher levels of well-being and resistance to long-term mental health conditions might be the preferred outcome, but this won't necessarily resemble an intervention designed to raise levels of achievement. Reconceptualising resilience as 'academic buoyancy', however, provides a useful framework to tackle specific issues surrounding underachievement and the fear of failure, as well as issues related to anxiety.

A second consideration is one of explicit training or the development of a nurturing environment. Few good longitudinal studies exist to support either of these options; however, studies by the likes of Rutter and Werner would certainly suggest that contributions to a resilient personality are multifaceted (e.g. Rutter, 2012; Werner, 2005). Data on resilience-building schemes is hard to come by, perhaps in part because many of these are offered by private providers who remain reluctant to release outcome data, and partly due to their relatively recent arrival on the educational stage. A specific scheme or intervention, however, might not be necessary; changes to school policies and creation of a nurturing environment is just as likely to reap benefits without the added cost to time and financial resources.

Finally, we shouldn't fall into the trap of thinking that underachievement is the result of a lack of resilience, character of grit. Neither should we assume that young people today are any less resilient than in the past. The danger is that we increase the pressure on young people and then argue that achievement and psychological distress are related to a lack of resilience, rather than the possibility that we have simply increased pressure beyond tolerable levels. Resilience interventions then become the bandage that attempts to repair the damage we, as teachers, parents and policymakers, have inflicted. Much of the evidence to date indicates that resilience is an emergent process rather than a taught behaviour.

Further reading

Fifteen Thousand Hours: Secondary Schools and Their Effects on Children by M. Rutter, B. Maughan, P. Mortimore and J. Ouston (Paul Chapman, 1979) One of the all-time classic texts on resilience, Rutter's work is as relevant today as it's ever been. Fascinating and insightful, this exploration of inner schools during the 1970s provides the best grounding for those wanting to understand how our children cope with adversity.

Building Classroom Success by A. Martin (Continuum, 2010) Andrew Martin's work has been making waves in Australia for some years now. A highly prolific researcher and writer, this book summarises many of the strategies that have arisen from his extensive work into resilience and academic buoyancy.

References

Anthony, E. J. and Cohler, B. (1987). *The Invulnerable Child*. New York: Guilford Press.

Bleuler, M. (1978). *The Schizophrenic Disorders: Long-Term Patient and Family Studies*. New Haven, CT: Yale University Press.

Duckworth, A. L., Peterson, C., Matthews, M. D. and Kelly, D. R. (2007). Grit: perseverance and passion for long-term goals. *Journal of Personality and Social Psychology*, 92(6), 1087–1101. doi: 10.1037/0022-3514.92.6.1087

Duckworth, A. L., Kirby, T. A., Tsukayama, E., Berstein, H. and Ericsson, K. A. (2011). Deliberate practice spells success: why grittier competitors triumph at the national spelling bee. *Social Psychological and Personality Science*, 2(2), 174–181. doi: 10.1177/1948550610385872

Fredrickson, B. L. (2004). The broaden-and-build theory of positive emotions. *Philosophical Transactions of the Royal Society of London. Series B, Biological Sciences*, 359(1449), 1367–1378.

Garmezy, N. (1991). Resiliency and vulnerability to adverse developmental outcomes associated with poverty. *American Behavioral Scientist*, 33(4), 416–430. doi: 10.1177/0002764291034004003

Hart, A. and Heaver, B. (2013). Evaluating resilience-based programs for schools using a systematic consultative review. *Journal of Child and Youth Development*, 1(1), 27–53. doi: 10.1186/2046-4053-1-28

Martin, A. J. (2013). Academic buoyancy and academic resilience: exploring 'everyday' and 'classic' resilience in the face of academic adversity. *School Psychology International*, 34(5), 488–500. doi: 10.1177/0143034312472759

Martin, A. J., Colmar, S. H., Davey, L. A. and Marsh, H. W. (2010). Longitudinal modelling of academic buoyancy and motivation: do the '5Cs' hold up over time? *British Journal of Educational Psychology*, 80(3), 473–496. doi: 10.1348/000709910X486376

Masten, A. (2001). Ordinary magic. *American Psychologist*, 56(3), 227–238. doi: 10.1037/0003-066X.56.3.227

O'Brien, T. (2016). *Inner Story: Understand Your Mind, Change Your World*. CreateSpace Independent Publishing Platform.

Perkins-Gough, D. (2013). The significance of grit: a conversation with Angela Lee Duckworth. *Resilience and Learning*, 71(1), 14–20.

Putwain, D. W., Nicholson, L. J., Connors, L. and Woods, K. (2013). Resilient children are less test anxious and perform better in tests at the end of primary schooling. *Learning and Individual Differences*, 28, 41–46. doi: 10.1016/j.lindif.2013.09.010

Rimfeld, K., Kovas, Y., Dale, P. S. and Plomin, R. (2016). True grit and genetics: predicting academic achievement from personality. *Journal of Personality and Social Psychology*, 111(5), 780–789. doi: 10.1037/pspp0000089

Rutter, M. (2012). Resilience as a dynamic concept. *Development and Psychopathology*, 24(2), 335–344. doi: 10.1017/S0954579412000028

Rutter, M., Maughan, B., Mortimore, P. and Ouston, J. (1979) *Fifteen Thousand Hours: Secondary Schools and Their Effects on Children*. London: Paul Chapman.

Sanders, J., Munford, R. and Thimasarn-Anwar, T. (2015). Staying on-track despite the odds: factors that assist young people facing adversity to continue with their education. *British Educational Research Journal*, 42(1), 56–73. doi: 10.1002/berj.3202

Seligman, M. E. P. (1975). *Helplessness: On Depression, Development, and Death*. San Francisco, CA: W. H. Freeman.

Urdan, T. and Midgley, C. (2001). Academic self-handicapping: what we know, what more there is to learn. *Educational Psychology Review*, 13(2), 115–138. doi: 10.1023/A:1009061303214

Werner, E. E. (2005). Resilience and recovery: findings from the Kauai longitudinal study. *Research, Policy, and Practice in Children's Mental Health*, 19(1), 11–14. doi: 10.1017/S095457940000612X

7 | Motivation

Motivation remains a problematic area for schools. This chapter aims to demystify the nature of motivation and critically examine methods that can be used to support it, both in the classroom and in the wider school environment.

- The main theories of motivation.
- Explanations of intrinsic and extrinsic motivation.
- How self-determination theory can enhance motivation.
- How teachers can internalise extrinsic motivation.
- Why extrinsic reward systems often fail.
- Ways in which teachers can motivate students.

Motivation has obvious impact on learning; students who are motivated learn faster and more efficiently than those who lack motivation. Motivation can be thought of as a combination of biological, emotional, cognitive and social factors that both direct and activate behaviour. Student motivation is also, of course, about the desire to be engaged in the learning process, but detecting this engagement in students is often highly problematic. It's perfectly possible for students to appear motivated yet still be disengaged, as well as for them to lack the outward signs of engagement while remaining highly motivated. Motivation is a complex construct, and nurturing motivation is more complex still. Further complications arise when teachers use certain motivational strategies that appear to be effective in the short term but often lead to lower levels of motivation and engagement further down the line.

Motivation is comprised of three basic characteristics:

- *Activation.* The initiation or the triggering of the specific behaviour. For example, we might feel hungry and go (or be motivated to go) to the kitchen to get some food.
- *Persistence.* The continued effort that we put into a task or how long we persevere. While some students might give up on a task quickly, others will keep going, even when the task becomes difficult or they experience repeated failure.
- *Intensity.* The strength of the response to the activity. Internal (intrinsic) factors such as personal interest might lead to greater intensity in the response to the task, as might certain extrinsic rewards. Alternatively, tasks that are not seen as personally interesting, useful or relevant, or where the extrinsic rewards are seen as inadequate, could result in less intense engagement.

Evolutionary theories of motivation

Evolutionary psychology proposes that genetic mutations are capable of altering both physical and behavioural traits. Mutations affecting behavioural traits can then help organisms to reproduce and allow these traits to be passed on to the next generation. People are therefore motivated to engage in behaviours that maximise genetic fitness (i.e. behaviours that improve their chances of survival).

Evolutionary psychology has been used to explain many behaviours and other psychological phenomena with varying degrees of success. It takes as its starting point the view that organisms capable of passing on certain behavioural traits are much more likely to survive and reproduce (survival of the fittest), and that such behavioural traits begin to manifest themselves across cultures. In other words, if certain behaviours convey an evolutionary advantage, they will be seen across diverse cultures; alternatively, if certain behaviours only manifest themselves within specific cultures or subcultures, it's more likely that the behaviour is sociocultural rather than evolutionary.

Take, for example, attachment. Attachment in psychological terms refers to the bond, both physical and emotional, between a child and its primary caregiver (usually, but not always, the mother). Certain aspects of attachment differ across cultures, but there remains certain common behavioural traits, such as crying and smiling, that either work to alert the caregiver that something is needed or as a way of increasing the bond (such behaviours are known *social releasers*). In the distant past, these behaviours would have made survival more likely, seeing as young humans are highly vulnerable. This behavioural trait would then have been passed on to the next generation, further ensuring survival.

Instinct theories

Instinct theories are based on the evolutionary view that people are motivated to engage in certain behaviours due to evolutionary mechanisms. William James (1842–1910) proposed a number of instincts that he believed were vital for survival, including attachment, disgust and shyness. These instincts compel us to behave in certain ways in order to survive. For example, ethnologist Konrad Lorenz was able to use *imprinting* on goslings to trick them into thinking he was their mother (Lorenz, 1935). The gosling would attach to the first living thing they came into contact with after hatching as a means of ensuring safety and protection; this would normally be the mother, but Lorenz ensured that the goslings imprinted on him instead. The goslings would follow Lorenz wherever he went, just as they would have done their mother. Psychologist William McDougall (1871–1938) was one of the first to develop an instinct theory of motivation. He proposed 18 different instincts, including curiosity, laughter, comfort, sex and hunger.

Instinct theory provides a less than adequate explanation of motivation, although more recent researchers have tried to incorporate environmental components into the biological model. Problems with the theory include its inability to explain all human behaviours and the unobservable nature of instincts themselves. Some instincts are certainly emotion-based, such as curiosity, but applying such a theory to student motivation and learning proves problematic.

Drive theories

Another biological-based theory of motivation is drive theory. Drive theories view behaviour as motivated by the desire to reduce internal tension caused by unmet biological needs such as hunger or thirst. These unmet biological needs 'drive' us to behave in certain ways to ensure our survival. The need for food or water makes us hungry or thirsty (the drive) and compels us towards drive-reducing behaviours, in this case to eat or drink something. The behaviour that reduced the drive is then reinforced and the cycle begins again.

Drives operate in this way because our bodies are biological systems that are delicately balanced to ensure survival. Our bodies strive for a state of homeostasis (the physiological equilibrium that the body strives to maintain), so when we are hot our body attempts to cool us down by sweating, and when our body is cold it will attempt to warm up by shivering. Motivation occurs because disruptions in homeostasis produce states of internal tension and these states produce behaviour that attempts to reduce the tension. Unlike drive theory, arousal theory is based on the assumption that people find very high and very low states of arousal unpleasant. When arousal is too low, people become motivated to increase the level by seeking out more stimulating experiences (e.g. when students are bored, they might misbehave in an attempt to alleviate the unpleasant feeling of boredom). If arousal is too high, people are motivated to reduce it by seeking out less stimulating environments.

Genetic factors in motivation

While we can attempt to explain motivation in terms of survival, we can also identify genetic similarities. The nature-nurture debate is widespread in psychological research and while biological and evolutionary perspectives claim that behaviour is largely innate, behaviourists argue that behaviour is learned. The view that all behaviour is learned may be preferable to teachers as it suggests that ability isn't fixed or constrained by factors we cannot change. The opposing view, however, suggests that much of human behaviour has a genetic base.

For example, behavioural genetics (a field of scientific research that attempts to identify genetic causes of individual differences) suggests certain abilities are highly heritable and points to studies using families and twins as evidence that everything from mental illness to intelligence is more to do with our genes than how we interact with the environment. Certain aspects of personality (including motivation), therefore, provide ample material to identify those aspects that are more likely to be genetic and those that are culturally specific.

In a 2015 study involving nearly 13,000 twin pairs in six different countries, researchers found that certain differences in motivation can be predicted genetically (Kovas et al., 2015). Twin studies provide a useful method because researchers can better understand genetic components due to identical twins sharing 100 per cent of their genes. If certain behaviours aren't present in both twins, the greater the likelihood that those behaviours are learned rather than inherited. The researchers were interested in two specific concepts related to motivation: enjoyment of learning (or intrinsic motivation) and self-perceived abilities. The study found that these two factors accounted for around 40 per cent of the variation and were no less heritable than cognitive abilities (for a discussion of cognition, see Chapter 2). Interestingly, however, environmental influences were wholly associated with individual experiences, indicating that some aspects of motivation are related to specific past events. For example, if students have positive memories of a specific school subject, they are more likely to approach that subject positively in the future. This has implications for early years teaching, where many of these experiences are formed.

Incentive theories

While evolutionary psychology would insist that motivation is all about biological drives and adapting to the environment for the purpose of survival, modern society doesn't necessarily operate in this way. We can therefore explain motivation in terms of rewards and punishment, a psychological approach known as behaviourism. Behaviourist approaches to motivation are certainly more relevant to the school environment than instinct theories, as many schools already apply incentive approaches to behaviour management. According to this view, behaviour is motivated by certain pull factors. These factors include money, recognition and other tangible rewards. The expectation of a reward for displaying an acceptable behaviour reinforces predetermined types of behaviour, while other behaviours are avoided because they result in punishment. Incentive strategies can be effective, especially with younger children, and sticker charts and naughty steps form much of the toolkit of super-nannies and many parents, while detentions and merit points can be found in most schools. However, incentive schemes don't work for all children, and are less effective with older children and teenagers. For incentives to work, the reward must be immediate, rather than being somewhere in the future; in other words, collecting merit points or similar in order to trade them in for a reward later down the line can prove highly ineffectual.

Motivation isn't always about survival

The above theories assume that motivation is a product of our evolutionary survival instincts (i.e. the reduction of uncomfortable feelings, such as hunger or boredom, and the desire to both be rewarded and to avoid being punished). What these theories fail to take into account is the desire for people to engage in behaviours and activities for their own sake. These theories can't account for the behaviour of a person who decides to take an evening class in a subject that has little practical value, or the person who decides to learn to play a musical instrument. An individual might decide to take a class about Victorian England not because this increases the possibility of external rewards or the relief of uncomfortable internal drives, but through pure interest. There are, of course, rewards attached, but these would more likely be internal in nature (i.e. the feeling of accomplishment or the feelings of the enjoyment the activity provides). Alternative theories of motivation have attempted to address these issues, often in terms of personal development and individual fulfilment.

Attribution theory and motivation

Attribution theory is a psychological concept about how people explain the causes of an event or behaviour. When we experience desirable and undesirable outcomes (such as success and failure), we can attribute the cause to something specific, which in turn can lead to increased or decreased motivational behaviour. Fritz Heider (1896–1988) stated that we are all 'naïve psychologists' with the innate desire to understand the causes of our behaviours and their outcomes. When people experience a particular outcome, attributions help them to understand what caused the event, so that if the outcome was desirable, they can do their best to experience it again (in psychology parlance, the event becomes positively reinforced). Alternatively, if the event is unpleasant or undesirable, they can try to avoid the behaviour that caused it. These attributions help to shape our emotional and behavioural responses to situations.

Attributions are classified along a dimension known as the locus of causality, from internal to external. If we attribute behaviour to an internal locus of causality, we assume that outcomes resulted from something within us, while if we attribute the outcomes to an external locus of causality, we view it as caused by something outside ourselves.

Attributions are also classified in terms of stability, from stable to unstable. Stable causes are those that are difficult to change, such as intelligence; unstable causes can be changed. For example, a student might fail a test because they didn't put enough effort into preparation. Effort therefore is an unstable cause of the failure (it can be changed); intelligence, however, is often thought of as stable, so if our student attributes lack of intelligence to their failure, they are more likely to believe that they cannot improve. Whether the student views their failure as either stable of unstable will then affect future expectations.

The problem is that attributions don't always accurately represent reality. Our student might, for example, attribute their failure to stable factors (intelligence) when in reality failure was caused by lack of effort (an unstable factor). This is what is known as a biased attributional style, and can lead to the increased likelihood that the student will succumb to false attributions.

Attributional style can have a major impact on motivation because the way we attribute cause affects future expectations. Researchers have identified three specific attributional styles: optimistic, pessimistic and hostile:

- *Optimistic.* A person holding an optimistic attributional style will attribute negative outcomes to external events and positive outcomes to internal events. This is known as a self-serving attributional style. A student therefore will attribute failure in an exam to something outside themselves; perhaps the exam paper was extraordinarily hard that year or the teachers hadn't covered the content in enough depth. Success, on the other hand, would be attributed to their own effort and superior preparation and stable measures, such as innate intelligence.

- *Pessimistic.* A person holding a pessimistic attributional style will tend towards explaining negative outcomes in terms of internal and stable factors. A student who fails an exam, therefore, would attribute their failure to something about themselves and to something they couldn't change (such as their level of intelligence). In the event of success, they would attribute the outcome to something external and unstable such as luck.

- *Hostile.* A hostile attributional style tends towards blaming external factors for undesirable outcomes. This blame can manifest itself in hostility towards the external entity seen to be responsible. Our student therefore might become hostile towards a teacher they believe is responsible for their failure.

Table 7.1 Summary of the main attributional styles

Attributional style	Impact	Example
Optimistic	Biased towards internal (often stable) attributions for positive outcomes External (often unstable) for negative outcomes	A student who attributes personal success to intelligence and failure to poor teaching
Pessimistic	Biased towards internal (often stable) attributions for negative outcomes External (often unstable) for positive outcomes	A student who attributes personal failure to their lack of ability and success to luck
Hostile	Biased towards external, stable attributions for negative outcomes	A student who displays aggression when confronted with academic problems Likely to blame others and seek revenge

Attributions and learned helplessness

Research into the phenomenon known as learned helplessness indicates that when people suffer repeated failure or punishments, they eventually become passive and unmotivated (for a more in-depth discussion, see Chapter 6). Studies conducted by Dweck also found that children who fail to complete a difficult task become reluctant to engage in easy tasks presented later (see Chapter 4). This is because they have formed an expectation of failure through their attributional process. Helplessness becomes a learned response, and even when individuals are presented with a way out, they rarely take it.

Learned helplessness in the classroom

School policies, the behaviour of school leaders, and individual teachers can all lead to students feeling that success is unobtainable, especially if effort is not appropriately recognised. Such behaviours create a feeling that nothing the student does will ever lead to success, and motivation and engagement decrease. Furthermore, teachers and school leaders who insist that the success of students is wholly the result of teaching and school policies are in danger of encouraging learned helplessness in their students. This behaviour, if adopted by school leaders, can also demotivate teachers in the same way.

From a wider perspective, schools that insist on implementing outdated or ineffective procedures may also find that teachers display little urgency or interest in their work. For example, the many teaching strategies that have been found to be highly erroneous (such as learning styles) are often well known by classroom teachers for their lack of empirical support, yet are still favoured by many school leaders. Teachers who understand this are less likely to engage in such practices (for good reason), but might also lose motivation for other aspects of the job.

The way in which people attribute the causes of events, therefore, impact on the motivation, due to the belief about the way future events will turn out. Those students who explain their failures in terms of internal and stable factors will view the future in the same way as the present: that nothing they do will make any difference. Success is dismissed as luck and effort rejected. Alternatively, those who view failure in terms of unstable factors (e.g. lack of effort rather than lack of intelligence) are better equipped to view failure and setback as things to be overcome.

Humanistic theories of motivation

While attribution theory views motivation as guided by our interpretation of the situation, humanistic psychology emphasises the role of free will and human beings' capacity for self-development, self-realisation and self-actualisation. It arose as a reaction against the narrow view of the behaviourists and the pessimism of Freudian psychodynamics, with its roots lying more in existential thought and Eastern philosophy than in traditional psychology. Although humanistic psychology has been highly criticised for its lack of scientific rigour, theories based on the humanistic paradigm have remained highly influential.

One of the most influential models of motivation that arose out of the humanistic tradition is Abraham Maslow's hierarchy of needs, first proposed in 1954, but subjected to several revisions and adaptations over the years.

Maslow suggested that there are two sets of motivational forces (or needs):

1 *Deficiency needs (D-needs)*. Those motivational forces that ensure survival by satisfying basic physical and psychological needs (e.g. safety, love, feelings of belonging).

2 *Needs related to self-actualisation (B-needs)*. Behaviours that are engaged for their own sake (i.e. they have no survival advantage) and are intrinsically satisfying.

According to the principles of the hierarchy, lower levels require satisfying before higher ones, so only once D-needs are satisfied does it become possible to take on those needs related to self-actualisation (B-needs). Self-actualisation represents the realisation of one's full potential or, according to Maslow, 'becoming everything that one is capable of becoming', especially in the intellectual and creative domains. B-needs represent the fulfilment of ambitions, the acquisition of admired skills, and the steady increase in understanding about people and oneself and the development of creativeness. Essentially, B-needs are concerned with our desire to be good human beings, and are thought to be a later evolutionary adaptation. For our ancestors, survival was the most important life component; there was little time for self-development or the pursuit of self-actualisation. Once our biological needs are satisfied, we can move on to these higher intellectual and self-development needs. Self-actualisation, however, will be different for all of us. In classroom settings, students learn better when their basic needs have been satisfied; hungry and exhausted children make poor learners.

Maslow's hierarchy does appear to make some intuitive sense; after all, how can we pursue higher personal goals if we lack food and shelter? Similarly, a child who is hungry, thirsty or lacking sleep would find it difficult to concentrate and engage in the learning process. Unfortunately, Maslow's theory lacks empirical support, with some claiming that there exists little evidence that behaviour is organised in such a hierarchical way. It's also accused of being ethnocentric, in that it ignores the differences between individualistic and collectivist societies. Generally, humanistic approaches have a tendency to lack the scientific rigour associated with other psychological approaches.

The role of intrinsic and extrinsic motivators

Although Maslow's theory of motivation lacks the empirical support necessary to make it tr.uly research-based, the suggestion that some forms of motivation are intrinsic (internal) and others are extrinsic (external) is supported by many studies. Extrinsic motivation assumes that there is some kind of external reward to be obtained from behaving in a particular way, while intrinsic motivation assumes that people engage in behaviours because they find them personally satisfying. Maslow's theory assumed that the path to self-actualisation isn't beholden to external rewards, but taps into intrinsic processes.

The promotion of extrinsic motivators has become common in school and educational settings, despite their negative consequences having been understood for some time. The basic idea is that students can be motivated by offering them an external, tangible reward. This reward could be something as simple as a positive comment or a merit, while more sophisticated systems allow students to accumulate points that can then be exchanged for anything from hair straighteners to Xbox games. The underlying assumption here is that most learning involves the study of material that is just too boring or undesirable to be able to develop a true passion for, so the only way to engage students is to offer them a reward for doing it. Extrinsic rewards can motivate, and when used well can be highly effective. At their worst, they can kill off any interest or passion that might have developed if the rewards were not offered. More importantly, when incentive schemes are withdrawn (perhaps due to financial constraints), behaviour and motivation drop to levels below those seen before the scheme was introduced.

Extrinsic rewards undermine intrinsic motivation

Lepper and his colleagues carried out a study with a group of children from the Stanford University nursery school to examine the way in which very young children respond to external rewards (Lepper et al., 1973). First, researchers spent time observing the children and identified those who chose to spend their free time on a drawing activity. They then selected a sample of children from their original observations and placed them into one of three experimental groups. The expected award group were asked to engage in a drawing activity and informed that they would receive a certificate and a ribbon for doing so. The unexpected award group were asked to carry out the same activity but were presented with the certificate without being told beforehand. The third group were neither awarded nor told to expect an award for carrying out the activity. The activity was then repeated a couple of weeks later with the same children. They used covert observation (they observed the behaviour through a one-way mirror) and collected measures of intrinsic motivation. They found that those children who had previously received the award spent less time drawing and were less interested in the drawing materials, while the children from the other two groups were still fully engaged in the activity. The children in the no-award group had never been given the opportunity to make the link between the activity and an external reward, and even the unexpected award group didn't appear to associate the activity with the award.

Studies such as those conducted by Lepper suggest that external reward system can have some unexpected negative side effects (although they can be effective in some circumstances). There remains little doubt that the expectation of a reward does motivate; the problem arises when such rewards are withdrawn, leading to a drop in motivation that is often lower than before the reward system was implemented. If such strategies are introduced as a means of behaviour management, again levels of poor behaviour can increase once the system is abandoned.

Other factors that are often viewed as best practice can also end up reducing intrinsic motivation, including threats of punishment and deadlines. Choice (or at least the illusion of choice) can increase it. Autonomy and intrinsic motivation are therefore closely linked, with increased levels of autonomy leading to higher-quality outcomes. The prospect of being formally evaluated (such as in an exam) diminishes the feeling of autonomy and can lead to reduced motivation, however counterintuitive this might seem. However, many of these problems can be tackled effectively with the use of good-quality feedback, which can often counter any negative consequences of loss of perceived autonomy.

Personal interests and memory

Students often recall a great deal about the topics that interest them but are often unable to do the same with topics related to school. Kou Murayama of the University of Reading uses an example from his own learning experience as he describes how he would memorise his entire Japanese history textbook in order to pass his exam. Once the exam was over, he would instantly forget the material. Comic books, however, were a different matter entirely, and he claims to still be able to recall by heart much of their content. Interest therefore plays a vital role in motivation, and the suggestion is that what interests us is more effectively remembered. Motivation is often related to goal setting and goal orientations: mastery versus performance goals.

Mastery goals rely on intrinsic motivation (the desire to develop knowledge), while performance goals rely on extrinsic motivation (the desire to be better than other people). Both approaches can facilitate elaborate learning processes, but are different for each type of goal. Because mastery-approach goals are linked to curiosity, exploration and an interest-based focus on learning, they facilitate a broad scope of attention beyond the to-be-learned material. Mastery-oriented goals lead to greater long-term consolidation of learning, while performance goals lead only to short-term learning.

In order to study the impact of different types of motivation on learning and memory, Murayama used a range of research methods that included behavioural experiments, longitudinal studies and neuroimaging (Murayama and Kuhbandner, 2011). In one study, participants were asked to learn a list of words followed by an immediate recall test. They were then asked to carry out another recall test a week later. One of the groups was given the following instructions: 'If you work on the task with the intention to develop your ability, you can develop your competence'. The second group was given the instructions: 'The aim of the task is to measure your cognitive ability in comparison with other university students'. The first instruction represents the mastery (intrinsic) goal condition; the second represents the performance (extrinsic) goal orientation.

There was very little difference between the scores for the first recall test, indicating that the instructions had little impact on short-term learning. However, when tested a week later, the mastery goal condition was found to produce a significantly higher recall rate than the performance goal condition (Murayama and Elliot, 2011).

As can be seen, it would appear that intrinsic-based belief systems lead to enhanced long-term learning, while extrinsic beliefs only help learning in the short term. What, therefore, is the impact on learning of extrinsic rewards such as money? Lepper (described previously) found that extrinsic rewards undermine motivation and task quality, especially when withdrawn, but Murayama, along with Christof Kuhbandner of the University of Munich, was more interested in how monetary rewards impact both motivation and memory consolidation (Murayama and Kuhbandner, 2011).

There is evidence indicating that monetary rewards promote memory consolidation by activating a part of the brain known as the mesolimbic reward pathway and increasing the release of the neurotransmitter dopamine into the hippocampal memory system. However, studies have found that hippocampal-dependent memory consolidation requires time to complete. This means that the effects of monetary rewards on learning aren't immediate; they take time. Another problem more pertinent to motivational psychology is that monetary rewards can undermine engagement in some circumstances. This is certainly the case when monetary rewards are offered for the completion of tasks already considered interesting. Extrinsic rewards *crowd out* the intrinsic value of the interesting task, a process known as the *undermining effect*.

To test the hypothesis, Murayama and Kuhbandner (2011) divided participants into two groups (monetary reward and no monetary reward) and presented them with a list of trivia questions. Some of the questions had been classified as uninteresting (e.g. 'What is the name of the author of the book *Nineteen Eighty-Four?*'), while others had been classified as interesting (e.g. 'What is the only consumable food that won't spoil forever?'). The classification of interesting and uninteresting had been decided by a panel of independent judges. The participants were tested on their recall ability of the question immediately and one week later.

Results indicated that:

- monetary rewards helped memory only after a delay;
- monetary rewards helped memory only when the material was uninteresting; and
- monetary rewards had little impact on memory when the material was considered interesting.

Using neuroimaging techniques, the researchers found that extrinsic rewards appeared to dampen down activation in an area of the brain called the striatum, which is responsible for executive functions, working memory and reward-induced memory consolidation, only when the task was considered to be interesting. Paying someone to do a task they love, it would appear, actually makes them less motivated and less successful at it. Extrinsic rewards do enhance learning and motivation for boring tasks, but not immediately.

Reward systems therefore fail when they represent a one-size-fits-all approach. Student motivation ebbs and flows and is often task-dependent. Furthermore, extrinsic rewards of a tangible nature operate in a different way to other forms such as praise and encouragement. In many ways, tangible, extrinsic rewards can be harmful to the most motivated students due to the undermining effect. How, then, do intrinsic and extrinsic motivators fit into our wider understanding of motivational psychology?

Self-determination theory and motivation

This distinction between intrinsic and extrinsic motivators forms the basis of self-determination theory (SDT), a model of motivation proposed by psychologists Edward Deci and Richard Ryan (Ryan and Deci, 2000). Self-determination theory stresses the importance of intrinsic motivators over extrinsic ones, but suggests that the differences are more nuanced than earlier research implied. SDT is a theory of human motivation, emotion and development, and attempts to explain factors related to assimilative and growth-oriented processes in people; in other words, it attempts to explain factors that promote or prevent people from intrinsically engaging in positive behaviours.

Psychologist Edward Deci has suggested that when a person expects a reward for carrying out an activity, they attribute their behaviour to the reward and not to the activity itself (Ryan and Deci, 2000). Initially, this might not matter too much, so long as the activity is completed. However, once the reward is linked to the activity, there arises an expectation that the activity will always be associated with a reward; once the reward is removed, people become much less inclined to participate in the activity in the future. In a study that illustrates this point, Deci asks a group of students to complete a puzzle. After dividing the students into two groups, one group was told that they would be paid to take part in the activity, while the second group would receive no reward. Once the payment stopped, the group who had previously been rewarded became less motivated and less inclined to participate.

In a second study, Deci located his experiment within a more realistic setting: a college newspaper. So-called field studies are often thought to be more valid than those taking place in laboratory settings, even though the experimental variables are more difficult to control. Participants were required to write headlines for a biweekly college newspaper but were unaware that the time in which it took them to write each headline was being recorded. Neither were they aware that their absences were also being logged. The experimenters used the time it took participants to write each headline as a measure of their motivation and their absences as a measure of attitude. One half of the group (the experimental condition group) were informed that they would receive 50 cents for each headline, but after three weeks were told that there was no more money left in the budget so the payment had to be withdrawn. It was found that withdrawing the payment decreased motivation, supporting the results of the earlier laboratory experiment.

But does the type of reward matter? Using the same experimental method as the first experiment, Deci found that replacing positive verbal encouragement and feedback increased intrinsic motivation, even when removed, unlike monetary rewards that, when removed, led to drops in intrinsic motivation. This is certainly more relevant to the classroom, as it suggests that verbal encouragement and positive feedback are more effective motivators than material rewards (Ryan and Deci, 2000). More recent studies continue to support the basic premise of self-determination theory in a number of settings, including education, addiction and environmental behaviour.

Self-determination theory assumes that all individuals have three basic needs: competence, relatedness and autonomy.

- *The need for competence.* Our desire to control or master the environment and outcomes. People want to know how things are going to turn out, and they want to know the results or consequences of their own actions.
- *The need for relatedness.* Our desire to interact with, be connected to and experience caring for other people. Everything we do in some way concerns others, and our actions impact on those around us. Through this need to build up a sense of belonging develops the feeling that we are part of a wider world beyond the limits of ourselves.
- *The need for autonomy.* The urge to be causal agents and have full volition and choice over what we do. If autonomous motivation concerns choice, then controlled motivation relates to the lack of choice. Ryan and Deci describe it as 'behaving with the experience of pressure or demand towards specific outcomes that come from forces perceived to be external to the self' (Ryan and Deci, 2000, p. 14). Autonomy doesn't necessarily mean acting independently; it merely means acting with choice, so it can mean acting alone but also acting interdependently with others.

One important point here is that motivation becomes entwined with emotional states, in that how motivated we feel is often related to how we feel emotionally. Motivation can ebb and flow in unison with our emotions; boredom can reduce motivation while curiosity can enhance it. This relationship is reciprocal in that not only can boredom reduce levels of motivation, but low levels of motivation can feed boredom (for a more in-depth analysis of the role of emotion on learning, see Chapter 3).

The opposing forces of autonomy and control often lead to heated debate among teachers. Some schools impose strict control over their pupils, while others are more relaxed in their approach, Similarly, individual teachers differ in their teaching styles and classroom management; some control their classrooms with an iron fist (so to speak), while others allow for a more liberal approach. The majority of teachers fall somewhere between these two extremes, and the control–autonomy distinction is handled differently under different circumstances.

The role of autonomy is an important factor in SDT, and it's vital to understand that while control per se isn't at issue, the nature of that control is. Highly controlled classroom environments undermine intrinsic motivation, while autonomy-supportive environments nurture it. This isn't to say that extrinsic reward systems don't work in the classroom – they often do, so long as the interpersonal classroom context remains informational and supportive, rather than critical and authoritarian. It therefore also follows that feedback given in a controlling context will also decrease intrinsic motivation. Those classroom environments that encourage autonomy (autonomy-supportive) result in greater levels of learning and performance outcomes than styles deemed to be more controlling. Research strongly indicates that practices and policies that attempt to motivate pupils through sanctions, rewards and evaluations undermine the quality of student engagement. Quality student engagement arises more often through intrinsic rather than extrinsic means, and because controlling classroom environments are more likely to employ extrinsic methods, they often stifle motivation. Autonomous-supportive classrooms, according to SDT advocates, foster interest, value and volition, encouraging greater persistence and better-quality engagement and learning.

Authoritarian teachers maintain that an approach that insists on things being done correctly, that students should be told what to do, and who use a number of controlling strategies, leads to more manageable classrooms and more positive outcomes in terms of exam results. Others emphasise the importance of allowing students to be more self-directed, to learn from their own successes and failures, and to solve problems for themselves. Early research conducted by Edward Deci found that in classrooms where teachers were more autonomy-supportive, students tended to be more intrinsically motivated, displaying behaviours such as curiosity, a preference towards challenge, and greater mastery orientations (i.e. they were motivated by the desire to learn rather than the desire to be seen as intelligent, especially among peers) (Ryan and Deci, 2000). They also felt more competent in their schoolwork and had higher levels of self-esteem.

Cross-cultural evaluations support this early research. Grolnick and Ryan (cited in Ryan and Deci, 2000) found that evaluative pressure undermined students' intrinsic motivation and their school performance in the US; Kage and Namiki (cited in Niemiec and Ryan, 2009) obtained similar results with Japanese students. Additional cross-cultural studies have found that interest is enhanced for lessons where the teacher is autonomy-supportive but diminished when the teacher is more controlling. Standage (cited in Niemiec and Ryan, 2009) compared student and teacher ratings of autonomy, autonomy support, confidence, relatedness, and self-determined motivation in physical education. Standage found that perceived autonomy support was associated with higher levels of autonomous self-regulation, including intrinsic motivation, and these in turn were associated with greater effort and persistence (for a comprehensive review of these findings, see Niemiec and Ryan, 2009).

We can therefore conclude that:

1   Teacher orientation and certain aspects of the learning task play a role in the development of intrinsic motivation. Teachers perceived as autonomous-supportive nurture students higher in intrinsic

motivation than those teachers with more authoritarian styles. Importantly, these results are consistent across cultures.

2   Children taught in classrooms where autonomy is supported display higher levels of intrinsic motivation. They also display a tendency towards better learning, especially on tasks requiring conceptual understanding.

3   When tasks promote the basic psychological needs of autonomy and competence, they allow for greater intrinsic motivation and deeper learning. Where these basic psychological needs are not met, intrinsic motivation and achievement suffer.

Sometimes learning just isn't interesting and intrinsic-related strategies will continually fail. Rather than attempt to instil intrinsic motivation in all students, teachers can try to internalise extrinsic factors. Some of these strategies might still lack the autonomy associated with intrinsic motivation, while others encourage greater autonomy and come closer to mimicking true intrinsic motivation. However, such forms of regulation still come with major problems, and might still only be effective in the short term:

- *External regulation.* This least autonomous form of extrinsic motivation is based firmly within the incentives camp. The main problem with this kind of extrinsic-based motivation is that it represents short-term rather than long-term achievement, with the reward resulting in the feeling that the task has been completed and doesn't need to be tackled again; motivation is shallow and unsatisfactory. Similarly, punishments for failing to complete homework increase the number of students completing it, yet do little to increase the quality of the homework. Once the work is handed in, the motivation dissolves until the same time next week. The importance of the task is solely influenced by the reward or the punishment, rather than the task itself; additionally, motivation is prompted by external factors rather than internal ones, and there is very little in the way of feelings of autonomy (or, it seems, competence).

- *Introjected regulation.* Like external regulation, introjected regulation is on the lower end of the autonomy scale. Here, behaviours are enacted in order to satisfy some internal contingency (i.e. to protect self-worth and self-esteem). A student might work hard in order to give the impression of dedication or to look intelligent. The student might also be thinking less about gaining knowledge and understanding, and be more concerned with protecting him or herself from looking unintelligent or avoiding the feelings of guilt for not working hard enough. This kind of motivation is about the protection of the ego, and can easily result in strategies related to the fear of failure, such as self-handicapping, defensive pessimism and defensive optimism.

- *Identified regulation.* We're now moving into the internal perceived locus of control and greater autonomy. Tasks, activities and subjects are now seen to have some kind of value and importance, rather than being based on reward or ego protection. A student might therefore work hard in a biology lesson because of a desire to become a doctor, or show motivation and dedication in order to get accepted into a specific university. This kind of motivation is still extrinsic because there is an ultimate external reward available (e.g. studying for a medical degree) rather than an internal desire for knowledge. However, the lines between extrinsic and intrinsic motivation are becoming blurred.

- *Integrated regulation.* The most autonomous kind of extrinsic motivation is integrated regulation; it also represents an internal locus of causation. Here, behaviours are integrated or synthesised with other aspects of our self, such as our desires, wishes and hopes; behaviour becomes consistent with our own values and interests. For example, our student doctor is motivated to work hard in biology in order to train as a doctor so that she can help people. She still might find some aspects of her studies boring, but motivation arises due to her long-term thinking and what needs to be done in order for her to eventually do what she intrinsically desires.

Grolnick found that students who scored higher on measures of self-regulation for learning were also rated by teachers as higher on measures of academic achievement and adjustment to the classroom, while Niemiec found that high school students who reported higher autonomous self-regulation for attending college reported higher well-being (in terms of vitality and life satisfaction), and lower levels of depression and externalising of problems. This indicates that the internalisation of extrinsic motivation plays an important role in both educational outcomes and psychological functioning. Promoting and nurturing internalisation, therefore, can help motivate in a more functional way when the only options available are extrinsic. Furthermore, because of the higher levels of general well-being found in students with higher internalisation of intrinsic motivation, the results go far beyond academic success.

Autonomy beyond the individual student

Autonomy-supportive classrooms encourage intrinsic motivation and can internalise more extrinsic factors; however, research indicates that teachers who feel more controlled and have to endure school procedures that limit autonomy are themselves more controlling. Roth (cited in Niemiec and Ryan, 2009) discovered that teachers who felt more controlled were themselves more controlling and less autonomy-supportive. Similarly, Luc Pelletier of the University of Ottawa (cited in Niemiec and Ryan, 2009) discovered that then when a sample of Canadian teachers perceived high levels of pressure and control from above, they were more controlling towards their students.

Interventions aimed at raising levels of motivation and engagement therefore need to be more than student-based. Indeed, any intervention that deals with psychological processes is likely to fail unless applied to the whole system (from students, to classroom teachers, and all levels of the management structure). Supporting and encouraging student autonomy is vital for the development of intrinsic motivation, yet teachers who feel that they have less autonomy and that control is being implemented from above are often unable to support and nurture independence in their own students. When teachers feel that they are being overly controlled, they become less enthusiastic and less motivated in the classroom, and are more likely to implement needless overtly controlling strategies in the classroom. Within a more controlling environment, teaching becomes less effective, less interesting and less inspiring.

Why extrinsic reward systems often fail

Reward systems implemented by schools are often based on outdated psychological principles. Research into learned helplessness strongly indicates that we are much more than simple stimulus-response machines, and that although human behaviour can indeed be predictable, it can as often as not be highly unpredictable. This is even more so in environments such as schools, where many students view rules as existing to be broken. Younger children are more likely to support extrinsic reward systems, but a complex interaction of neurological and social development later on means that teenagers are less likely to benefit. Furthermore, academic achievement can be adversely affected in students with higher levels of intrinsic motivation who are also often the more able. Students who find learning interesting and relevant don't necessarily require extrinsic rewards, and in many cases will experience a drop in motivation if such rewards are offered.

Another issue to consider when implementing reward systems relates to their possible future withdrawal. Systems offered by external companies might not be sustainable in the long term for many reasons. Research is consistent in the conclusion that withdrawing reward systems can lead to drops in both behaviour and attainment, often below the level that existed prior to the implementation of the intervention. This has been evidenced both in experimental studies and within real-world school environments.

Using the theories of motivation

Students are motivated for many different reasons, making the topic of motivation and engagement challenging. Some students are motivated by grades, others by interest, and some of these will be intrinsic while others will be more extrinsic in nature.

Students respond positively to a number of elements, regardless of their intrinsic and extrinsic orientation. These include:

- a well-designed and well-organised course of study;
- teachers who are enthusiastic and knowledgeable;
- teachers who display caring attitudes towards students and learning; and
- teachers who instil feelings of autonomy in students.

In addition, there are a number of strategies that can help promote motivation, in particular the all-important intrinsic kind. These include:

- setting realistic short- and long-term goals with guidance on how to move forward towards them;
- wherever possible, making tasks relevant to current and future goals;
- encouraging personal best goals that emphasise a better-than-before approach, rather than aiming directly for a long-term goal such as a target grade;
- emphasising mastery goals over performance goals (growth rather than fixed mindset); and
- using praise strategically; when praise is overused or students are praised without sufficient justification, motivation is reduced – praise should be reserved for when effort is matched to the challenge, rather than to make students feel good about themselves.

Using extrinsic rewards

Despite the problems associated with extrinsic reward systems, if they are used appropriately they can still prove highly successful. This is especially the case when such rewards help to foster identified regulation rather than attempting to preserve intrinsic motivation. It would therefore prove counterproductive to suspend the use of extrinsic rewards due to the fear that this would undermine existing intrinsic motivation. Many students are motivated by both extrinsic and intrinsic rewards, while others can show a preference to a specific type of reward or display immunity to all kinds of rewards. Despite these problems, the important thing for teachers to know is how and when to use extrinsic rewards.

Some important points about extrinsic rewards:

- Extrinsic rewards can increase the intensity and duration of a task, but do not improve the quality of the outcomes.
- Extrinsic rewards prove more effective in supporting learning only when there is a clear goal and a clear set of stages to follow in achieving that goal.

Extrinsic rewards are more effective when tasks:

- are routine rather than novel;
- are intentional, rather than unintentional, research-based or involve discovery learning;
- require steady performance rather than creativity;
- require rote learning and practice; and
- are repetitive or considered boring.

Extrinsic rewards are ineffective when:

- students are expected to continue the task on their own (such as carrying out online research after the initial learning episode has concluded); and
- when the initial level of interest is low and the value or interesting parts of the task only become apparent at a later stage (e.g. learning to play a musical instrument).

Applying extrinsic rewards

Extrinsic rewards will only motivate if students believe that they have a real chance of being awarded them. Students need to be aware that if they put in the effort, they stand the same chance of being given the reward as any other member of the class.

Teachers must ensure that:

- rewards are not reserved only for the high achievers or the 'good kids';
- all students have equal access to the rewards;
- rewards are offered for appropriate progression based on previously defined achievement goals or maintaining the previous level of progress;
- students understand why they have been given the reward and how the reward is related to personal goals or progress;
- rewards are never offered for what is expected of all students (e.g. turning up to a lesson or handing in homework); and
- when rewards are offered for a specific task or piece of homework, always include opportunities for redoing the task if the result doesn't meet the standard required for the reward.

Motivating low achievers

Despite the best efforts of teachers to motivate all students, some learners will struggle for a variety of reasons. Such motivational issues may be specific to learning difficulties that negatively impact on their progress. Students who struggle academically often compare themselves to more able peers and lose motivation often due to the mechanisms of learned helplessness. Studies have identified a number of strategies that help to motivate low-achieving students, including:

- *Individualising activities (where possible).* This can include reducing the length of the task or tweaking the difficulty level so that tasks are more appropriately challenging. One useful strategy is to make the first part of the task less challenging and then build up the level of difficulty gradually. Early success is often a precursor of later motivation, while early failure inhibits it.

- *Provide more detailed instructions and guidance.* Ask students to recite the instructions back to the teacher or a work partner to ensure that they understand what is expected. Teachers and students can model the task and help to clear up any ambiguities that might arise. If possible, avoid strict time limits and allow for some flexibility, but don't ask them to complete any unfinished task as homework.

- *Provide extra assistance.* Use teaching assistants and other students who can provide extra help. Sit the student next to an average student (avoid sitting them next to high achievers) or peers with whom they are on friendly terms.

- *Maintain motivation.* Use encouragement and positive comments to ensure that struggling students don't feel left out or are seen as less deserving of positive attention.

Promoting autonomy, competence and relatedness

Feelings of autonomy promote internalisation, but teachers also need to satisfy students' need for competence and relatedness. This can be achieved in a number of ways, including:

- *Minimising the salience of evaluative pressure.* By evaluative pressure, we essentially mean the pressure of tests, exams and any other activity that is used for formal or informal performance tracking. Unfortunately, for some students, terms such as test and exam can create pressure and anxiety (much of which is illusionary). While the likes of tests and exams are very much here to stay, deferring to regular low-stakes testing can relieve some of this pressure. Regular low-stakes testing helps to normalise the test environment. One of the reasons students are fearful of exams and tests is that they don't necessarily represent the usual day-to-day aspects of learning and are seen as something out of the ordinary; by including them regularly (even in every lesson), they become part of the everyday environment. These tests or quizzes need not be formal all of the time, and can include regular multiple-choice exercises.

- *Reducing coercion in the classroom and maximising students' perceptions of choice in activities.* Students who believe they have a choice in what and how they learn feel more responsible for this learning. By providing choice within predetermined parameters, teachers reduce the likelihood that students will feel coerced or controlled. This does not necessarily mean that students should be given absolute control, but rather they should feel that there is flexibility.

- *Ensuring that tasks and activities are appropriately challenging.* Boredom and frustration often arise because the learning task is either too challenging or not challenging enough. In addition, in such circumstances, extrinsic methods are more likely to fail so internalisation is harder. When students feel appropriately challenged, they are more likely to internalise extrinsic factors. If tasks are too challenging, then students are more likely to fall into the trap of learned helplessness because they are unable to match their effort with their progress. If tasks aren't challenging enough, students begin to view the task as irrelevant and become fully aware that the task doesn't represent individual progress, and motivation falls. Extrinsic rewards therefore become redundant if the task is either too hard or too easy.

- *Providing support and feedback throughout the learning process.* Process-oriented feedback, rather than goal-oriented feedback, has been found to both nurture mastery orientations and intrinsic motivation. It can also aid in the internalisation of extrinsic motivation by focusing on skills rather than grades. Feedback should be based on how to improve rather than on how to get a higher grade, and while the two might seem synonymous, the subtle differences can lead to greater engagement and heightened skills.

- *Nurturing positive teacher–pupils and pupil–pupil relationships.* Feelings of relatedness increase our sense of belonging (a basic psychological need). Classrooms are full of people we are or would like to be connected to; teachers and other students are the obvious inhabitants of such environments, and those inhabitants we like, respect and value create greater opportunities for internalisation. A student might have little intrinsic motivations towards history and might find the content uninteresting or difficult. This student will lack intrinsic motivation and will have to rely on extrinsic behaviours in order to engage in lessons. However, the teacher is passionate about history, is highly skilled, supportive and nurtures positive relationships with students. While our unmotivated student will never have a true passion for the subject, they are able to internalise extrinsic components as a result of the teacher–student relationship. Students who report such relatedness are more likely to work harder on more difficult tasks, while being disconnected or feeling rejected by teachers encourages students to rely more heavily on external contingencies such as rewards and punishments.

Conclusions

Motivating students can be difficult. Intrinsic motivation is preferable to extrinsic motivation, but ultimately in the real world teachers will often fall back on simple reward and punishment. There is nothing inherently wrong with extrinsic motivators, so long as they are effective and sustainable over the long term.

The belief in the individual as an autonomous agent can also help to nurture intrinsic motivation in many students. Intrinsic motivation cannot thrive in authoritarian environments, and that is why authoritarianism often relies on extrinsic methods. Autonomy shouldn't be interpreted as giving students freedom over what they study and when they study it, but rather ensuring that students feel as if they have some control over their own learning by perhaps offering homework from a menu of choices rather than simply issuing a single task. This is more difficult within the classroom because of time constraints and increasing workloads; however, by ensuring that students are working towards certain goals that have a specified time frame, it can encourage many to self-motivate through the desire to reach that goal. Keeping goals short-term is preferable to working towards long-term goals because they are more likely to be viewed as unachievable.

Finally, there is no foolproof method for motivating all students; some will be more motivated than others, but much of what motivates people is intricately entwined with personal beliefs about what is within our capabilities, and this is why ensuring that students are appropriately challenged is so important; they will lose motivation if they are both under- and over-challenged.

Further reading

Self-Determination Theory: Basic Psychological Needs in Motivation, Development, and Wellness by R. Ryan and E. Deci (Guildford Press, 2017)
The result of decades of research into motivation from those who first brought us self-determination theory.

Drive by D. Pink (Canongate, 2010)
A highly accessible and entertaining read that draws on much of the research conducted by Ryan and Deci.

References

Kovas, Y., Garon-Carrier, G., Boivin, M., Petrill, S. A., Plomin, R., Malykh, S. B., et al. (2015). Why children differ in motivation to learn: insights from over 13,000 twins from 6 countries. *Personality and Individual Differences*, 80 (July), 51–63. doi: 10.1016/j.paid.2015.02.006

Lepper, M. R., Greene, D. and Nisbett, R. E. (1973). Undermining children's intrinsic interest with extrinsic reward: a test of the 'overjustification' hypothesis. *Journal of Personality and Social Psychology*, 28(1), 129–137. doi: 10.1037/h0035519

Lorenz, K. (1935). Der Kumpan in der Umwelt des Vogels. Der Artgenosse als auslösendes Moment sozialer Verhaltensweisen. *Journal für Ornithologie*, 83, 137–215, 289–413.

Maslow, A. H. (1954). *Motivation and Personality*. New York: Harper.

Murayama, K. and Elliot, A. J. (2011). Achievement motivation and memory: achievement goals differentially influence immediate and delayed remember-know recognition memory. *Personality and Social Psychology Bulletin*, 37(10), 1339–1348. doi: 10.1177/0146167211410575

Murayama, K. and Kuhbandner, C. (2011). Money enhances memory consolidation – but only for boring material. *Cognition*, 119(1), 120–124. doi: 10.1016/j.cognition.2011.01.001

Niemiec, C. P. and Ryan, R. M. (2009). Autonomy, competence, and relatedness in the classroom: applying self-determination theory to educational practice. *Theory and Research in Education*, 7(2), 133–144. doi: 10.1177/1477878509104318

Ryan, R. M. and Deci, E. L. (2000). Self-determination theory and the facilitation of intrinsic motivation, social development, and well-being. *The American Psychologist*, 55(1), 68–78. doi: 10.1037/0003-066X.55.1.68

8 Independent learning

What can psychology tell us about when and how learners should study independently? This chapter explains these processes from the perspective of psychological concepts and research. From the debates over discovery learning to the issue of homework, it tackles the most common situations in which learners may have to work partly or entirely on their own. In particular, it covers:

- The timing and quality of homework.
- The generation effect.
- What are active learning and discovery learning, and do they work?
- The 'region of proximal learning' model of self-study, and its implications for learner revision.
- Structuring and supporting project work via planning and metacognitive awareness.
- Guidance on the psychology of effective revision.

Independent learning is where learners work with reduced input from a teacher, and the course of their learning process is consequently less predictable and more governed by individual curiosity. Examples include project work, open-ended art/technology/writing projects, and autonomous reading. These activities begin in primary school or even before, and in many educational settings they increase in scale and complexity as a learner progresses through the system. Homework can also, to a large extent, be classified as a form of independent learning.

Approaches to student independent learning often involve giving pupils a task and a period of time in which to do it, with reduced structure and guidance (or none at all). This chapter will look at the psychology of learning independently, how to make the process educationally effective, and at the issues over when and whether it is a good use of classroom time.

Why learn independently?

Independent learning might sound a little threatening to the teacher – if our pupils can truly learn independently, then what are we needed for? Perhaps there is a worry that at some point, everyone will be learning using online resources and computerised schemes of work, and the professional teacher will become obsolete.

Of course, children are – almost by definition – not independent learners. The whole concept of school is based on the idea that children need help to learn, and although school as a cultural institution is modern, the idea of learning from elders is very old. Hunter-gatherer societies, for example, use direct instruction of children, and those children then practise and refine their skills with considerable supervision and input from adults. Indeed, arguably one reason that humans have such long childhoods compared to other species is because it gives a great deal of behaviourally flexible time to learn skills before becoming able to cope with the world as an adult (Bjorklund, 2007).

Over time, though, young learners become increasingly independent, start to set their own goals, and put themselves in the position to teach themselves and others, as well as to be taught. Being a lifelong independent learner can therefore be seen as a desirable outcome from the schooling process, but also a gradual process, encompassing skills that take time and patience to develop.

As teachers are well aware, it is important to prepare learners for life beyond the exam. Previous chapters in this book have emphasised the importance of encoding knowledge to LTM, but also of the ability to transfer it to new learning situations. Being good at exams is less important for higher education than the ability to find things out autonomously or in teams (Gopnik, 2016). In both the workplace and everyday life as a citizen, we don't simply rely on the knowledge and skills gained in school, but use this as a foundation for new learning.

What are the characteristics of an independent learner?

According to Otero and Graesser (2001, pp. 143–144), an ideal learner 'asks deep questions and searches for answers to thought-provoking questions'. This description is appealing, but not immediately recognisable in many pupils, even (or perhaps especially) towards the final stages of their school careers. It's probably best to see such skills as ranging along a scale rather than 'all or nothing' – not something that a learner has or does not have, but a target that they will be closer to or further away from at different points within their schooling and when working on different kinds of tasks. A worthy aim of teaching, therefore, would be to move our learners closer to this 'ideal' by motivating them to take the necessary steps towards it, and by equipping them with the skills to overcome obstacles.

A specific learning experience, likewise, could be considered on a scale from more to less independent – it's not simply one or the other. Even a very teacher-led task may have elements of independence where the teacher steps back and allows a learner to think something through or attempt a step by themselves.

Benefits and efficiency

Why choose independent learning – and are there other methods with which we could achieve as much or more within the same amount of learning time? This question of efficiency has led some educationalists, such as Christodoulou (2014), to criticise the use of project work in education, preferring direct instruction as the default method of imparting knowledge. At the other extreme, education that is informed by a social constructivist framework may seem to disavow the idea that learners should ever be taught directly; this philosophy, drawing heavily on the work of Bruner and Vygotsky, states that learning is a process of actively building knowledge in the social context.

While evidence-based approaches to education arguments may appear to be taking a side in this debate, a great deal depends on the purpose of the task. There are undoubtedly cases where the most efficient way to impart learning is to tell another person directly, but more independent approaches may offer psychological benefits related to curiosity and motivation, foster research skills and resilience, and prompt active retrieval of prior learning. And as Bransford et al. (2000) note, using social constructivism as an argument against direct instruction confuses a theory of knowledge with a methodology for teaching: the assumption that learners actively construct knowledge and connect to their existing cultural schemas does not preclude the use of activities such as lectures or silent reading. The evidence relating to independent learning activities can be weighed up objectively, but the choice of task ultimately depends on what the teacher or school are aiming to achieve.

Practicalities

If independent learning tasks involve practical research, it's important to keep an eye on ethical issues, and where appropriate refer to institutional guidelines on research ethics. If in any doubt at all, it's best to guide learners away from project ideas that involve gathering primary data from human participants or animals.

What are the key principles of independent learning?

Generation

Generation means creating something rather than receiving it passively. Laboratory studies have shown that a list of items that is read out or shown to a participant is less well remembered than words that they generate themselves (e.g. by stating a word that they associate with each word from a list) (Slamecka and Graf, 1978).

While caution is needed in applying this result given that the task is rather different from most classroom activities, it could imply that responses that pupils come up with will be more memorable than what is told to them or read. So, for example, asking pupils in a history lesson to think of and write down reasons why the population of a country may have supported or opposed going to war could be more memorable than hearing these points from the teacher (this could be a good example of the use of brainstorming; see Chapter 4).

Of course, such a strategy needs to be balanced against the quality of the ideas – there can be little doubt that in many situations, such as the example above, the ideas of the pupils, however interesting, will have more inaccuracies; Zamary et al. (2016) note that learners who generate examples of technical concepts do so poorly, and tend to be unaware of their own mistakes.

One way to promote generation but keep down the number of mistakes would be to provide a prompt, such as a partially completed sentence or initial letter. Alternatively, preparatory reading could be done in advance, so that generation focuses more on recall from memory rather than guesswork. Richland et al. (2009) have found that even if learners make mistakes, guessing beforehand can be advantageous to memory for new material, compared to hearing it directly without preparation – an effect that can be distinguished from the benefits of simply paying more attention to the material. This would imply that brief generative activities at the start of a topic can be very helpful (e.g. group discussions and/or learners individually writing down their thoughts). Such a task could help to highlight differences between their assumptions/beliefs and the material that is being taught, and to 'activate' schema knowledge. In any case, prompt teacher review of any mistakes or misunderstandings would seem to make sense.

Other generation-type activities that have been found to be effective include the acting out of example actions (Guttentag and Hunt, 1988), suggesting that the generative development of a key concept could have benefits even if the concept itself is provided directly by the teacher; Rawson and Dunlosky (2016) found that generating examples of concepts was more effective than restudying definitions, suggesting that this could be a good revision strategy (but studying teacher-provided examples may be even more effective due to greater speed and accuracy; Zamary and Rawson, 2017).

Wammes et al. (2016) found that sketching/drawing new ideas was more helpful for memory than writing them down as traditional notes, perhaps because it promoted the integration of both visual and verbal information with the meaningful concepts being learned. This is a simple strategy, easily applied to many teaching contexts.

Task

Think of ways in which a learner could generate ideas in a lesson that you teach.

Active learning

It is worth considering what exactly is meant when educators refer to 'active' learning. Most obviously, the term is used to contrast with passive forms of learning – in particular, reading or listening to 'teacher talk'. Wooldridge et al. (2016) state that active learning 'refers to any number of activities through which students participate in the learning process instead of passively listening to or watching transmitted information'. While it could be viewed more broadly as any task that allows pupils to become mentally engaged (Prince, 2004), such a definition would include almost everything that happens in the classroom, and also depends more on the pupil than on the task. This section therefore focuses on a moderately broad definition, including all tasks that cause pupils to take initiative in their learning and to engage in problem-solving and similar processes, rather than following a teacher's lead. Active learning could therefore include discovery learning (see below), but it also includes a much larger group of possible school tasks: discussion, generative or creative tasks, independent reading, answering questions, essay writing, and much more.

Being self-directed affects the level of attention a learner pays to a task, making it less likely that they will engage in mind-wandering. As Risko et al. (2012) have suggested, a learner's attention, and consequently their learning of facts, declines during a lecture-type activity, while Phillips et al. (2016) have linked the ineffective nature of rereading as a learning strategy to increased mind-wandering. Inserting an element of learner input – such as doing a gap-fill or answering questions periodically throughout a video – can help learners to stay focused (Szpunar et al., 2013).

Retrieval practice (see Chapter 1) is another example of active learning because it involves pupils making a mental effort. Together with generation, the efficacy of quiz-type tasks suggests that the greater attention and/or cognitive processing involved in active learning could link to improved performance, in comparison with more passive tasks such as rereading or relistening.

However, the benefits of active or passive learning may depend on the specific task. Carvalho and Goldstone (2015) gave learners a task where they had to discriminate between similar novel objects, and were either told which category the object belonged to (passive) or had to work it out for themselves (active). Learners who saw the objects mixed up (i.e. interleaved; see Chapter 1) learned better in the active learning condition, but when objects were presented together in a group, the passive learning condition was superior with one of the tasks used (with the other, learners still did worse in passive learning condition, but the difference was reduced). The researchers suggested that passive learning can help to draw learners' attention to similarities and patterns that they might not otherwise notice.

Expertise may also play a role, given that novice learners tend to struggle to discriminate between items, especially where the differences are subtle, and therefore school pupils may benefit from some passive approaches in the early stages of learning in order to establish basic schema knowledge, which they can later draw on during active tasks. Among university students in 'STEM' subjects, a meta-analysis by Freeman et al. (2014) found an overall benefit of active learning approaches, with those experiencing passive lecturing 1.5 times more likely to fail.

Active learning therefore encompasses a broad range of tasks, and is best seen as a dimension on which any task or lesson can be judged. It may be more helpful for some learning tasks than for others, but can generally boost learner engagement and the active retrieval of information.

Most independent learning tasks will be active by definition, but given the broad scope of 'active' discussed above, it is likely that most primary and secondary classes are already doing a range of relatively active learning, in that pupils are responding to questions and working at their own pace on writing and problem-solving. It is useful for the teacher to bear in mind that lengthy talks, texts and videos are likely to lead to more mind-wandering, but that interpolating short activities, such as answering two or three questions, could be enough to boost their engagement and retention.

Tasks that are more passive such as teacher explanations appear to be appropriate towards the early stages of a topic where learners' knowledge levels are low. This can link to the points made about cognitive load (see Chapter 2), where it was suggested that a worked example can be more effective for novices than solving problems. The level of independent control over an activity can be gradually increased as learners' basic skills develop and simple procedures become more automatic.

Discovery learning

Discovery learning is a particular type of active learning that involves pupils discovering information or concepts through enquiry rather than being given it directly (and is therefore often contrasted with direct instruction). For example, a primary teacher might directly teach a spelling rule such as 'i before e, except after c', or alternatively could provide pupils with a list of words such as shield, relief, chief, niece, deceive, field, and then ask the pupils to come up with a rule. Learners are therefore given independence within the learning process, which could be guided to a greater or a lesser extent.

The main arguments usually put forward in favour of a discovery approach are that it is more engaging and memorable to work something out for yourself (i.e. it is a form of active learning), and that it fits children's natural tendencies to work things out. Essentially, we have all been programmed by evolution to be curious about our surroundings, to find out useful information and to discard inaccurate theories about the world (Gopnik, 2010; Piaget, 1962). Applying this to education, Bruner (1961, p. 2) stated that learning works best as a process of discovery, arguing that 'it goes without saying that, left to himself [sic], the child will go about discovering things'. He notes that like a scientist with a hypothesis, it is necessary to have knowledge and expectations to know that you have made a discovery. In this way, via exploration, experimentation and discovery, new ideas can be linked to what is already known.

More broadly, discovery learning sits well with the social constructivist philosophy of education discussed above, which suggests that children actively build up meaningful knowledge linked to their context and prior learning. However, it has been criticised for placing too great an emphasis on practical tasks and group work (Bransford et al., 2000). Mayer (2004, p. 17), focusing on what he refers to as 'pure discovery learning', states that 'the formula constructivism = hands-on activity is a formula for educational disaster'. He argues instead that teachers can promote cognitive discoveries in their pupils by a process of guided discovery, using their classroom experience to know what to say at just the right time.

Discovery is just one form of active learning. Free exploration of a new topic area via unstructured hands-on activities (e.g. finding out about a piece of electronic apparatus) can be highly memorable, leading to learners forming episodic long-term memories for the events themselves – and can promote curiosity. However, teachers will want to curtail the amount of time spent on such 'pure' discovery – it is inefficient, as learners are unlikely to happen upon solutions by chance.

Ways of guiding discovery learning could include prior (passive) teaching of how to tackle a hands-on discovery task, or periodic input/feedback from the teacher. These approaches allow learners to gain the motivational benefits of 'discovering' rather than simply being told information, while minimizing the inefficiencies inherent in freer discovery.

The example given above of the 'ie' words involves guided discovery, for it involves drawing learners' attention to a particular set of words that have something in common. The key feature for the teacher is to step back and allow learners to notice this pattern, rather than telling it to them in advance.

Older learners are likely to make a great many 'discoveries' during research tasks (e.g. via their independent reading). It is worth bearing in mind, though, that such learners are not novices, and have already amassed the schema knowledge and research skills that allow them to make good use of such opportunities.

Homework

Homework is perhaps the classic form of independent learning, and can of course be structured in a huge number of ways. It also takes up a lot of a young person's time out of school (e.g. a common policy in the US is to assign 10 minutes of work per night in first grade – approximately age 6 – and increase this by a further 10 minutes per night each year, up to an eventual total of around two hours per night; Weir, 2016).

Evidence that regular homework helps to develop good study or time-management habits is inconsistent, and research has therefore focused on its efficacy in consolidating learning; if we are impacting on family time and causing stress for parents and children and extra workload for the teacher, is it worth it? Reviews have suggested that primary school pupils gain very little from homework tasks – it just isn't a major factor in attainment, statistically – but are more positive about secondary/high school homework (Cooper et al., 2006).

Even then, there can be diminishing returns – Fernández-Alonso et al. (2015) found that one hour of work per night (inclusive of all subjects) was optimal, after which increased fatigue counteracted any benefits. More importantly, they found that it was not the amount or difficulty of the homework that mattered (in terms of improving grades), but the level of autonomy, with learners who persevered and received little help gaining more advantage. This may well be because they were gaining independent learning skills and confidence in themselves as learners, with benefits beyond the tasks.

Unsurprisingly, there is still a great deal of debate over the value of homework; previous research has been criticised on the basis of its methodology, and much will depend on the nature of the homework tasks themselves. From a psychological point of view, an understanding of LTM (see Chapter 1) has great potential to be applied to this area in the coming years.

Homework is largely an expectation in schools, so teachers may not have the option of abandoning it altogether, even if they have little faith in its efficacy. An alternative could be to modify the type and amount, using short active tasks that synthesise the key points from previous lessons rather than repeating recent class exercises. Homework should not be simply about 'reinforcing' classroom lessons and content, as this approach leads to less engagement and poorer attainment (Trautwein et al., 2002; see also discussion of repetition/rehearsal in Chapter 2).

As Fernández-Alonso et al. (2015) argue, the data on the duration of homework indicate that it is not useful as an extension of lesson time, but it can be useful for practising the ability to persevere without teacher assistance. 'Talking homework', where learners explain concepts that they have learned to family members, can be a regular low-stress task that boosts engagements and helps to get family more involved. Such tasks are likely to involve retrieval practice, the development of schema knowledge by linking real-world examples, and forming associations in a different context.

Quality of homework is a major issue at all levels. If we are going to give tasks, what can we do to ensure they are effective? A simple investigation would be to set different types of homework and later compare the benefits via snap tests, providing the teacher with feedback on the design of the homework tasks.

Timing may also play a role; greater spacing and interleaving helps memory, an effect that could be applied to homework, although teachers should be wary that while such 'desirable difficulties' can boost learning, they can also make the task harder, with potential effects on motivation and task completion that could be more problematic when learning independently than in the classroom.

Finally, the impact on both the teacher (in terms of marking) and on the family must be weighed up. Wapole (2013) parodies the latter impact by suggesting that family chores be brought into the classroom! To minimise its negative impact and for learners to get the greatest benefit, arguments about evidence-based effectiveness and time-efficiency are particularly crucial in the context of homework.

Physical activity

Active learning (see above) is sometimes assumed to require an element of physical activity, and there has been pressure put on teachers to include more movement-based activities in their teaching. Simple activities of this kind could include matching up physical objects or cards, groups taking it in turns to write ideas on the board, passing a ball from one pupil to another while reciting items such as quotes or times tables, or even just standing up to give a short talk. More elaborate versions can include class outings, finding objects that have been hidden around the classroom, or parachute games.

What is the evidence that movement actually helps with learning, beyond subjects that inherently involve movement, such as sports and drama? The largely discredited 'learning styles' concept suggests that some pupils are 'kinaesthetic learners' who learn better if taught via movement rather than sound or images, but as Pashler et al. (2008) note in a comprehensive review, there is simply no evidence that tailoring a learner's classwork to their supposed style actually helps. However, learners can benefit from using various modalities rather than just one (e.g. using both verbal and visual stimuli is more effective when it comes to encoding and retrieving a set of items from memory than using words alone) (Clark and Paivio, 1991; see Chapter 1). From this perspective, a movement-based task as part of a learning process has potential to vary the way that items are represented in memory, as it would be processed by the visual component of working memory, distinct from any verbal elements of the task.

There is some evidence that movement can also be beneficial in and of itself. Embodied cognition means the association of movement and thinking (e.g. the idea that someone might be able to think better if they move around or if they move their hands when speaking). Cook et al. (2008) compared children's recollection of maths, with and without the opportunity to mimic a gesture that complemented the instruction, a form of embodied cognition. Those who gestured did better in a delayed test. This is despite the fact that doing so could increase the complexity, and therefore the cognitive load, of the task (Fiorella and Mayer, 2016). It also seems to work better for more advanced learners, suggesting that it could link to our ability to integrate different modalities into a more abstract mental representation.

A key final consideration is the extent to which physical actions are required in the real-world contexts to which learning is intended to transfer. As Robert Bjork (1994, p. 188) has noted:

> One chance to actually put on, fasten, and inflate an inflatable life vest, for example, would be of more value – in terms of the likelihood that one could actually perform that procedure correctly in an emergency – than the multitude of times any frequent flier has sat on an airplane and been shown the process by a steward or stewardess.

Movement-based tasks can vary the way that items are represented in memory, and may also help to boost engagement and alertness. Physical actions are particularly relevant in some topics and subjects – in others, a physically active task can be a distraction. If things are not set up in a clear way whereby the learning is an integral part of the movement activity, it can be the case that the activity is remembered while the learning outcomes are missed – the kids remember the day they did the parachute game, but don't remember why they did it. The purpose of the activity needs to be clear, and teachers should ask whether it is the most efficient way of learning.

The embodied cognition research could be easily applied to a number of tasks (e.g. associating gestures or movements with sets of information or skills, from elements of the periodic table to types of plant cells). Regardless of the more philosophical debate behind some of this research, these kinds of classroom tasks are likely to be better remembered due to being both more visual and more distinctive – and perhaps more fun – than a verbal-only version.

Self-regulation and self-study

Learning via the Internet continues to grow in importance, from global open-access MOOCs ('massive online open courses') to everyday use of websites for information, to a host of other resources such as online quizzing apps and YouTube. Online access to schools and universities is also becoming standard; the whole concept of learning as being inherently classroom-based is arguably changing, with more flexible, partially home- or library-based models emerging. Indeed, some school pupils learn entirely online (a trend that is growing rapidly; Levinson, 2015), while many conventional classrooms have begun to adopt a 'flipped' model whereby traditional homework-type tasks are done in class with the aid of the teacher, and exposition-type tasks (e.g. watching a lecture or video) are done at home (Lo and Hew, 2017). In this context, it is becoming more important than ever for learners to have the skills needed to take in information effectively via more autonomous modes of study (Rice and Carter, 2016).

On a bio-psychological level, self-regulation is an executive function regulated by the frontal lobe of the brain. Adolescents are easily diverted by irrelevant social information, more influenced by peer behaviour than older adults, and worse at blocking out distractions (Blakemore and Mills, 2014; see Chapter 2). We therefore can't expect all pupils to self-regulate or organise themselves as well as adults – a failure to do so is not a matter of character. Lengthy and complex projects for learners in late primary school or early secondary school can provide valuable learning experiences, but it is unlikely that even the more diligent individuals will be able to manage the cognitive demands of such projects without help from teachers, from parents, or from support materials (or all three). The temptation to allocate projects as homework because they are time-consuming can have equity implications in terms of pupils who have less well-supported home settings.

The ability to plan and regulate independent work varies between individuals, but generally increases through childhood and adolescence. Significant individual differences are to be expected in terms of how much support learners require to stay on track (including sex differences; males hit puberty two years later than females, and changes in frontal lobe structure show a similar delay). Self-regulation interacts with personality too; those who are more conscientious tend to persevere longer with a task (see Chapter 6).

Furthermore, learners are not always good at deciding what tasks are most beneficial for them at a given time, tending instead to rely on their naive mental model of how memory works. They have many biases in how they perceive learning, and typically fail to recognise the benefits of such tactics as spacing and self-testing – the very fact that such techniques lead to difficulties will cause learners to avoid them (Kornell and Bjork, 2007). A teacher may rightly worry that if a pupil is given freedom to study however they wish, they are likely to be misled by short-term improvements and to avoid important but challenging tasks.

An important metacognitive phenomenon here is the 'stability bias' – the tendency for a learner to fail to account for past learning and future forgetting, and thus viewing their knowledge and ability level as relatively stable over time. This phenomenon makes it harder for them to plan their learning autonomously across the year. They may also view recent test scores as a reliable guide to their knowledge level (Finn and Metcalfe, 2007), ignoring issues such as the difficulty of the particular test and any more recent learning.

Teachers can support self-study by putting structures in place whereby learners are expected to test themselves regularly and record scores, drawing their attention to areas of weakness not just from recent work, but also from previous study sessions. Brief tests and quizzes, especially when given frequently without warning, can be a useful awareness-raising technique – try giving a snap test on material that learners studied three or four weeks ago, followed by a reflective discussion of how rapidly forgetting occurs, and what steps can be taken to tackle it. Learners' study plans could also be submitted to their teacher for feedback at the start of a revision process. And although the learning sessions may take place independently, teachers could ask to see the evidence of these sessions in the form of notes, flash cards, responses to quizzes, etc. These can give a good indication of the strategies that a learner has been using.

Research and project work

Student research or project tasks have great potential for a number of reasons. However, they have also been criticised, the main objection being that they are less efficient than direct instruction. While there is good evidence that direct instruction helps to improve learner attainment (e.g. Hattie, 2008), most schools also encourage project work to supplement this, both for variety and due to concerns that direct instruction alone does not provide a sufficiently diverse learning experience (e.g. Tweed, 2004).

From a psychological point of view, what benefits could a project have? They have the potential to be motivating, especially where pupils can focus on particular aspects of a topic that appeal to them (Ito et al., 2013). They can also be cross-curricular in a way that is difficult within more structured tasks, and can be used to engage with real-world issues (Egan, 2014). Motivation can be boosted because the outcome of research is novel, at least to the learner – even a simple science project such as growing a plant under various lighting conditions has an element of unpredictability that helps to prompt curiosity and excitement.

Davis and Fullerton (2016) have described the benefits of after-school projects to better engage students from vulnerable backgrounds via tasks with obvious relevance to their interests.

It is also possible that project work, while perhaps less time-efficient over the short term, has certain cognitive benefits. As well as generation (see above), items learned during a project could be better remembered due to the richly meaningful context and the relatively unusual experiences involved. Research tasks also tend to be spaced out over time, with multiple opportunities for active retrieval of previous learning. Additionally, practical research typically develops and integrates a range of skills, including group work, planning, data handling, ethical and safety practices, and metacognitive awareness. Comparisons with the efficiency of learning via direct teaching may not fully take account of the durability of learning, as well as of incidental learning that can take place via projects.

Teachers could first consider the most appropriate times to impart or consolidate content and skills via projects and research. Research tasks may gain the benefits of active learning discussed above, as well as being memorable, but they also share some of the same concerns – they will ideally be guided rather than totally free, and require a certain level of prior learning.

Teachers have an important role in guiding project topic choice and monitoring progress. Learners often make two key mistakes when planning: overambitious aims, and fixed ideas about the eventual findings. In terms of aims, it can be best to begin with a small-scale project and allow time for expansion if possible; as with any form of research, it is best to have definite but limited results than to tackle something so ambitious that it never comes to fruition. Allowing a free choice of project topics is motivating, but can cause difficulties, because learners may all pick a similar topic and/or because they avoid challenging but important areas of the syllabus. A halfway house could be to give small groups of pupils a selection of options and allow them to negotiate about who does what, if necessary allowing them to pair up on a single task.

At times, the educational aims of project work will be less about content and more about research skills, such as the use of online and library sources, evaluating evidence, sourcing legal/free-to-use images, summarising, avoiding plagiarism, etc. – all skills that will be of use throughout their academic careers.

A theory: Kornell and Metcalfe's region of proximal learning model

How do learners decide what to study in an independent situation? This might seem to be a near-impossible question, as there are so many individual differences in study habits that could affect study plans and preferences. However, research by Kornell and Bjork (2007) suggests that the topics learners choose to revise are actually quite predictable – when in a hurry, people tend to opt for something they find easy and can therefore master quickly, while with more time available, they will tackle something that they find challenging.

Furthermore, researchers have looked at the question of how long learners persist when studying a particular item or set of items before moving on. The obvious assumption might seem to be that they will continue studying until they know it fairly well (i.e. until they reach their goal or a standard that fits the norms for their class). However, such a theory would predict that learners would study impossible items indefinitely! To address this, Kornell and Metcalfe (2006) suggested that instead of working towards a particular internal goal, learners will persist in studying something until they feel they are no longer making progress. If they feel they are making gains, they continue. If progress slows, they switch to a different item.

Developing this idea, Kornell and Metcalfe developed a theory of metacognition called the *region of proximal learning (RPL) model* of learners' study choices – a metacognitive development of the classic 'zone of proximal development' concept. It explains that learners do not necessarily choose to study the most difficult material or the easiest – what they do is select items for which they will be making the fastest progress. If they feel they have learned, they will stop or switch. Likewise, if they feel that the item is so hard that they are learning little or nothing, then they will stop or switch.

Importantly, the model depends on a learner's belief about how well they know something, and this can be biased by a number of factors, including their memory of past test scores. It can even be biased by something as apparently trivial as how fluently a teacher has explained it (Carpenter et al., 2013). Finally, learners tend to be misled by short-term improvements (Soderstrom and Bjork, 2015), mistakenly thinking that mastery of a topic within a single study session indicates permanent learning.

These biases can lead to major flaws in a learner's developing knowledge and understanding. In the absence of good feedback and accurate metacognition about the study process, they are likely to choose items on the basis of a relatively superficial sense of difficulty. Their choices can also link to pragmatic aspects such as the study time available and the date of the test or exam that they are preparing for (Metcalfe, 2002).

The RPL model essentially focuses on revision as a cognitive and metacognitive task. As such, it concerns key executive functions such

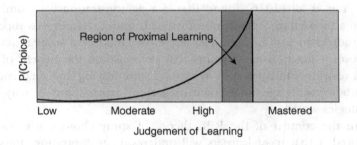

Figure 8.1 The region of proximal learning model helps to explain why students stick with or give up on different topics when revising. The darker line indicates that study items in the region of proximal learning are more frequently chosen, but dropped when the learner perceives mastery.
Source: Metcalfe, J. (2009). Metacognitive judgments and control of study. *Current Directions in Psychological Science*, 18(3), 159–163. doi: 10.1111/j.1467-8721.2009.01628.x

as task monitoring and decision-making (see Chapter 2), as well as a metacognitive awareness of one's own comprehension (Serra and Metcalfe, 2009). These skills are difficult even for experienced learners.

Although a learner's judgement of how well they know and understand individual items improves with practice, their sense of overall ability level in the subject remains quite poor (Koriat et al., 2004). As mentioned above, this can lead to a 'stability bias' where they underestimate both potential progress and the likelihood of forgetting over time.

Using the theory

The RPL model suggests that the vital process of self-directed study is subject to flawed thinking, with learners guided by a subjective sense of how much progress they are making. What's more, they avoid beneficial techniques such as spacing out their study – even when they have actually done better with spacing in the past, they tend to still retain the opinion that massing is a superior strategy (Zechmeister and Shaughnessy, 1980). Such assumptions can be difficult to overcome, but Yan et al. (2016) found that if a demonstration was combined with a theoretical explanation of why a learning strategy was superior, attitude change did occur. This therefore could be a strategy used in schools – practical experiments that demonstrate the benefit of certain revision strategies such as spacing, interleaving and dual coding, combined with age-appropriate theoretical explanations of why such strategies work.

In the context of the RPL theory of study choices, it's possible to predict that most learners will underestimate forgetting, miss out key content, and spend too little revision/study time going back to materials that they learned earlier in the course. Teachers could try to influence this process by specifying which topics to revise, and how and when it should be done. As learner biases are partly based on beliefs about learning, it will be helpful if teachers can tackle inaccurate ideas and instead promote evidence-based approaches to learning, such as the concepts covered in this book.

Using the principles of independent learning

The following section looks in more detail about how the psychological principles underlying independent learning can be used to inform key teacher decisions.

Lesson planning

Given the pressure in many school systems for teachers to include more active learning in their lessons, it is important to be mindful of what 'active' really means, and avoid conflating it with group activities or movement-based tasks. It may be helpful to ask yourself how you will know that a learner is engaging actively – what will make these processes 'visible' to the learners themselves and to you as teacher?

It's not a bad thing at all to include physically active tasks, especially where this promotes visual processing of information, but given what we know about the importance of meaningful processing and LTM, the emphasis should be on activities that promote active thinking and curiosity by creating a 'knowledge gap', and which build on previous learning. These will include tasks that prompt learners to reflect and criticise, to make comparisons, and to process examples of concepts. Peer teaching, teacher-led discussions, and short presentations can help them to see each other's analytical thinking at work, while quizzes can help to boost LTM for key facts and concepts while improving metacognitive awareness of how quickly details are forgotten.

A specific example of how a more mentally active strategy can be beneficial comes from the work of Mueller and Oppenheimer (2014), who looked at student note taking on laptops versus by hand. Students who were typing tended to take much more detailed notes, but this was found to lead to poorer recall. It appeared that the brevity of notes taken by hand prompted deep processing of the new information, with learners writing summaries rather than copying texts verbatim.

Materials and course design

Learning materials are typically designed with an emphasis on providing information and structuring classroom tasks within a single lesson or set of lessons. However, the structure of materials can (and arguably should) take account of the issues we know that learners are likely to face when revising and reviewing concepts independently. This could include providing revision activities or quizzes that are intended to be completed at a later date – and even suggesting a suitable date.

As we have seen, learners are often poor at judging how well they are learning. A useful attempt to explain this issue was provided by Koriat (1997), who noted that learners draw on three main cues when judging how well they are learning: the perceived difficulty of the task, the number of opportunities to learn, and how well they feel they know the information at the present moment. However, they tend to emphasise the first of these – perceived difficulty – and greatly underestimate the role of the second cue – opportunities for practice. This problem can be partly overcome by providing homework tasks that interleave questions from previous topics with newer material, prompting review in situations where it is unlikely to be undertaken autonomously. As the perceived difficulty of the material is biased by the difficulty of a specific task, it's worth considering how material is first presented – most teachers begin an activity with a simple and engaging task, but after this it is worth increasing the difficulty level relatively rapidly so that learners do not develop a false sense of security.

These considerations apply to review lessons in the classroom too. While more intensive, direct instruction is ideal in the early stages of learning, consolidation tasks should interleave material from various topics to promote meaningful connections as well as discrimination between easily confused areas (Kang, 2016). Such tasks can also help to promote transfer to real-world situations too, by varying contextual associations. To do this, teachers will need to develop a motivating scenario that prompts learners to retrieve essential knowledge/skills, combine learning from more than one topic in meaningful ways, and then apply this. One example could be giving learners who have been studying prejudice a role-play task where they have to make recommendations to a school or local government. This will prompt them to draw on and analyse the concepts and evidence that they have learned throughout the topic, and allow them to use this in a realistic situation (which could lead to a real outcome if their recommendations are then passed on by the teacher, rather than remaining as a simulation).

Planning research homework and projects

According to the work of Fernández-Alonso et al. (2015), homework should be regular, and should emphasise motivation and independence rather than seeking to extend class time. Tasks could be structured in a way that makes the initial stages easy, and overall should promote accomplishment without taking a long time for learners. A simple strategy for ongoing improvement is for teachers to include a feedback box, asking pupils and/or parents how long a task took and how its clarity could have been improved.

As discussed above, the metacognitive abilities involved in managing independent learning are challenging for younger learners. Specific project materials could eschew some of the nice (distracting) visuals and instead place a flow chart on every page, indicating where in the process the learner is. This can help to promote time management – most learners, even older ones, have poor judgement of how long a task is likely to take, a phenomenon that researchers have termed the 'planning fallacy', and which seems to take place even when they have experience or when advice is given (Buehler et al., 1994). As well as supporting learners, this strategy will help to build a sense of how a project can effectively develop over a series of weeks – and avoid the risk of it all being done the night before the deadline with substantial parental help.

The aims of homework are often extraneous to the end product, and may include developing a learner's broad general knowledge, fostering curiosity, and improving research skills. Such things can fall by the wayside, however, when the emphasis is on the attractive outcome (e.g. a leaflet or PowerPoint to present in class). Breaking a homework task into a series of stages emphasises the process, and allows multiple opportunities for feedback and support, as in the following example.

Project on an area of the world, with end product to produce leaflet about the area's history and culture

- Week 1: Read overview text on several possible areas in class; homework is to choose one area and write a one-paragraph summary stating which one they have chosen and why.
- Week 2: Find two sources (e.g. books or websites; this could be done with staff guidance in class/library, especially with younger learners). Write a brief explanation of how you found it, and why you think it is a suitable source. Note down one other source that you intend to find.
- Week 3: Using sources collected the previous week, write one A4 page of initial notes under headings (e.g. 'historical events', 'famous people', 'important places', 'culture'), and bring these notes in for feedback/corrections from classmates and teacher. Include bibliography/references.
- Week 4: Guidance in class on forming ideas from notes into a four-page leaflet, cutting down and summarising. Completion of a draft leaflet for homework.
- Week 5: Feedback on draft; completion of final leaflet set as homework task.

As can be seen, some of the most challenging aspects of structuring the research and the design could be done during class time with teacher oversight, with more straightforward aspects that require time and reflective reading left to later. By ensuring that learners leave the classroom with the key ingredients of the task, as well as a plan (the method or recipe of the homework), autonomous success becomes more likely. Feedback on the research processes also presents opportunities to develop metacognitive awareness of strengths and weaknesses, which is why the 'assessment for learning' approach recommends peer marking based on comment and discussion, rather than traditional grading (Black et al., 2004).

Planning for revision

Revision is different in nature to projects or extension tasks in that the aim is to consolidate prior learning, but it may occupy similar times of day outside class and be done in a similar context. Some schools set dedicated study periods, and provide materials and booklets to work through; most have spaces such as the school library that are well-suited to quiet work. Having said that, learners often believe they can revise effectively while watching TV, talking to friends, and regularly checking their phone – in practice, this is likely to be largely ineffective as it causes attention to be divided.

Regardless of the setting, it is clear that students need help in making their study time effective. Learners' assumptions about what helps to make information stick in memory tend to be inaccurate (Schwartz and Efklides, 2012). In a simple but powerful example of this, Rhodes and Castel (2008) found that learners judged themselves to have learned better when items were shown in larger-sized text, even though it made no difference to recall. More broadly, learners are more likely to make use of ineffective strategies such as rereading and highlighting than more effective ones such as self-testing (Hartwig and Dunlosky, 2012). Highlighting large sections of notes or textbooks is also ineffective, although a more discriminating approach to highlighting – focusing on key terms or short phrases, or highlighting different types of information with different colours – is an active task that can promote helpful deep processing (Yue et al., 2015).

Shorter learning sessions involving active tasks are also likely to be more effective than more lengthy sessions, during which attention levels are likely to dip. Learners may benefit from self-testing towards the beginning of their study time, followed by working at tackling any particular weaknesses, rather than testing themselves at the end, which could lead to stress.

Finally, as many students have found over the years, mnemonics can greatly aid retrieval of information at a later date (e.g. in exams). Tullis and Benjamin (2015) looked at how people make mnemonic cues, and found that most cues created were effective and meaningful, but it helps if learners are made aware of which items are easily forgotten or confused. Some of the most effective mnemonic cues are visual or even multisensory. These tricks don't do much to encode new information, but they can help to organise and retrieve it under the stress of a test or exam, and therefore have the potential to act as a scaffold for learning.

The guide below will be a useful guide for learners about how to revise.

Brief evidence-based guide to revision for students

- Avoid distractions, as attention is limited and essential for memorisation. Switch your phone off and find somewhere quiet.
- Use flash cards or other questions/prompts, and test yourself frequently.
- Use several study locations where possible. Perhaps you can even move around as you revise (e.g. when looking through flash cards).
- Delay revision/restudy *of the same topic* by two to four weeks where possible – in other words, not too soon, but not so long that you have totally forgotten the information.
- Study the same items in several different ways and switch between topics frequently. Look for ways in which topics connect and overlap, and find or think of real-world examples/uses of concepts.
- Make memory cues for yourself, such as phrases that link the key ideas or visual images based on hard-to-remember words or names.

- For easily confused items (e.g. two plays or poems that you tend to mix up), it may help to study them side by side.
- Keep study sessions short but focused. The 'pomodoro technique' involves 25 minutes of intensive study followed by a five-minute break.
- Don't try to do too much in a single day – the brain needs time (and sleep) in order to consolidate new information. If you must do a lot in one day, then take longer breaks, study in more than one location, and test yourself on the key points within the next couple of days to minimise forgetting.
- Above all, don't underestimate how much you will forget! You might know something today, but you should aim to test yourself another three times in subsequent weeks.

Conclusions

Independent learning is undoubtedly a fixture of education today, from self-study and revision to research projects with pupils of all ages. For the educator, it is important to understand the psychological processes involved in order to make sure that pupils are learning successfully when working more independently, and to identify what support may be needed.

The psychology of independent learning suggests that there are reasons to be cautious, but also great opportunities to connect learning to more realistic contexts:

- On the one hand, learners' metacognitive awareness is open to simplistic biases, and when studying in a self-directed fashion they often make bad choices guided by inaccurate assumptions about their learning. Free discovery learning also has serious questions to answer about both its efficacy and time-efficiency.
- On the other hand, guided discovery learning and project work can tap into motivational processes that are beneficial for learning and

promote the integration of knowledge across varied contexts, promoting far transfer (see Chapter 4). It can provide a stimulus for many of the principles that are known to benefit LTM and understanding (e.g. spontaneous retrieval of information, spacing out relearning, and integrating knowledge with elaborate real-world examples).

Research, revision, homework and projects which are designed in a way that takes account of psychological evidence can provide motivating and effective learning experiences throughout the school years, supplementing other forms of learning.

Further reading

Handbook of Metacognition in Education edited by D. J. Hacker, J. Dunlosky and A. C. Graesser (Routledge, 2009)
A comprehensive guide to metacognition, covering issues as diverse as children's literacy and scientific enquiry.

Enquiry and Project Based Learning: Students, School and Society edited by D. Leat (Routledge, 2017)
This book argues for enquiry-based learning in preference to more direct teaching of curriculum content. Several example projects are described by different authors.

Connected Learning: An Agenda for Research and Design by M. K. Ito and colleagues (Digital Media and Learning Research Hub, 2013)
A compelling argument for 'connected learning' – the value of practical projects that are rooted in learners' interests and life experience. Available as an ebook via http://eprints.lse.ac.uk/48114/

Whole School Projects: Engaging Imaginations Through Interdisciplinary Inquiry by K. Egan (Teachers College Press, 2015)
This is a broader take on the concept of student independent learning via projects, focusing on how to build a school-wide research agenda that student projects can form a part of.

Free Voluntary Reading by S. D. Krashen (Libraries Unlimited, 2011)
Linguistics researcher Krashen makes the case for students to engage in extensive interest-based independent reading as a way of broadening knowledge and vocabulary – an argument that has implications for memory and cognition too.

References

Bjork, R. A. (1994). Memory and metamemory considerations in the training of human beings. In J. Metcalfe and A. P. Shimamura (eds), *Metacognition: Knowing About Knowing* (pp. 185–205). Cambridge, MA: MIT Press.

Bjorklund, D. F. (2007). *Why Youth Is Not Wasted on the Young: Immaturity in Human Development*. Oxford: Blackwell.

Black, P., Harrison, C., Lee, C., Marshall, B. and Wiliam, D. (2004). Working inside the black box: assessment for learning in the classroom. *Phi Delta Kappan*, 86(1), 8–21. doi: 10.1177/003172170408600105

Blakemore, S. J. and Mills, K. L. (2014). Is adolescence a sensitive period for sociocultural processing? *Annual Review of Psychology*, 65, 187–207. doi: 10.1146/annurev-psych-010213-115202

Bransford, J. D., Brown, A. L. and Cocking, R. R. (2000). *How People Learn: Brain, Mind, Experience and School*. Washington, DC: National Academy Press.

Bruner, J. S. (1961). The act of discovery. *Harvard Educational Review*, 31, 21–32.

Buehler, R., Griffin, D. and Ross, M. (1994). Exploring the 'planning fallacy': why people underestimate their task completion times. *Journal of Personality and Social Psychology*, 67(3), 366–381. doi: 10.1037/0022-3514.67.3.366

Carpenter, S. K., Wilford, M. M., Kornell, N. and Mullaney, K. M. (2013). Appearances can be deceiving: instructor fluency increases perceptions of learning without increasing actual learning. *Psychonomic Bulletin & Review*, 20(6), 1350–1356. doi: 10.3758/s13423-013-0442-z

Carvalho, P. F. and Goldstone, R. L. (2015). The benefits of interleaved and blocked study: different tasks benefit from different schedules of study. *Psychonomic Bulletin & Review*, 22(1), 281–288. doi: 10.3758/s13423-014-0676-4

Christodoulou, D. (2014). *Seven Myths About Education*. Abingdon: Routledge.

Clark, J. M. and Paivio, A. (1991). Dual coding theory and education. *Educational Psychology Review*, 3(3), 149–210. doi: 10.1007/BF01320076

Cook, S. W., Mitchell, Z. and Goldin-Meadow, S. (2008). Gesturing makes learning last. *Cognition*, 106(2), 1047–1058. doi: 10.1016/j.cognition.2007.04.010.

Cooper, H., Robinson, J. C. and Patall, E. (2006). Does homework improve academic achievement? A synthesis of research, 1987–2003. *Review of Educational Research*, 76(1), 1–62. doi: 10.3102/00346543076001001

Davis, K. and Fullerton, S. (2016). Connected learning in and after school: exploring technology's role in the learning experiences of diverse high school students. *The Information Society*, 32(2), 98–116. doi: 10.1080/01972243.2016.1130498

Egan, K. (2014). *Whole School Projects: Engaging Imaginations Through Interdisciplinary Inquiry*. New York: Teachers College Press.

Fernández-Alonso, R., Suárez-Álvarez, J. and Muñiz, J. (2015). Adolescents' homework performance in mathematics and science: personal factors and teaching practices. *Journal of Educational Psychology*, 107(4), 1075–1085. doi: 10.1037/edu0000032

Finn, B. and Metcalfe, J. (2007). The role of memory for past test in the underconfidence with practice effect. *Journal of Experimental Psychology: Learning, Memory, and Cognition*, 33(1), 238–244. doi: 10.1037/0278-7393.33.1.238

Fiorella, L. and Mayer, R. E. (2016). Eight ways to promote generative learning. *Educational Psychology Review*, 28(4), 717–741. doi: 10.1007/s10648-015-9348-9

Freeman, S., Eddy, S. L., McDonough, M., Smith, M. K., Okoroafor, N., Jordt, H., et al. (2014). Active learning increases student performance in science, engineering, and mathematics. *PNAS*, 111(23), 8410–8415. doi: 10.1073/pnas.1319030111

Gopnik, A. (2010). How babies think. *Scientific American*, 303(1), 76–81.

Gopnik, A. (2016). *The Gardener and the Carpenter: What the New Science of Child Development Tells Us About the Relationship Between Parents and Children*. London: Bodley Head.

Guttentag, R. E. and Hunt, R. R. (1988). Adult age differences in memory for imagined and performed actions. *Journal of Gerontology*, 43(4), P107–P108. doi: 10.1093/geronj/43.4.P107

Hartwig, M. K. and Dunlosky, J. (2012). Study strategies of college students: are self-testing and scheduling related to achievement? *Psychonomic Bulletin & Review*, 19(1), 126–134. doi: 10.3758/s13423-011-0181-y

Hattie, J. (2008). *Visible Learning: A Synthesis of Over 800 Meta-Analyses Relating to Achievement*. London: Routledge.

Ito, M.K., Gutiérrez, K., Livingstone, S., Penuel, B., Rhodes, J., Salen, K., et al. (2013). Connected learning: an agenda for research and design. *Digital Media and Learning Research Hub*. Retrieved 12 November 2015 from http://eprints.lse.ac.uk/48114/

Kang, S. H. (2016). The benefits of interleaved practice for learning. In J. C. Horvath, J. M. Lodge and J. Hattie (eds), *From the Laboratory to the Classroom: Translating Science of Learning for Teachers* (pp. 79–93). London: Routledge.

Koriat, A. (1997). Monitoring one's own knowledge during study: a cue-utilization approach to judgments of learning. *Journal of Experimental Psychology: General*, 126(4), 349–370. doi: 10.1037/0096-3445.126.4.349

Koriat, A., Bjork, R. A., Sheffer, L. and Bar, S. K. (2004). Predicting one's own forgetting: the role of experience-based and theory-based processes. *Journal of Experimental Psychology: General*, 133(4), 643–656. doi: 10.1037/0096-3445.133.4.643

Kornell, N. and Bjork, R. A. (2007). The promise and perils of self-regulated study. *Psychonomic Bulletin & Review*, 14(2), 219–224. doi: 10.3758/BF03194055

Kornell, N. and Metcalfe, J. (2006). Study efficacy and the region of proximal learning framework. *Journal of Experimental Psychology: Learning, Memory, & Cognition*, 32, 609–622. doi: 10.1037/0278-7393.32.3.609

Levinson, M. (2015). Face-to-face vs. online learning: why is it either/or? *Edutopia*. Retrieved 15 April 2017 from www.edutopia.org/blog/face-to-face-vs-online-why-either-or-matt-levinson

Lo, C. K. and Hew, K. F. (2017). A critical review of flipped classroom challenges in K-12 education: possible solutions and recommendations for future research. *Research and Practice in Technology Enhanced Learning*, 12(4). doi: 10.1186/s41039-016-0044-2.

Mayer, R. E. (2004). Should there be a three-strikes rule against pure discovery learning? *American Psychologist*, 59(1), 14–19. doi: 10.1037/0003-066X.59.1.14

Metcalfe, J. (2002). Is study time allocated selectively to a region of proximal learning? *Journal of Experimental Psychology: General*, 131(3), 349–363. doi: 10.1037//0096-3445.131.3.349

Mueller, P. A. and Oppenheimer, D. M. (2014). The pen is mightier than the keyboard: advantages of longhand over laptop note taking. *Psychological Science*, 25(6), 1159–1168. doi: 10.1177/0956797614524581

Otero, J. and Graesser, A. C. (2001). PREG: elements of a model of question asking. *Cognition and Instruction*, 19(2), 143–175. doi: 10.1207/S1532690XCI1902_01

Pashler, H., McDaniel, M., Rohrer, D. and Bjork, R. A. (2008). Learning styles: concepts and evidence. *Psychological Science in the Public Interest*, 9(3), 105–119. doi: 10.1111/j.1539-6053.2009.01038.x

Phillips, N. E., Mills, C., D'Mello, S. and Risko, E. F. (2016). On the influence of re-reading on mind wandering. *Quarterly Journal of Experimental Psychology*, 69(12), 2338–2357. doi: 10.1080/17470218.2015.1107109

Piaget, J. (1962). *Play, Dreams and Imitation in Childhood*. New York: Norton.

Prince, M. (2004). Does active learning work? A review of the research. *Journal of Engineering Education*, 93(3), 223–231. doi: 10.1002/j.2168-9830.2004.tb00809.x

Rawson, K. A. and Dunlosky, J. (2016). How effective is example generation for learning declarative concepts? *Educational Psychology Review*, 3(28), 649–672. doi: 10.1007/s10648-016-9377-z

Rhodes, M. G. and Castel, A. D. (2008). Memory predictions are influenced by perceptual information: evidence for metacognitive illusions. *Journal of Experimental Psychology: General*, 137(4), 615–625. doi: 10.1037/a0013684

Rice, M. F. and Carter Jr, R. A. (2016). Online teacher work to support self-regulation of learning in students with disabilities at a fully online state virtual school. *Online Learning*, 20(4), 118–135.

Richland, L. E., Kornell, N. and Kao, L. S. (2009). The pretesting effect: do unsuccessful retrieval attempts enhance learning? *Journal of Experimental Psychology: Applied*, 15(3), 243–257. doi: 10.1037/a0016496

Risko, E. F., Anderson, N., Sarwal, A., Engelhardt, M. and Kingstone, A. (2012). Everyday attention: variation in mind wandering and memory in a lecture. *Applied Cognitive Psychology*, 26(2), 234–242. doi: 10.1002/acp.1814

Schwartz, B. L. and Efklides, A. (2012). Metamemory and memory efficiency: implications for student learning. *Journal of Applied Research in Memory and Cognition*, 1, 145–151. doi: 10.1016/j.jarmac.2012.06.002

Serra, M. J. and Metcalfe, J. (2009). Effective implementation of metacognition. In D. J. Hacker, J. Dunlosky and A. C. Graesser (eds), *Handbook of Metacognition in Education* (pp. 278–298). New York: Routledge.

Slamecka, N. J. and Graf, P. (1978). The generation effect: delineation of a phenomenon. *Journal of Experimental Psychology: Human Learning and Memory*, 4(6), 592–604. doi: 10.1037/0278-7393.4.6.592

Soderstrom, N. C. and Bjork, R. A. (2015). Learning versus performance: an integrative review. *Perspectives on Psychological Science*, 10(2), 176–199. doi: 10.1177/1745691615569000

Szpunar, K. K., Khan, N. Y. and Schacter, D. L. (2013). Interpolated memory tests reduce mind wandering and improve learning of online lectures. *PNAS*, 110(16), 6313–6317. doi: 10.1073/pnas.1221764110

Trautwein, U., Köller, O., Schmitz, B. and Baumert, J. (2002). Do homework assignments enhance achievement? A multilevel analysis in 7th grade mathematics. *Contemporary Educational Psychology*, 27(1), 26–50. doi: 10.1006/ceps.2001.1084

Tullis, J. G. and Benjamin, A. S. (2015). Cue generation: how learners flexibly support future retrieval. *Memory & Cognition*, 43(6), 922–938. doi: 10.3758/s13421-015-0517-3

Tweed, A. (2004). Direct instruction: is it the most effective science teaching strategy? *NSTA Reports, 15 December*. Retrieved 21 March 2017 from www.nsta.org/publications/news/story.aspx?id=50045

Wammes, J. D., Meade, M. E. and Fernandes, M. A. (2016). The drawing effect: evidence for reliable and robust memory benefits in free recall. *Quarterly Journal of Experimental Psychology*, 69(9), 1752–1776. doi: 10.1080/17470218.2015.1094494

Wapole, C. (2013). Thirty minutes tops. *Huffington Post – The Blog*, 3 November. Retrieved 7 June 2017 from www.huffingtonpost.com/claire-wapole/thirty-minutes-tops_b_3861853.html

Weir, K. (2016). Is homework a necessary evil? *APA Monitor on Psychology*, 47(3), 36.

Wooldridge, C., Smith, M. and Weinstein, Y. (2016). Incorporating (good) active learning in the classroom. *Learning Scientists Blog.* Retrieved 8 September 2016 from www.learningscientists.org/blog/2016/9/8-1

Yan, V. X., Bjork, E. L. and Bjork, R. A. (2016). On the difficulty of mending metacognitive illusions: a priori theories, fluency effects, and misattributions of the interleaving benefit. *Journal of Experimental Psychology: General*, 145(7), 918–933. doi: 10.1037/xge0000177

Yue, C. L., Storm, B. C., Kornell, N. and Bjork, E. L. (2015). Highlighting and its relation to distributed study and students' metacognitive beliefs. *Educational Psychology Review*, 27(1), 69–78. doi:10.1007/s10648-014-9277-z

Zamary, A. and Rawson, K. A. (2017). Which technique is most effective for learning declarative concepts – provided examples, generated examples, or both? *Educational Psychology Review.* doi: 10.1007/s10648-016-9396-9

Zamary, A., Rawson, K. A. and Dunlosky, J. (2016). How accurately can students evaluate the quality of self-generated examples of declarative concepts? Not well, and feedback does not help. *Learning and Instruction*, 46, 12–20. doi: 10.1016/j.learninstruc.2016.08.002

Zechmeister, E. B. and Shaughnessy, J. J. (1980). When you know that you know and when you think that you know but you don't. *Bulletin of the Psychonomic Society*, 15(1), 41–44. doi: 10.3758/BF03329756

Index

Bold page numbers indicate where a term appears in a table.